WILD EARTH

WILD EARTH

WILD IDEAS FOR A WORLD OUT OF BALANCE

EDITED BY TOM BUTLER

MILKWEED
EDITIONS

Published 2002 by Milkweed Editions
Printed in Canada
Cover and interior design by Dale Cooney
Cover art, "The Eyes Have It (Wolf)," by Dennis Logsdon.
Cover photograph by Gen/Photonica.
Art on p. ii, "Table Rock—November," by Davis Te Selle
Art on p. 3, "Alligator Mother and Young," © 1992, and on p. 243, "Grizzly Bear in Huckleberry
Bushes," © 1981, by Diana Dee Tyler
Art on p. 127, "American Sycamore—Bark, Leaves, and Fruit," by Heather Lenz
The text of this book is set in Bembo.
02 03 04 05 06   5 4 3 2 1
First Edition

Special underwriting for this book from Furthermore, a program of the J. M. Kaplan Fund.

Milkweed Editions, a nonprofit publisher, gratefully acknowledges support from our World As Home
funder, Reader's Legacy underwriter Elly Sturgis. Other support has been provided by the Elmer L.
and Eleanor J. Andersen Foundation; Bush Foundation; Faegre and Benson Foundation; General
Mills Foundation; Marshall Field's Project Imagine with support from the Target Foundation;
McKnight Foundation; Minnesota State Arts Board through an appropriation by the Minnesota
State Legislature and a grant from the National Endowment for the Arts, and a grant from the
Wells Fargo Foundation Minnesota; A Resource for Change technology grant from the National
Endowment for the Arts; Lawrence and Elizabeth Ann O'Shaughnessy Charitable Income Trust in
honor of Lawrence M. O'Shaughnessy; Oswald Family Foundation; Ritz Foundation on behalf of
Mr. and Mrs. E. J. Phelps Jr.; John and Beverly Rollwagen Fund of the Minneapolis Foundation;
St. Paul Companies, Inc.; Target Stores; U.S. Bancorp Foundation; and generous individuals.

Library of Congress Cataloging-in-Publication Data

    Wild earth : wild ideas for a world out of balance / edited by Tom Butler.— 1st ed.
      p. cm.
      ISBN 1-57131-262-5 (pbk.)
        1. Biological diversity conservation. 2. Environmental protection. I. Butler, Tom, 1963–

    QH75 .W47 2002
    333.95'16—dc21

                              2001032689

This book is printed on acid-free, recycled paper.

For the loons of Rock Pond,
and John Davis

—T.B.

WILD EARTH

FOREWORD *by Bill McKibben* **x**

INTRODUCTION, "A RIVER OF WORDS FOR WILDERNESS," *by Tom Butler* **xiii**

WILD SCIENCE AND STRATEGY

"WOOD ANEMONE" *by Walt Franklin* **5**

"AROUND THE CAMPFIRE (VOL. 1, NO. 1)" *by Dave Foreman* **7**

"THE WILDLANDS PROJECT MISSION, VISION, AND PURPOSE" **10**

"WILDERNESS: FROM SCENERY TO NATURE" *by Dave Foreman* **15**

"FEATHERS AND FOSSILS: HAWAIIAN EXTINCTIONS AND MODERN
    CONSERVATION" *by Lyanda Lynn Haupt* **34**

"THE GREAT DENIAL: PUNCTURING PRONATALIST MYTHS"
    by Sandy Irvine **45**

"NULLIPARITY AND A CRUEL HOAX REVISITED" *by Stephanie Mills* **63**

"PHILANTHROPY AND NATIONAL PARKS: AN AMERICAN TRADITION"
    by Robin W. Winks **70**

"BEAR NECESSITIES: GRIZZLIES, WILDERNESS, AND THE SCIENCE OF
    EXTINCTION" *by Louisa Willcox* **72**

"REWILDING FOR EVOLUTION" *by Connie Barlow* **83**

"BRING BACK THE ELEPHANTS!" *by Paul S. Martin and David A. Burney* **89**

"AND I WILL BE HEARD: ABOLITIONISM AND PRESERVATIONISM IN OUR TIME"
    by Jamie Sayen **105**

WILD THINKING

"LANGUAGE AND EXPERIENCE" *by Pattiann Rogers*   **129**

"ISLAND CIVILIZATION: A VISION FOR PLANET EARTH IN THE YEAR 2992"
   by Roderick Frazier Nash   **131**

"A MINORITY VIEW: REJOINDER TO 'ISLAND CIVILIZATION'" *by John Davis*   **139**

"CONSERVATION IS GOOD WORK" *by Wendell Berry*   **142**

"NIGHT AND FOG: THE BACKLASH AGAINST THE ENDANGERED SPECIES ACT"
   by R. Wills Flowers   **156**

"ECOPORN AND THE MANIPULATION OF DESIRE" *by José Knighton*   **165**

"A CRITIQUE OF AND AN ALTERNATIVE TO THE WILDERNESS IDEA"
   by J. Baird Callicott   **172**

"WILDERNESS—NOW MORE THAN EVER: A RESPONSE TO CALLICOTT"
   by Reed F. Noss   **187**

"IS NATURE REAL?" *by Gary Snyder*   **195**

"ECOFORESTRY OR PROTECTED STATUS? SOME WORDS IN DEFENSE OF PARKS"
   by Ken Wu   **199**

"RETURNING TO OUR ANIMAL SENSES" *by David Abram*   **209**

"CONTACT AND THE SOLID EARTH" *by Christopher Manes*   **216**

"THE WILDERNESS OF HISTORY" *by Donald Worster*   **221**

"THE MYTHS WE LIVE BY" *by George Wuerthner*   **230**

"COMING HOME TO THE WILD" *by Florence R. Shepard*   **233**

WILD PLACES AND CREATURES

"ISLE ROYALE FRAGMENTS" *by Gary Lawless*   **245**

"FELLOW TRAVELERS" *by Mollie Yoneko Matteson*   **247**

"LOSS OF PLACE" *by Howie Wolke*   **251**

"THE POLLINATOR AND THE PREDATOR" *by Gary Paul Nabhan* **256**

"TRAVELING THE LOGGING ROAD, COAST RANGE"
    by Kathleen Dean Moore **261**

"EXTINCTION: PASSENGER PIGEON CHEWING LOUSE *(COLUMBICOLA EXTINCTA)*"
    by Peter Friederici **267**

"FIELD REPORT: YELLOWSTONE BISON SLAUGHTER" *by Doug Peacock* **272**

"THE GIFT OF SILENCE" *by Anne LaBastille* **285**

"JOB AND WILDERNESS" *by Bill McKibben* **287**

"THE LEAST NAVIGABLE CRAFT: WHALES AT THE MILLENNIUM"
    by Phoebe Wray **290**

"THE LANGUAGE OF ANIMALS" *by Barry Lopez* **296**

"GRIZZLY FEARS" *by Glendon Brunk* **306**

AFTERWORD, "EARTH VERSE," *by Gary Snyder* **319**

ABOUT THE CONTRIBUTORS **321**

ABOUT THE WILDLANDS PROJECT AND *WILD EARTH* **328**

ACKNOWLEDGMENTS **329**

CONTRIBUTOR ACKNOWLEDGMENTS **331**

FOREWORD

When the original issue of *Wild Earth* arrived, the first thing I noticed was how it looked—which is to say, markedly different from any "environmental magazine" I'd ever seen. Where were the glossy shots of aspens quaking in the Rocky Mountain breeze? Where were the close-ups of wolf pups mewling and play-fighting?

Nowhere could I find a grizzly bear spearing a salmon in midjump. There were some very lovely line drawings, but for me the absence of *Nikonicry* made me sit up and take notice, even before I started reading the contents. In many ways, *Wild Earth* was the first postscenic environmental magazine, the first work of serious journalism born in the very teeth of the various cataclysms haunting the planet.

And yet, at the same time, it was the least grim conservation journal ever published. It has paid full heed to global warming, to extinction, to population growth, to all the myriad degradations visited on the planet, but its tone has never been defensive. It's been on the offensive from the beginning, less concerned with lamenting the decline of wildness than in planning for its resurgence. It focuses on the Wild Earth that we were born into and are now destroying, but it also imagines the Wild Earth we might yet create.

Perhaps that flowed naturally from the staff's decision to locate back east, first in the Adirondack Mountains where I make my home, and then just across Lake Champlain in the northlands of Vermont. It's not Ansel Adams country: the peaks are shorter than the Sierra or the Cascades, the trees stubbier; save for the last two weeks of September, its grandeur is quieter. On the other hand, the Adirondacks are the

Alaska of ecological recovery; left for clear-cut dead a century ago, the forest has resurrected itself. Most, though not all, of its creatures have returned. These mountains, and the hills of Vermont, are the right place to imagine what might happen if people took a step back—they allow one to dream responsibly of a revived tallgrass prairie, a rain forest covering the Pacific Northwest, of the longleaf pine that early American naturalist William Bartram saw rampant in the Southeast.

Wild Earth has never shied away from the hardest cases; if anything, it's sought them out. Bring back the grizzly! Hell, bring back the mammoth! And yet the mood from the beginning has been mature and tactically flexible. As Jamie Sayen points out in these pages, the battle for environmental salvation will demand at least the energy, and the long-term commitment, of the battle to abolish slavery. That doesn't mean patience with destruction; it does mean planning for the long haul.

In very few other publications could one find spirited arguments over what the right size human population should be a thousand years hence, or how best to draw the maps of a green continent seven generations ahead. David Abram is surely right when he says we've spent millennia learning how not to see, how not to feel. But in these pages, issue after issue, are at least the seeds of reborn possibility.

Those seeds are nourished with the water of art, the sunlight of poetry.

Though *Wild Earth* has fought the good fight in the various debates that have roiled the conservation community—particularly the battles over environmental historian William Cronon's disparagement of the wilderness idea—it has never descended to academic abstraction. Instead, piece after piece begins in real places, amid real creatures: "The steep riverine valley I live within . . ." "As I camp alone in a narrow canyon . . ." "Like milk poured in water, morning fog moves through the trees and along the course of the narrow road." We are not living on the abstract earth of the philosophers, but on the real earth of sun and water, photosynthesis and predation, a planet governed by an emotional gravity that our intellect ignores at its peril.

The first essay I wrote for *Wild Earth,* a short discussion of global warming that appeared in the premier issue, was, frankly, gloomy. I remain, frankly, gloomy. We seem bent on testing every limit our planet knows; the next fifty years will be a tight squeeze through a narrow hole, and less glory will emerge from that slot canyon than started through it. Our species may simply never back off, never let up, never give anything else the room to breathe.

In that case, *Wild Earth* will have been a noble witness to other possibilities, a refutation of the inevitability argument too often used as an excuse for inaction. But just imagine we made the radical turn— return, actually—toward wildness. Imagine that conviction, or more likely, catastrophe, forced us in an entirely new direction. If that ever happened, then this stouthearted journal will have been one of the chief maps toward a new old future. Four times a year, anyway, we can hope.

—BILL MCKIBBEN

INTRODUCTION
A RIVER OF WORDS FOR WILDERNESS

We abuse land because we regard it as a commodity belonging to us. When we begin to see land as a community to which we belong, we may begin to use it with love and respect.

—ALDO LEOPOLD

One glorious autumn day some years ago, I hiked with a friend in wild country, not far from the Canadian border. It was a warm day, and while the mountains that towered above us were white, the ground we covered was mostly free of snow. We spoke quietly or not at all, ascending through a long valley toward an alpine lake ringed by a half circle of mountain—a classic glacial cirque. This was bear country, though, and I took care to raise my voice when we walked through thick, streamside forest where startling a grizzly would have been, well, even more of a wilderness experience than we had sought.

The land was exquisitely beautiful, and full of life. A flock of ruby-crowned kinglets chattered in the treetops. The hillsides were dotted with mountain goats, moving nimbly through fractured cliff bands. As the trail crossed just uphill from a small lake, we heard something—something big—snuffling and crashing through the scrub. I froze, then began to back away slowly from the sound. A massive bull moose emerged just feet ahead of us, his rack still dripping. As much as I'd hoped to see bears, in that moment I was relieved to meet *Alces alces,* not *Ursus arctos.*

Like your first love, you don't forget your first grizzly. We could quibble over whether or not Aldo Leopold was speaking metaphorically when he began *A Sand County Almanac* with these words: "There are some who can live without wild things, and some who cannot. These essays are the delights and dilemmas of one who cannot."

But ask anyone who's been in a truly wild place, a place where the land community is still intact (and some members of that community can eat you): ask them if they didn't feel more fully human, more alive *then and there* than ever before.

I felt alive that day. And I saw a bear.

It wasn't dramatic. We weren't charged. The details aren't especially important, and perhaps, as in recollecting any intimate encounter, discretion is warranted. But I will say that the fifteen or twenty minutes we spent watching a female grizzly were memorable, not simply because it was a first for me, but because the scene seemed so normal. *This is what the world should look like,* I thought.

That bear was busy foraging, putting on fat stores for the winter. She was at home—just having lunch—and never knew of our presence. But I remember exactly how I felt.

I felt at home, too.

To people who cannot live, or at least wouldn't care to live, in a world devoid of wild things and goose music, interactions with our wild kin are demarcations in life as central as a love affair, a graduation, a first Springsteen concert. I have no idea what I did on my birthday last year, but I can describe the scene exactly, after many years, of canoeing around a bend on the Marion River in the heart of the Adirondacks and spying a fisher.

Fishers—bushy-tailed, midsized mustelids (members of the weasel family)—have made a remarkable comeback in the recovering forests of New England and New York, and to catch sight of one is not the rare event it once was. Certainly not as rare as seeing its smaller cousin the pine marten, which seems to have even narrower habitat requirements, needing large blocks of interior, mature forest. (Outside the Adirondacks, such wild forests are still rare in the Northeast, and I've yet to meet a marten.)

I can recall precisely where I was when I first saw a blackburnian warbler, and what I was thinking one morning when, deep in a canyon in Dinosaur National Monument, I watched a peregrine falcon—the fastest living thing on Earth—streaking through a brilliant blue sky. ("Wow. That is fast!")

OK, so I'm no Annie Dillard. My response to the numinous event is sure to be less than profound. Heck, I may not even recognize my numinous events. These encounters with wildness are personal landmarks, yes, but they are also prosaic—the by-product of time spent outside in the real world, getting to know my neighbors in the ecological community. Moreover, for active conservationists, particularly those of us who are daily immersed in the literature of ecological cataclysm, excursions into wild nature are an antidote to despair.

Where was I that fall day hiking in the company of kinglets and mountain goats, moose and bears?

In *wilderness.* In a place where the land is "self-willed"—where natural processes, not human agency, direct the ebb and flow of life.

To be precise, we were exploring the backcountry of Glacier National Park and the terrain was *de facto,* not *designated,* wilderness (the park has no formally protected wilderness areas). The landscape was characterized both by what it contained—a largely intact native biota, including large carnivores such as grizzly bears and wolves—and by what it did not: No roads. No logging operations. No permanent human residents. No infrastructure of any kind save a footpath and an occasional sign.

For over a century, conservationists have worked to save places like this—to set aside swaths of primeval America from economic exploitation. Their success is written on the landscape most notably in our National Park System and National Wilderness Preservation System, but also in various types of protected natural areas in both public and private ownership. In the beginning, the American conservation movement emphasized:

- *Aesthetics.* Early parks were proposed for areas of great scenic beauty such as Yosemite and Yellowstone; they "monumentalized" the grand spectacles of nature.

- *Recreation.* Early wilderness proponents stressed the value of wildlands for primitive recreation, particularly for sportsmen. Wilderness areas were in part a reaction to road-building and settlement of the West, and were promoted as places where frontier skills could be maintained.

- *Solitude and spiritual renewal.* John Muir, patron saint of the American wilderness movement, described nature in overtly religious language; parks and wilderness areas would provide opportunities for solitude and reflection in God's untouched handiwork.

Today's conservation movement has not abandoned these foundational arguments but has built upon them, and now stresses:

- *Ecology.* Wilderness provides habitat for shy and sensitive and wide-ranging wildlife, and canvas for natural processes that create and shape biodiversity.

- *Evolution.* Wild nature is the context in which life has blossomed and flourished. Well over a century before Dave Foreman expressed this sentiment in the phrase "wilderness is the arena of evolution," Henry David Thoreau said essentially the same thing in his famous dictum: "In wildness is the preservation of the world."

- *Intrinsic value.* All species, regardless of their utility to humans and including those that require large blocks of self-willed land to thrive, have a right to exist and fulfill their evolutionary potentials.

- *Science.* Wild, unmanaged lands provide a control or benchmark— "a base datum of normality," as Aldo Leopold said—against which we can measure our progress toward sustainable use of the managed landscape.

In 1991 a small group of wilderness activists and conservation biologists founded *Wild Earth* journal to articulate and advance these modern wilderness values. We hoped to communicate conservation science to a broad audience of activists, policy makers, academics in the biological and social sciences, and conservation professionals, and to provide a forum for discussion within the conservation movement on strategy, philosophy, and tactics. I believe that we have been successful in helping move ecological and evolutionary arguments for wildlands protection to the forefront of the conservation agenda.

Some future historian may well borrow a metaphor from evolutionary biology and describe the 1990s as a punctuation in the equilibrium—marked by a rapid change in our conception of parks and wilderness. The burgeoning disciplines of conservation biology and landscape ecology, manifest in the growth of professional societies such as the Natural Areas Association, the Society for Ecological Restoration, and the Society for Conservation Biology, provided the scientific context for this sea change in thinking.

In the 1980s and 1990s, scientific consensus among ecologists became clear: We had entered the sixth major extinction spasm in Earth history, this time due not to an asteroid strike or a geological event, but to human action—*Homo sapiens'* explosive population growth and concomitant conversion and destruction of natural habitats.

Wild Earth put this insight into context for activists: all land conservation, be it concerned with a few acres or a few million, is now practiced against the backdrop of a global extinction crisis, a contraction in life's diversity unprecedented in 65 million years. Protecting parks and wilderness is no longer about saving a pretty place to picnic or a playground for backcountry sports—it's about forestalling extinction and ensuring that the full membership in the ecological community will survive humanity's assault on wild nature. Indeed, it's an absolutely critical step toward reversing that assault.

Wild Earth has been instrumental in catalyzing this cognitive revolution. We've made conservation biology accessible to nonscientists, most notably, the insights that:

- existing parks, wilderness areas, and wildlife refuges are too small and disconnected to sustain the diversity of life;

- fragmentation and isolation is a recipe for extinction, and to fully protect biodiversity we must restore functional connectivity of habitats across the landscape;

- systems of protected natural areas—variously called ecological reserves, conservation areas, or wildlands networks—are necessary to restore and maintain healthy ecosystems.

Along with our sister organization, the Wildlands Project (which was founded in 1992 to engage directly in regional conservation planning and implementation), we've articulated a new vision of parks and wilderness areas—as the central building blocks of wildlands networks designed to protect the full range of native biodiversity. Our overarching message has been that with time, the healing powers of nature, and restorative action by conservationists, we can *rewild* the land.

We've challenged advocates for wild nature to address the deep, systemic causes of the ecological crisis and begin playing offense for a change: to articulate a positive vision of what an ecologically and culturally vibrant North America might look like, and develop effective strategies to move us there.

To be sure, a total shift from defense to offense would be unwise. There are still daily outrages to be fought—logging, livestock grazing, mining, and motorized recreation abuses of our public land, industrial exploitation of nature's richness at every level of biological organization and across most of the world. But our vision, a science-based agenda for continent-wide wildlands recovery and protection, has now percolated through the conservation movement.

While helping to drive this evolution in thinking about the

goals and scale of biodiversity conservation, *Wild Earth* has itself evolved, maturing from a rough-around-the-edges, start-up publication with a bold vision (produced on a shoestring budget) to an award-winning, established periodical with a bold vision (alas, still produced on a shoestring budget). Production values and graphic appearance have steadily improved. The editorial content has shifted slightly over time; we now pay more attention to protecting biodiversity on private lands and through private philanthropy than we did in the past, for example, and have published more articles on conservation movement history in recent years. But *Wild Earth*'s focus remains constant: to communicate and help shape the latest thinking in conservation science, strategy, philosophy, and activism.

Completing its first decade, *Wild Earth* has become the journal of record for the wilderness wing of the American conservation movement and has published over 2 million words on these subjects—a river of words for wilderness. Choosing a representative sample from such riches was difficult. Many leading biologists, activists, and writers whose work has appeared in the journal could not be included in this collection, given the book's space constraints. Making these choices has been painful.

Within the wealth of material, I have endeavored to select articles and essays that reflect the diversity of topics and voices—some scholarly, some highly personal—we have published. Readers well acquainted with our backlist will note that this book's content is somewhat skewed toward matters philosophical, particularly the debates over the wilderness idea that engaged the conservation movement through the 1990s. Conservation science and strategy, the heart of *Wild Earth*'s mission, are less well represented.

This is in part due to the intended broader audience of this anthology, and in part done with an eye toward avoiding redundancy. A collection of the conservation biology–related articles from *Wild Earth*'s first decade has been suggested and would be fun to compile, but would add relatively little to the knowledge of a reader familiar with *The Diversity of Life* by E. O. Wilson (Norton, 1992), *Saving Nature's Legacy* by Reed Noss and Allen Cooperrider (Island Press, 1994), *The Song of the Dodo* by David Quammen (Scribner, 1996), and *Continental Conservation* edited by Michael Soulé and John Terborgh (Island Press, 1999). (Anyone who has not already done so—most especially members of Congress!—should read these four superb books.)

Moreover, the particulars of science and strategy may change with changing circumstances. An article from early in the decade on the Greater Yellowstone ecosystem, for example, is now dated; with wolf recovery in Yellowstone a considerable, albeit incomplete, success, the political and ecological landscape has changed. Similarly, Reed Noss's landmark paper, "The Wildlands Project Land Conservation Strategy," from *Wild Earth*'s 1992 special issue introducing the Wildlands Project, while still an important article, is somewhat dated. Noss, *Wild Earth*'s science editor since its inception and past president of the Society for Conservation Biology, has refined his preferred methodology for desiging networks of conservation lands in subsequent years.

The Wildlands Project, too, has evolved, and now emphasizes *rewilding*—protecting core wilderness areas connected by habitat linkages, with a goal of recovering and sustaining populations of wideranging top predators: cores, carnivores, and connectivity, for short. This complements other initiatives, including the Nature Conservancy's ecoregional planning, which seeks to represent all the vegetative communities native to a given area within a system of nature reserves. While methodological approaches to science-based conservation planning vary among scientists and organizations, the consensus among conservation biologists is clear: think big and connected.

That a piecemeal approach to conservation has given way to landscape-level thinking is cause for optimism. Applying conservation science to society's land-use decisions, though, is but one part of a comprehensive solution—we might call it a "whole landscape of the heart" solution—to the crisis of culture that has precipitated a global extinction spasm.

Ultimately, whether we value wild nature and allow all members of the land community their rightful places and spaces is an ethical question. Half a century after Aldo Leopold framed the question this way, we continue to wrestle with the fundamental decision of whether to treat the natural world as a commodity—a collection of "resources" for human use, enjoyment, and profit—or as a community to which we belong.

This is an ongoing conversation, with roots as ancient as human history. For ten years, we have carried it on with spirited dialogue in the pages of *Wild Earth*. Little snippets of that conversation are swirling about in the wider culture—in politics, history, science, and religion—and the fruits of that dialogue have profound consequences for the future.

Will the evolutionary lineage of that beautiful brown bear I watched in Glacier National Park continue? Will humanity grant her ursine daughters equivalent rights to life, liberty, and the pursuit of happiness as are accorded my daughter? Will we bequeath to our children, human and wild, a world of steadily diminishing beauty and complexity—a planet of weeds—or leave a legacy of wildness and diversity?

Commodity. Or community.

With the scientists, activists, scholars, writers, and artists whose work in sum have been *Wild Earth* in its first ten years, I trust that the conversation has been helpful in moving us toward the latter. May this river of words lead to a forever wild Earth!

—TOM BUTLER, Editor, *Wild Earth*

WILD EARTH

WILD SCIENCE AND STRATEGY

WOOD ANEMONE
(FOR THE PINE CREEK WATERSHED)

Only the winds of spring
can open the anemone
wrote Pliny

Windflower
mayflower
nimbleweed
Anemone quinquefolia
the wind god's
name in spring

Five white petals
three-part leaves—
the ancients picked them
chanting prayers

      Help us
         to protect these waters
these wild lands you open on
instill in us
         the powers
         to contain the ooze
            of mines
the excrement of greed

Protect these
aquifers and springs
         of highland rock
the breath of winds
we blossom by

       —WALT FRANKLIN

Around the Campfire
(VOL. 1, NO. 1)

Dave Foreman *(1991)*

More than a decade ago, ecologist Raymond Dasmann of the
University of California declared that World War Three had already
begun—it was the war of industrial humans against the Earth. With
that warning in mind, we can begin to understand what the environmental crisis is and what it is not. Too often we look on ecological
issues as affecting us only incidentally. The preservation of national
parks and wilderness areas is characterized in terms of monumental
scenery, primitive outdoor recreation, or "watchable wildlife."

But the truth is far different. Ecocatastrophe is not some remote
possibility in the future. It is here now. We are currently embroiled in
the greatest crisis in four billion years of life on Earth. Never before—
not even 65 million years ago at the end of the Cretaceous when dinosaurs became extinct—has there been an extinction rate comparable
to today's. The world's leading field ecologists warn us that one-third
of all species living may become extinct in the next twenty or thirty
years, that by the middle of the twenty-first century the only large
mammals remaining will be those we humans choose to allow to exist.

Not only are we devastating biological diversity through habitat
destruction, pollution, and slaughter of other species, but for the first
time human beings are having a systemic impact on the life support
system of Earth—through the destruction of the ozone layer, the
greenhouse effect, acid precipitation, and worldwide radioactive and
toxic pollution.

For over 3.5 billion years, life has been blossoming, diversifying, and expanding into incredible forms and unimaginably complex relationships. And now, in the space of a human generation, we will truncate this flowering.

Human overpopulation and overconsumption lead to this unprecedented destruction of life. But it is caused most fundamentally by an idea—the idea that human beings are separate from and superior to the natural world. Gifford Pinchot, founder of the United States Forest Service, summarized it this way: *There are only two things in the world— human beings and natural resources.* We seem to believe the living Earth is a smorgasbord table, continually replenished by a magic kitchen, for the exclusive use of humans. That attitude is what is destroying life on Earth—including human beings.

Mere reform of industrial civilization will not suffice. Grappling with the ecological crisis requires a rethinking of the role of humans within the life community. We must recognize with John Muir that all things are connected, that humans are only one of many millions of species that have been produced by evolution. We have no divine right to treat all other life as "resources" for our use. Other beings have value independent of their worth to humans; they live for their own sake.

On a practical level, this means that conservationists must no longer look on national parks, wilderness areas, and other protective classifications as natural museums, outdoor gymnasiums, scenic art galleries—as islands of nature in a sea of development. We must rethink the role of wilderness areas and parks, and consciously design them so they maintain and help restore biological diversity.

During the 1980s, new conservation groups have sprung up like owl clover in the desert after a wet winter. These groups, ranging from the Society for Conservation Biology to the Association of Forest Service Employees for Environmental Ethics to the grassroots Alliance for the Wild Rockies and Preserve Appalachian Wilderness, are working in a variety of ways for the preservation of natural diversity and the careful design of preserves to protect that diversity. Scenery and primitive recreation are incidental to their agenda. Traditional mainstream conservation groups like the Wilderness Society and the Oregon Natural Resources Council are also replacing the old scenery and recreation arguments with those for biodiversity.

Wild Earth is being launched to encourage this new approach to wilderness preservation. Our magazine exists as a forum for serious discussion of the ideas and methods of ecological preservation. We are here to help translate the theories and information of conservation biology into grassroots preservation activism. We are here to help all groups and individuals working to protect biological diversity.

In doing that, we will consciously be advocates for nonhuman nature. We will speak for wolf, orca, gila monster, saguaro.

If you like the talk and the company around this campfire, join us. Sit down and share your ideas. But if this campfire doesn't feel like home to you, please look for another one. There are lots of good groups out there. *Wild Earth* is not for everyone. We are conservationists. We believe in wilderness for its own sake. With John Muir, we are on the side of the bears in the war industrial humans have declared against wild nature.

The Wildlands Project Mission, Vision, and Purpose

(1992; revised 2000)

THE PROBLEM

As the new millennium begins, humanity approaches a watershed for wildlife and wilderness. Human activity is undoing creation; the remaining degraded and fragmented lands will not sustain their biological diversity and evolutionary processes. We need a bold plan to halt and reverse the destruction. Healing the land means reconnecting the parts so that vital flows can be renewed.

OUR MISSION

The mission of the Wildlands Project is to protect and restore the natural heritage of North America through the establishment of a connected system of wildlands. The idea is simple. To stem the disappearance of wildlife and wilderness we must allow the recovery of whole ecosystems and landscapes in every region of North America. Recovery on this scale will take time—a hundred years or more in some places. This vision for continental renewal rests on the spirit of social responsibility that has built so many great institutions in the past and acknowledges that the health of our society and its institutions depends on wildness. The land has given much to us; now it is time to give something back—to allow nature to thrive once more and to restore the links that will sustain both wilderness and the foundations of human communities.

OUR VISION

We are ambitious: we live for the day when grizzlies in Chihuahua have an unbroken connection to grizzlies in Alaska; when wolf populations are restored from Mexico to the Yukon; when vast forests and flowing prairies again thrive and support their full assemblage of native plants and animals; when humans dwell on the land with respect, humility, and affection; when we come to live no longer as conquerors but as respectful citizens in the land community.

OUR CHALLENGE

We are called to our task by the inability of existing parks, wilderness areas, and wildlife refuges to adequately protect life in North America in the face of increasing human numbers and technological change. While these areas preserve spectacular scenery and provide outstanding recreational opportunities, they are too small, too isolated, and represent too few types of ecosystems to perpetuate the continent's biological wealth. Despite the establishment of parks and reserves from Canada to Central America, true wilderness and native, wildland-dependent species are in precipitous decline.

• Grand predators including the grizzly bear, gray wolf, wolverine, jaguar, and American crocodile have been exterminated from large parts of their pre-Columbian range and are imperiled in much of their remaining habitat.

• The disappearance of these top predators and other keystone species hastens the unraveling of ecosystems and impoverishes the lives of human beings.

• Forests have been over-cut, cleared, and fragmented, leaving only scattered remnants of once vast ecosystems. Even extensive habitats, such as the boreal forest, face imminent destruction.

- Tall- and shortgrass prairie, historically the most extensive community type in North America, and once home to an extraordinary concentration of large mammals, has been almost entirely destroyed or domesticated.

- Deserts, coastal areas, and mountains are imperiled by sprawling subdivisions and second-home development.

- Motorized vehicles penetrate the few remaining roadless areas on illegal roads and tracks.

- A rising tide of invasive exotic species—ecological opportunists of the global economy—threatens a new wave of extinction and the eventual homogenization of ecosystems everywhere.

- Climate change adds to the vulnerability of wildlands that remain.

These trends, acting globally, are among the notable causes of the current and sixth major extinction event to occur since the first large organisms appeared on Earth a half-billion years ago. The Wildlands Project, as a remedy, is working to create regional and continental networks of conservation areas that will protect wild habitat, biodiversity, ecological integrity, ecological services, and evolutionary processes.

THE MEANING OF WILDERNESS

We reject the notion that wilderness is merely a remote destination suitable only for backpacking. We see wilderness as a wild home for unfettered life. Wilderness means:

- Extensive roadless areas—vast, self-regulated landscapes—free of mechanized human use and the sounds and constructions of modern civilization;

- Viable, self-reproducing populations of all native species, including large predators;

• Natural patterns of diversity at the genetic, species, ecosystem, and landscape levels.

Such wilderness is absolutely essential. It is not the solution to every ecological problem, but without wilderness the planet will sink further into biological poverty, and humanity's communion with its roots will be lost forever.

OUR METHOD

We seek partnerships with grassroots and national conservation organizations, government agencies, indigenous peoples, private landowners, and with naturalists, scientists, and conservationists across the continent to create networks of wildlands from Central America to Alaska and from Nova Scotia to California. We seek to heal nature's wounds by designing and creating wildlands networks and by restoring critical species and ecological processes to the land.

The wildlands networks will:

• Support the repatriation of top predators where they have been extirpated from present and future wilderness areas and national parks;

• Establish large areas of wild habitat where plants and animals are unrestrained, where native species thrive, and where nature, not technology, determines their evolutionary fate;

• Establish extensive linkages between large natural areas to ensure the continuation of migrations and other movements vital for the survival of healthy populations;

• Enable the recovery of natural processes such as fire.

We will implement these networks by:

• Supporting the designation of new conservation areas and improving the management of existing public lands;

- Campaigning both for the removal of public subsidies that maintain abusive land-use practices and for positive incentives that encourage responsible land management;

- Assisting landowners and land trusts in the voluntary protection of critical parcels of private land;

- Cooperating with transportation agencies to help remove or mitigate barriers to wildlife movement;

- Working with planners at all levels to create a balance between the needs of nature and human society;

- Promoting the restoration of disturbed lands and waters until that time when nature has recovered and can manage itself.

- Inspiring the people of North America to care for their home—for its own sake and for the sake of those yet to come.

WILDERNESS
FROM SCENERY TO NATURE

DAVE FOREMAN *(1995)*

Two scenes, only months apart:

October 31, 1994. President Bill Clinton lifts his pen from the California Desert Protection Act, and the acreage of the National Wilderness Preservation System soars to over 100 million acres, nearly half of which is outside Alaska, and the acreage of the National Park System jumps to almost 90 million acres, over one-third outside Alaska. American wilderness areas and national parks—the world's finest nature reserve system—are a legacy of citizen conservationists from Barrow to Key West, of courageous federal agency employees, and of farsighted elected officials. One hundred million acres is more than I thought we would ever protect when I enlisted in the wilderness wars (and I'm far from a hoary old warhorse like Dave Brower or Ed Wayburn—I've only been fighting for a quarter of a century).

February 14, 1995. The *New York Times* reports on a National Biological Service study done by three distinguished biologists. Reed Noss, editor of the widely cited scientific journal *Conservation Biology* and one of the report's authors, says, "We're not just losing single species here and there, we're losing entire assemblages of species and their habitats." The comprehensive review shows that ecosystems covering half the area of the forty-eight states are endangered or threatened. The longleaf pine ecosystem, for example, once the dominant vegetation of the coastal plain from Virginia to Texas and covering more than 60 million acres, remains only in dabs and scraps covering less than 2 percent of its original sprawl. Ninety-nine percent of the native grassland of California has been lost. There has been a 90 percent loss of riparian ecosystems in Arizona and New Mexico. Of the various natural ecosystem types in the United States, fifty-eight have declined by 85 percent or more and thirty-eight by 70 to 84 percent.

The dissonance between these two events is as jarring as chain saws in the forest, dirt bikes in the desert, the exploding of harpoons in the polar sea.

How have we lost so much while we have protected so much?

The answer lies in the goals, arguments, and process used to establish wilderness areas and national parks over the past century.

In his epochal study, *National Parks: The American Experience* (University of Nebraska Press, 1979), Alfred Runte discusses the arguments crafted to support establishment of the early national parks. Foremost was what Runte terms *monumentalism*—preservation of inspirational scenic grandeur like the Grand Canyon or Yosemite Valley and protection of the curiosities of nature like Yellowstone's hot pots and geysers. Later proposals for national parks had to measure up to the scenic quality of Mount Rainier or Crater Lake. Even the heavily glaciated Olympic Mountains were denied national park designation for many years because they weren't deemed up to snuff. Then, after the icy mountains were grudgingly accepted as national park material, the National Park Service and even some conservation groups bristled over including the lush temperate rain forests of the Hoh and Quinalt Valleys in the new park, seeing them as mere trees unworthy of national park designation. National park status was only for the "crown jewels" of American nature, an award akin to the Congressional Medal of Honor. If a substandard area became a national park, it would tarnish the *idea* of national parks as well as diminish all other national parks. (In our slightly more enlightened age, the stupendous conifers are the most celebrated feature of Olympic National Park.)

A second argument for new national parks, Runte explains, was based on *"worthless lands."* Areas proposed for protection, conservationists argued, were unsuitable for agriculture, mining, grazing, logging, and other make-a-buck uses. Yellowstone could be set aside because no one in his right mind would try to grow corn there; no one wanted to mine the glaciers of Mount Rainier or log the sheer cliffs of the Grand Canyon. The "worthless lands" argument often led park advocates to agree to boundaries gerrymandered around economically valuable forests eyed by timber interests, or simply to avoid proposing timbered lands altogether. Where parks were designated over industry objections (such as California's Kings Canyon National Park, which was coveted as a reservoir site by Central Valley irrigators), protection prevailed only because of the dogged efforts of the Sierra Club and allied groups. Such campaigns took decades.

When the great conservationist Aldo Leopold and fellow rangers called for protecting wilderness areas on the national forests in the 1920s and 1930s, they adapted the monumentalism and worthless lands arguments with success. The Forest Service's enthusiasm for Leopold's wilderness idea was, in fact, partly an attempt to head off the Park Service's raid on the more scenic chunks of the national forests. "Why transfer this land to the Park Service?" the Forest Service asked. "We have our own system to recognize and protect the crown jewels of American scenery!" Wilderness advocates also reiterated the *utilitarian* arguments used decades earlier for land protection. The Adirondack Forest Preserve in New York, for example, had been set aside to protect the watershed for booming New York City. The first forest reserves in the West had been established to protect watersheds above towns and agricultural regions. Such utilitarian arguments became standard for wilderness area advocacy in the twentieth century.

The most common argument for designating wilderness areas, though, touted their *recreational* values. Leopold, who railed against "Ford dust" in the backcountry, feared that growing automobile access to the national forests would supplant the pioneer skills of early foresters. "Wilderness areas are first of all a series of sanctuaries for the primitive arts of wilderness travel, especially canoeing and packing," said Leopold. He defined wilderness areas as scenic roadless areas suitable for pack trips of two weeks' duration without crossing a road. Bob Marshall in the 1930s elaborated on the recreation arguments. Wilderness areas were reservoirs of freedom and inspiration for those willing to hike the trails and climb the peaks. John Muir, of course, had used similar recreation arguments for the first national parks.

In the final analysis, most areas in the National Wilderness Preservation System and the National Park System were (and are) decreed because they had friends. Conservationists know that the way to protect an area is to develop a constituency for it. We create those advocates by getting them into the area. Members of a Sierra Club group or individual hikers discover a wild place on public land. They hike the trails, run the rivers, climb the peaks, camp near its lakes. They photograph the area and show slides to others to persuade them to write letters in its support. We backcountry recreationists fall in love with wild places that appeal to our sense of natural beauty. Conservationists also know the many political compromises made in establishing boundaries by chopping off areas coveted by industry for lumber, forage, minerals, oil and gas, irrigation water, and other natural resources—"worthless" lands coming back to haunt us.

The character of the National Wilderness Preservation and National Park Systems is formed by these monumental, worthless, utilitarian, and recreational arguments. Wilderness areas and national parks are generally scenic, have rough terrain that prevented easy resource exploitation or lack valuable natural resources (timber and minerals especially), and are popular for nonmotorized recreation.

So, in 1995, despite the protection of nearly 50 million acres of wilderness areas and about 30 million acres of national parks in the United States outside of Alaska, we see true wilderness—biological diversity with integrity—in precipitous decline. In 1992 the Wildlands Project cited some of these losses in its mission statement:

• Wide-ranging, large carnivores like the grizzly bear, gray wolf, mountain lion, lynx, wolverine, and jaguar have been exterminated from many parts of their pre-European settlement ranges and are in decline elsewhere.

• Populations of many songbirds are crashing.

• Waterfowl and shorebird populations are approaching record lows.

• Native forests have been extensively cleared and degraded, leaving only remnants of most forest types—such as the grand California redwoods and the low-elevation coniferous forests of the Pacific Northwest. Forest types with significant natural acreages, such as those of the Northern Rockies, face imminent destruction.

• Tallgrass and shortgrass prairies, once the habitats of the most spectacular large mammal concentrations on the continent, have been almost entirely converted to agriculture or other human uses.

It is important to note, however, that *ecological integrity* has always been at least a minor goal and secondary justification in wilderness area and national park advocacy. At the Sierra Club Biennial Wilderness Conferences from 1949 to 1973, scientists and others presented ecological arguments for wilderness preservation and discussed the scientific values of wilderness areas and national parks. In the 1920s and 1930s, the Ecological Society of America and the American Society of Mammalogists developed proposals for ecological reserves on the public lands. The eminent ecologist Victor Shelford was an early proponent of protected wildlands big enough to sustain populations of large carnivores.

Some of this country's greatest conservationists have been scientists, too. One of the many hats John Muir wore was that of a scientist. Aldo Leopold was a pioneer in the sciences of wildlife management and ecology, and he argued for wilderness areas as ecological baselines. Bob Marshall had a Ph.D. in plant physiology. Olaus Murie, longtime president of the Wilderness Society, was an early wildlife ecologist and one of the first to defend the wolf.

Moreover, not all national parks were protected primarily for their scenery. Mount McKinley National Park was set aside in 1917 not for its stunning mountain but as a wildlife reserve. Everglades National Park, finally established in 1947, was specifically protected as a wilderness ecosystem. Even the Forest Service used ecosystem representation to recommend areas for wilderness designation in the Second Roadless Area Review and Evaluation (RARE II) in 1977–79.

Somehow, though, professional biologists and advocates for wilderness preservation drifted apart—never far apart, but far enough so that the United States Forest Service lumped its wilderness program under the division of recreation.

That drifting apart was brought to an abrupt halt when the most important—and most depressing—scientific insight of the twentieth century was recognized. During the 1970s, field biologists had grown increasingly alarmed at population losses in myriad species and by the loss of ecosystems of all kinds around the world. Tropical rain forests were falling to saw and torch. Coral reefs were dying from god knows what. Ocean fish stocks were crashing. Elephants, rhinos, gorillas, tigers, and other charismatic megafauna were being slaughtered. Frogs every-where were vanishing. These staggering losses were in oceans and on the highest peaks; they were in deserts and in rivers, in tropical rain forests and arctic tundra alike.

A few scientists—like Michael Soulé, later a cofounder of the Society for Conservation Biology, and Harvard's famed entomologist E. O. Wilson—put these disturbing anecdotes and bits of data together. They knew, through studies of the fossil record, that in the 500 million years or so of terrestrial evolution there had been five great extinction events—the hard punctuations in the equilibrium. The last occurred 65 million years ago at the end of the Cretaceous when dinosaurs became extinct. Wilson and company calculated that the current rate of extinction was 1,000 to 10,000 times the background rate of extinction in the fossil record. That discovery hit with all the subtlety of an asteroid striking Earth:

RIGHT NOW, TODAY, LIFE FACES THE SIXTH GREAT EXTINCTION EVENT IN EARTH HISTORY.

The cause is just as disturbing: eating, manufacturing, traveling, warring, and breeding by 5.5 billion human beings.

The crisis we face is biological meltdown. Wilson warns that one-third of all species on Earth could become extinct in forty years. Soulé says that for all practical purposes "the evolution of new species of large vertebrates has come to a screeching halt."

That 1980 realization shook the daylights out of biology and conservation. Biology could no longer be removed from activism, if scientists wished their research subjects to survive. Conservation could no longer be about protecting outdoor museums and art galleries, and setting aside backpacking parks and open-air zoos. Biologists and conservationists began to understand that species can't be brought back from the brink of extinction one by one. Nature reserves have to protect entire ecosystems, guarding the flow and dance of evolution.

A new branch of applied biology was launched. Conservation biology, Michael Soulé declared, is a *crisis* discipline.

Conservation biologists immediately turned their attention to nature reserves. Why hadn't national parks, wilderness areas, and other reserves prevented the extinction crisis? How could reserves be better designed and managed in the future to protect biological diversity? Looking back, we see that four lines of scientific inquiry led to the sort of reserve design now proposed by the Wildlands Project and our allies.

Conservation biologists first drew on an obscure corner of population biology called *island biogeography* for insights. In the 1960s, E. O. Wilson and Robert MacArthur studied colonization and extinction rates in oceanic islands like the Hawaiian chain. They hoped to devise a mathematical formula for the number of species an island can hold, based on factors such as the island's size and its distance from mainland.

They also looked at continental islands. Oceanic islands have never been connected to the continents. Hawaii, for example, is a group of volcanic peaks rising from the sea floor. Any plants or animals had to get there from somewhere else. But continental islands, like Borneo or Vancouver or Ireland, were once part of nearby continents. When the glaciers melted 10,000 years ago and the sea level rose, these high spots were cut off from the rest of the continents and became islands. Over the years, continental islands invariably lose species of plants and animals that remain on their parent continents, a process called *relaxation*. On continental islands, island biogeographers tried to develop formulas for the rate of species loss and for future colonization, and to determine whether equilibrium would someday be reached.

Certain generalities jumped out at the researchers. The first species to vanish from continental islands are the big guys. Tigers. Elephants. Bears. The larger the island, the slower the rate at which species disappear. The farther an island is from the mainland, the more species it loses; the closer, the fewer. An isolated island loses more species than one in an archipelago.

In 1985, as Soulé, David Ehrenfeld, Jared Diamond, William Conway, Peter Brussard, and other top biologists were forming the Society for Conservation Biology, ecologist William Newmark looked at a map of the western United States and realized that its national parks were also islands. As the sea of development had swept over North America, national parks had become islands of natural habitat. Did island biogeography apply?

Newmark found that the smaller the national park and the more isolated it was from other wildlands, the more species it had lost. The first species to go had been the large, wide-ranging critters—gray wolf, grizzly bear, wolverine. Faunal relaxation had occurred, *and was still occurring.* Newmark predicted that all national parks would continue to lose species. Even Yellowstone National Park isn't big enough to maintain viable populations of all the large wide-ranging mammals. Only the complex of national parks in the Canadian Rockies is substantial enough to ensure their survival.

While Newmark was applying island biogeography to national parks, Reed Noss and Larry Harris at the University of Florida were using the *metapopulation* concept to design reserves for the Florida panther, an endangered subspecies, and the Florida black bear, a threatened subspecies. Metapopulations are populations of subpopulations. A small, isolated population of bears or panthers faces genetic and stochastic (random) threats. With few members of the population, inbreeding is likely, and this can lead to all kinds of genetic weirdness. Also, a small population is more vulnerable than a large one to local extinction (*winking out,* in ecological jargon). If the animals are isolated, their habitat can't be recolonized by members of the species from another population. But if habitats are connected so that animals can move between them—even as little as one horny adolescent every ten years— then inbreeding is usually avoided, and a habitat whose population winks out can be recolonized by dispersers from a nearby population.

Noss and Harris designed a nature reserve system for Florida consisting of core reserves surrounded by buffer zones and linked by habitat corridors. Florida had the fastest-growing population in the nation. When the Noss proposal, calling for 60 percent of Florida to be protected in such a nature reserve network, was published in 1985, it was considered . . . well, impractical. But over the past decade this visionary application of conservation biology has been refined by the state of Florida, and now state agencies and the Nature Conservancy are using the refinement to set priorities for land acquisition and protection of key areas.

In 1994 the Florida Game and Fresh Water Fish Commission

published a 239-page document, *Closing the Gaps in Florida's Wildlife Habitat Conservation System*. Using computer mapping technology, *Closing the Gaps* identified biodiversity hot spots for Florida. The study looked in detail at range occurrences and habitat needs for thirty-three sensitive species, from the Florida panther to the pine barrens treefrog, and at 25,000 known locations of rare plants, animals, and natural communities. Existing conservation lands in Florida cover 6.95 million acres. The hot spots—called Strategic Habitat Conservation Areas—encompass an additional 4.82 million acres. Once a new Ph.D.'s pie-in-the-sky, a conservation biology–based reserve system is now the master plan for land protection in Florida.

While metapopulation dynamics and island biogeography theory were being applied to nature reserve design, biologists were beginning to recognize the value of large carnivores to their ecosystems. Previously, scientists had tended to see wolves and wolverines and jaguars as relatively unimportant species perched on top of the food chain. They really didn't have that much influence on the overall functioning of the natural system, biologists thought. Until the 1930s, in fact, the National Park Service used guns, traps, and poison to exterminate gray wolves and mountain lions from Yellowstone and other parks (they succeeded with the wolf). Early in his career, even Aldo Leopold beat the drum for killing predators.

Today, biologists know that lions and bears and wolves are ecologically essential, in addition to being important for a sense of wildness in the landscape. For example, the eastern United States is overrun with white-tailed deer. Their predation on trees is preventing forest regeneration and altering species composition, according to University of Wisconsin botanists Don Waller, Steve Solheim, and William Alverson. If wolves and mountain lions were allowed to return, they would scatter deer from their concentrated wintering yards and reduce their numbers, thereby allowing the forest to return to more natural patterns of succession and species composition.

Large herds of elk are overgrazing Yellowstone National Park. Conservation biologists hope that the recent reintroduction of the gray wolf will control elk numbers and keep large herds from loafing in open grasslands.

Michael Soulé has shown that native songbirds survive in suburban San Diego canyons where coyotes remain; they disappear when coyotes disappear. Coyotes eat foxes and prowling house cats. Foxes and cats eat quail, cactus wrens, gnatcatchers, and their nestlings. Soulé calls this phenomenon of increasing midsized carnivores because of decreasing large carnivores *mesopredator release.*

In the East, David Wilcove, staff ecologist for the Environmental Defense Fund, has found that songbirds are victims of the extirpation of wolves and cougars. Neotropical migrant songbirds such as warblers, thrushes, and flycatchers winter in Central America and breed in the United States and Canada. The adverse effects of forest fragmentation on songbird populations are well documented; but Wilcove has suggested that songbird declines are partly due to the absence of large carnivores in the East. Cougars and gray wolves don't eat warblers or their eggs, but raccoons, foxes, and possums do, and the cougars and wolves eat these midsize predators. When the big guys were hunted out, the populations of the middling guys exploded—with dire results for the birds. Soulé's mesopredator release rears its ugly head again.

On the Great Plains, the tiny swift fox is endangered. Why? Because the wolf is gone. Swift foxes scavenged on wolf kills but wolves didn't bother their little cousins. Coyotes, however, eat swift foxes. Wolves eat coyotes. Get rid of the wolf and swift foxes don't have wolf kills to clean up, and abundant coyotes eat up the foxes.

John Terborgh of Duke University (in my mind the dean of tropical ecology) is currently studying the ecological effects of eliminating large carnivores from tropical forests. He tells us that large carnivores are major regulators of prey species numbers—the opposite of once-upon-a-time ecological orthodoxy. He has also found that the removal or population decline of large carnivores can alter plant species composition, particularly the balance between large- and small-seeded plants, due to increased plant predation by animals normally preyed upon by large carnivores.

In addition to being critical players in various eat-or-be-eaten schemes, large carnivores are valuable as *umbrella species.* Simply put, if enough habitat is protected to maintain viable populations of top predators like wolverines or harpy eagles, then most of the other species in the region will also be protected. Those that aren't, such as rare plants with very restricted habitats, can usually be protected with vest-pocket preserves of the old Nature Conservancy variety.

A final piece in conservation biology's big-picture puzzle is the importance of natural disturbances. Caribbean forests are adapted to periodic hurricanes. Many plant communities in North America evolved with wildfire. Floods are crucial to new trees sprouting in riparian forests. To be viable, habitats must be large enough to absorb major natural disturbances (types of *stochastic events,* in ecologist lingo). When Yellowstone burned in 1988, there was a great hue and cry over the imagined destruction; but ecologists tell us that the fire was natural and beneficial. Because Yellowstone National Park covers 2 million acres and is surrounded by several million acres more of national forest wilderness areas and roadless areas, the extensive fires affected only relatively small portions of the total reserve area.

Things didn't turn out so well when the Nature Conservancy's Cathedral Pines Preserve in Connecticut was hammered by tornadoes in 1989. In this tiny patch of remnant old-growth white pine forest (with some trees 150 feet tall), 70 percent of the trees were knocked flat, devastating the entire forest patch. Had the tornadoes ripped through an old-growth forest of hundreds of thousands of acres, they instead would have played a positive role by opening up small sections to new forest growth.

These four areas of recent ecological research—island biogeography, metapopulation theory, large carnivore ecology, and natural disturbance dynamics—are the foundation for the Wildlands Project. We used insights from these four fields to set our goals for protecting nature in a reserve network. For a conservation strategy to succeed, it must have clearly defined goals. These goals should be scientifically justifiable, and they should be visionary and idealistic. Reed Noss set out the four fundamental goals of the Wildlands Project in 1992:

1. Represent, in a system of protected areas, all native ecosystem types and seral stages across their natural range of variation and abundance.

2. Maintain viable populations of all native species in natural patterns of abundance and distribution.

3. Maintain ecological and evolutionary processes, such as disturbance regimes, hydrological processes, nutrient cycles, and biotic interactions, including predation.

4. Design and manage the system to be responsive to short-term and long-term environmental change and to maintain the evolutionary potential of lineages.

   With the criteria embodied in these goals, we can look closely at existing wilderness areas and national parks and answer our original question: Why has the world's greatest nature reserve system failed to prevent biological meltdown in the United States?

   As we have seen, wilderness areas and national parks are generally islands of wild habitat in a matrix of human-altered landscapes. By fragmenting wildlife habitat, we imperil species from grizzlies to warblers who need large, intact ecosystems. Because they have been chosen largely for their scenic and recreational values, and to minimize resource conflicts with extractive industries, wilderness areas and national parks are often "rock and ice"—high-elevation, arid, or rough areas that are beautiful and are popular for backpacking, but also are *relatively* unproductive habitats. For the most part, the richer deep forests, rolling grasslands, and fertile river valleys on which a disproportionate number of rare and endangered species depend have passed into private ownership or, if they are public, have been "released" for development and resource exploitation. To make matters worse, the elimination of large carnivores, suppression of natural fire, and live-stock grazing have degraded even the largest and most remote wilderness areas and national parks in the lower forty-eight states.

To achieve the Wildland Project's four reserve design goals, we must go beyond current national park, wildlife refuge, and wilderness area systems. Our ecological model for nature reserves consists of large wilderness cores, buffer zones, and biological corridors. The core wilderness areas would be strictly managed to protect and, where necessary, to restore native biological diversity and natural processes. Traditional wilderness recreation is entirely compatible, so long as ecological considerations come first. Biological corridors would provide secure routes between core reserves for the dispersal of wide-ranging species, for genetic exchange between populations, and for migration of plants and animals in response to climate change. Surrounding the core reserves, buffer zones would allow increasing levels of compatible human activity away from the cores. Active intervention or protective management, depending on the area, would aid in the restoration of extirpated species and natural conditions.

Admittedly, there has been some debate among scientists about reserve design. Some aspects of corridors have been criticized. Several "scientists" representing the anticonservation "wise use"/militia movement have misstated these controversies, ignoring the general consensus that has emerged among reputable scientists on all sides of these discussions.

This emerging consensus has been summarized in several forms. In 1990, with the Conservation Strategy for the Northern Spotted Owl, Jack Ward Thomas, later chief of the Forest Service, set forth five reserve design principles "widely accepted among specialists in the fields of ecology and conservation biology." In 1992 Reed Noss updated those five and added an important sixth principle:

1. Species well distributed across their native range are less susceptible to extinction than species confined to small portions of their range.

2. Large blocks of habitat containing large populations of a target species are superior to small blocks of habitat containing small populations.

3. Blocks of habitat close together are better than blocks far apart.

4. Habitat in contiguous blocks is better than fragmented habitat.

5. Interconnected blocks of habitat are better than isolated blocks; corridors or linkages function better when habitat within them resembles that preferred by target species.

6. Blocks of habitat that are roadless or otherwise inaccessible to humans are better than roaded and accessible habitat blocks.

Based on his studies of faunal extinctions in fragmented chaparral habitats in San Diego County, Michael Soulé summarized some reserve design principles in a very understandable way for us layfolk:

• Bigger is better.

• Single large is usually better than several small.

• Large native carnivores are better than no large carnivores.

• Intact habitat is better than artificially disturbed.

• Connected habitat is usually better than fragmented.

In a 1995 report for the World Wildlife Fund, *Maintaining Ecological Integrity in Representative Reserve Networks,* Noss added several more fundamental principles:

- Ecosystems are not only more complex than we think, but more complex than we *can* think.

- The less data or more uncertainty involved, the more conservative a conservation plan must be (i.e., the more protection it must offer).

- Natural is not an absolute, but a relative concept.

- In order to be comprehensive, biodiversity conservation must be concerned with multiple levels of biological organization and with many different spatial and temporal scales.

- Conservation biology is interdisciplinary, but biology must determine the bottom line (for instance, where conflicts with socioeconomic objectives occur).

- Conservation strategy must not treat all species as equal but must focus on species and habitats threatened by human activities.

- Ecosystem boundaries should be determined by reference to ecology, not politics.

- Because conservation value varies across a regional landscape, zoning is a useful approach to land-use planning and reserve network design.

- Ecosystem health and integrity depend on the maintenance of ecological processes.

- Human disturbances that mimic or simulate natural disturbances are less likely to threaten ecological integrity than are disturbances radically different from the natural regime.

- Ecosystem management requires cooperation among agencies and landowners and coordination of inventory, research, monitoring, and management activities.

- Management must be adaptive.

• Natural areas have a critical role to play as benchmarks or control areas for management experiments, and as refugia from which areas being restored can be recolonized by native species.

Now what? Where do we go with all this? Conservation biology has shown us the crisis we face (and it *is* a crisis despite the sugary "What, me worry?" attitude of eco-Pollyannas like Gregg Easterbrook); conservation biology has developed the theory supporting the protection of biological diversity; and conservation biology has set out a new model of how nature reserves should be designed. It is up to citizen conservationists to apply conservation biology to specific land-use decisions and wilderness area proposals. We have the political expertise, the love for the land, and the ability to mobilize support that an ambitious nature protection campaign demands.

There is wide agreement among conservation biologists that existing wilderness areas, national parks, and other federal and state reserves are the building blocks for an ecological reserve system. Inspired by Noss's and Soulé's work, conservationists in the U.S. Northern Rockies, led by the Alliance for the Wild Rockies, applied conservation biology principles there as early as 1990. Biologists like pioneer grizzly bear researcher John Craighead and conservationists like former Wilderness Society head Stewart Brandborg reckoned that if Yellowstone is not large enough to maintain viable populations of grizzlies and wolverines, then we need to link Yellowstone with the big wilderness areas of central Idaho, the Glacier National Park/Bob Marshall Wilderness complex in northern Montana, and on into Canada's Banff/Jasper National Park complex. Maintaining metapopulations of wide-ranging species means landscape connectivity must be protected throughout the entire Northern Rockies.

The Northern Rockies Ecosystem Protection Act (NREPA), which would designate 20 million acres of new wilderness areas in the United States and protect corridors between areas, has been introduced into Congress and drew over sixty cosponsors in 1994. Scores of grass-roots wilderness groups have helped advance the legislation. The Sierra Club was the first major national conservation organization to endorse NREPA. Passing this landmark legislation is one major step toward creating a Yellowstone to Yukon reserve system.

Other conservation groups are using conservation biology to develop alternative proposals for the next generation of national forest management plans. They are seeking to identify biological hot spots including habitat for sensitive species, remaining natural forest, and travel corridors for wide-ranging species. With such maps they will argue for expanding existing wilderness areas into ecologically rich habitats and for protecting wildlife linkages. In many areas roads need to be closed in sensitive ecosystems, once-present species like wolves and mountain lions reintroduced, and damaged watersheds restored. The Southern Rockies Ecosystem Project is coordinating several groups in a comprehensive conservation biology approach to new national forest plans in Colorado. The Southern Appalachian Forest Coalition is developing a conservation biology management strategy for all national forests in its region. These are good examples of regional coalitions working from conservation biology principles.

One of the central messages of conservation biology is that ecosystems and wildlife ranges do not follow political boundaries. Many nature reserves will need to cross international borders. The best application of this so far is in Central America, where a consortium of government agencies, scientists, and private groups is working with the Wildlife Conservation Society to link existing national parks and other reserves from Panama to Mexico's Yucatan. This proposed nature reserve network, called *Paseo Pantera* (Path of the Panther), would allow jaguars and mountain lions to move between core reserves throughout Central America. [It is now more often referred to as the Meso-American Biological Corridor.]

To the north, the Canadian Parks and Wilderness Society and

World Wildlife Fund Canada are incorporating conservation biology in their Endangered Spaces campaign throughout Canada. In every province and territory, scientists and activists are working to identify core reserves and connecting corridors based on the needs of large carnivores, biological hot spots, and "enduring features" on the land-scape. The Canadians are working with conservationists in Alaska and the northern part of the lower forty-eight states on cross-border reserves and linkages.

National U.S. conservation groups like the Sierra Club, the Wilderness Society, Defenders of Wildlife, World Wildlife Fund, and American Wildlands have been influenced by the Wildlands Project and are seeking to incorporate conservation biology into their work.

In fifteen years, conservation biology has wrought a revolution. The goal for nature reserves has moved beyond protecting scenery to protecting all nature—the diversity of genes, species, ecosystems, and natural processes. No longer are conservationists content with protecting remnant and isolated roadless areas; more and more biologists have come to agree with Reed Noss, who says, "Wilderness recovery, I firmly believe, is the most important task of our generation." Recycling, living more simply, and protecting human health through pollution control are all important. But it is only by encouraging wilderness recovery that we can learn humility and respect; that we can come home, at last. And that the grand dance of life will continue in all its beauty, integrity, and evolutionary potential.

FEATHERS AND FOSSILS
HAWAIIAN EXTINCTIONS AND MODERN CONSERVATION

LYANDA LYNN HAUPT *(1996)*

The textbooks render a terrific indictment of the Europeans' Hawaiian settlement. Captain Cook arrived with his entourage in 1778, we are told, surveying a pristine tropical landscape in which the native people had lived harmoniously for over a millennium. Norwegian rats, modern weaponry, and foreign diseases in tow, Cook and his mates proceeded to set up permanent European residence, destroy the native fauna, and lay waste the land. The Rousseauian bliss and spiritual-ecological balance that characterized the native culture were lost forever. It comes as a recent surprise (and a sore source of denial in much of Hawaii) that over half of Hawaii's endemic bird species went extinct at human hands *before* the arrival of a single European.

Since the late 1970s, avian paleontologist Helen James and her husband, Storrs Olson (ornithological curator at the Smithsonian), have been excavating fossil birds in Hawaii. Incredibly, they have unearthed at least fifty previously unknown species of birds that went extinct before the advent of "modern" ornithological record-keeping instituted upon Cook's arrival. Stratigraphy, radiocarbon dating, and archaeological associations place the majority of the extinctions within the last 1,500 years of the Recent geological epoch. Bones found in archaeological sites link the extinctions categorically to the time period of human presence. Despite the temptation to delve into the theoretical implications of their findings, Olson and James doggedly bent their effort toward the painstaking taxonomical tasks their work demanded. If any meaningful discussion was to emerge from their research, the fossils had to be described, categorized, numbered, and named.

This is not just more meaningless scientific data to litter the dusty annals of academe. On some level we *owe* these birds a name. We will never know the special behaviors, the flashes of brilliantly colored plumage, the songs and habits that meaningfully defined these animals. Having robbed them of their life histories, their continuation as both individuals and lineages, we must give these species some attention— justice demands it. At this point, taxonomic recognition may be the best we can do.

Olson and James established excavation sites on the islands of Oahu, Molokai, Kauai, Maui, and Hawaii. The locales were varied, including lava tubes, sinkholes, caverns, kitchen middens, and other archaeological sites. They uncovered an astonishing variety of extinct birds: a small petrel, nine flightless rails, three species of a new genus of long-legged owl, an accipiter hawk, a *Haliaeetus* eagle (same genus as the bald eagle), two large crows, and fifteen drepanidines (endemic Hawaiian "honeycreepers"—a subfamily of the finches). Among the more unusual finds were four strange species of flightless geese with oversized mandibles and thick, powerful hind limbs. Olson named them *moa-nolas*. They were evidently suited to the ecological role played by large tortoises on some other oceanic islands. Three flightless ibises were a surprise, as no endemic ibises from the islands were previously known.

In 1991 Olson and James published a slim ornithological monograph that catalogued the names and taxonomic details of the "new" species. I imagine other readers were overcome with the mixed emotions I experienced while poring over the technical descriptions that accompany the photographs of neatly arranged bones. Each thrill (an endemic *ibis!!!*) is tempered, and shaken. Knowledge of a bird's existence and of its extinction hit simultaneously.

Apropos of the academic monograph as a literary form, the

work gained a singular kind of popularity. It was certainly read by the country's small cadre of avian paleontologists. Other academic fossil-finders and interested ornithologists found their way to the monograph, as well. E. O. Wilson mentioned the work in his best-seller *The Diversity of Life*. But as knowledge of conservation issues in Hawaii continues to grow among biologists interested in the region, this amazing work on the Hawaiian fossils remains popularly unknown.

Conservation biologists and paleontologists live in different buildings. It is unsettling that academic compartmentalization can keep cloistered such keen lessons regarding animals that went extinct recently, under human impact, in *extant ecosystems*. As conservation biologists undertake a frenzied eleventh-hour census of the world's biota in order to apprehend what must be accomplished to preserve biodiversity, this work offers a broader perspective on ecological systems that long surpass present data-input techniques. Ecosystems are older than computer models. We can plug numbers into our mathematical models with great practical results; but nothing in the modern repertoire can rival the epochal field of ecological vision that these Hawaiian fossils give us. Their relevance for modern conservation cannot be overstated.

The Polynesians arrived in Hawaii somewhere around 400 A.D. They swiftly went to work setting up an island economy and culture based on agriculture and hunting. Notwithstanding its romanticized image, native Hawaiian society was based on a rigid caste system, replete with slavery and ritual human sacrifice. The flora and fauna were quickly transformed as the Polynesians planted their introduced crops, including coconut, sugarcane, sweet potatoes, bamboo, and gourds. Enormous tracts of land, mostly lowland scrub forest, were burned for conversion to agricultural purposes. Despite the pride with which most Hawaiians regard the ecological harmony achieved by their ancestors, the activities of the early Hawaiians led directly to the extinction of more than half of the endemic avifauna.

Outright overhunting is the most obvious explanation for the disappearance of many species. The flightless moa-nolas, ponderous of gait and unaccustomed to predators, were likely to have been easy meals. With them, the flightless ibises, rails, and burrow-nesting petrel were probably just too slow and too naive to escape the formidable and versatile predator *Homo sapiens.*

We can reasonably conjecture that the avian predators and scavengers in the Hawaiian Islands were hit by ecological domino effects after the arrival of humans. Their food base was wiped out. Though none of the avian meat eaters were large enough to carry off adult geese, the eagle and owls probably fed on the young of these species. The crows and the eagle scavenged their sizable adult corpses. Unlike continents, the tropical islands did not support a mammalian fauna, so big birds were what a large predator or scavenger had to eat. As the geese and rails disappeared, they took their ecological codependents with them.

Conversely, the rampant extinctions among the passerines (so-called "songbirds") cannot be explained by overhunting. Lacking BB guns, it is unlikely that the Polynesians stalked the forests in search of small birds, especially when they were obviously so well fed on goose. In the Passeriform order, the specialized drepanidines suffered most severely. The beaks of the Hawaiian drepanidines demonstrate a diversity, a monument to adaptive radiation, that would make Darwin's Galapagos finches look like evolutionary child's play. The array of slim, curved bills, perfectly coevolved to suit the native Hawaiian flora, has led ornithologists to believe that this subfamily is mainly nectarivorous, and to dub them the "honeycreepers." Surprisingly, the recent work shows many finchlike beaks—clearly suited to seeds and insects.

The cause of the pre-European extinctions in this group was probably outright habitat destruction, as the lowland forests were destroyed by burning for agricultural use. These birds had coevolved with specific plants and insects over the lengthy course of geological time. They were highly and specifically adapted. Most species could not simply "move" to the higher-elevation wet montane forests. Diaries from the Cook expedition lead us to believe that most of the scrub forest was wiped out before European arrival. This unique ecosystem survives only in remnants today.

Passerines of other species were decimated for the creation of ceremonial robes—sometimes as many as 80,000 individuals for a single garment—a practice that continued into the early 1900s, when the chiefs ran out of birds. The extent and ecological impact of this practice is unknown, but several species that went extinct during European settlement, such as the lusciously plumed o'os, had been used for these purposes. It is possible that their populations had dropped to barely viable numbers, and the further human impacts dealt the death knell.

The Norwegian rat, introduced by the Europeans, has fallen into rightful infamy. Its ubiquitous presence on most Pacific islands is blamed for the extinction of several vulnerable species, and its rampage contin- ues today. But the destructiveness of *Rattus norvegicus* to Hawaii's native fauna is directly rivaled by that of *Rattus exulans,* the Polynesian rat, which arrived 1,500 years earlier, on the boats of the first Hawaiians. Proliferating wildly in tropical conditions, the rat devoured the eggs and nestlings of the native birds. The endemic species were at particu- larly high risk, having evolved in a habitat that boasted no rats or species with similar niches, like the land crabs that inhabit some Pacific islands. The passerines and all ground-nesting birds (which probably included the *Haliaeetus* eagle) were at tremendous risk from rat predation.

In short, a sudden convulsion of human activity—overhunting, habitat conversion, and introduction of alien predators—rapidly deci- mated Hawaii's native avian fauna. At least fifty species of birds disap- peared in just a thousand years. This is many thousands of times the natural extinction rate.

The discovery of the fossils and their unique context offers strong support for Paul Martin's "Overkill Hypothesis" on Quaternary period extinctions (see Martin's "Last Entire Earth"). Martin's research pertains largely to the North American megafauna, which was likely overhunted into extinction during recent geological history. Martin favors a "blitzkrieg" model, in which human hunters wiped out the lumbering behemoths that populated this continent in a brief, several-thousand-year period. The model continues to be hotly debated, rivaled by climatic models for the mass Quaternary extinctions.

It is easy to imagine a first-order "blitzkrieg" in Hawaii, as the early settlers stumbled over the literal sitting ducks that meant easy dinners. By itself, a "blitzkrieg" cannot accommodate the complex factors that contributed to the Hawaiian extinctions, but Martin's model is more subtle than the military metaphor suggests. *Overkill* has come to be an umbrella term, encompassing the variety of human activities that together led to the decimation of nonhuman species.

Recent epoch extinctions in Hawaii undermine the climatic model. At odds with that model is the preponderance of flightless bird fossils. Clearly, the number of flightless species that evolved in insular habitats demonstrates the advantage of this adaptation in environments lacking predators of large birds. This character evolved over geological time, during which climatic oscillations were often tremendous. Yet half the extinctions are of flightless birds. Scientists know of nothing in the minor climatic upheavals of the Recent epoch that could have selected specifically against flightlessness. The same argument applies to the proportionately high number of endemic extinctions. Add the fact that all of these birds survived the relatively tumultuous climatic conditions of the preceding Pleistocene epoch, and the climatic model loses almost all credibility. A broad version of overkill, on the other hand, explains all of these factors.

Recent overkill extinctions offer commentary on present models for conservation. To begin, we need to expand the temporal framework in which we consider the ecology of species. Our view of the

Hawaiian avifauna was skewed by differential extinction. The loss of all but one raptor (an endemic buteo, the Hawaiian hawk) led us to imagine an avifauna that evolved without any predation at all. Now we know there were several large predacious birds. We imagined a simple lower-elevation ecosystem, with most radiation of the avifauna occurring in wet montane forests. We have learned from recent studies of remnants that the lowland scrub forest contained more species of trees than the complex montane systems and supported its own avifauna, now lost forever. We have learned that the drepanidines, an important group in Hawaiian ecology, had habits and diets surpassing the imagination of modern ornithology. Changes in our understanding of native flora have grown around these discoveries. When we consider modern species in the freeze-frame of the present, we may miss an evolutionary foundation that has tremendous relevance for conservation efforts. Species and populations do not exist in a static present.

E. O. Wilson, Murray Gell-Mann, and other prominent scientists are advocating a global biotic census. While this might be timely and important, it is also politically naive and *late*. Obviously, conservation of biodiversity cannot wait for twenty years of data collection. In this light, it is amazing that we are overlooking a veritable blueprint for conservation at our fingertips. The Hawaiian work does not stand alone. Similar paleontological projects in New Zealand, the Chathams, New Caledonia, Madagascar, Fiji, St. Helena, the West Indies, and other Pacific islands yield similar results. Though the contexts differ somewhat, the impacts of overhunting, introduced predators, and habitat conversion have led to incredible avian extinction levels in the past 2,000 years.

Most ecological experiments are short-term. They involve small areas and few species. They are bound to fall short of the needs of applied ecology, which addresses systems over years—systems that have evolved over *epochs*. A conservationist's eye on the Hawaiian fossils will reveal descriptive correlations that span geological time and may be even more useful than the complex analysis of modern models. The parallel understanding of conservation biologists and paleontologists can be twined for a deeper approach to modern conservation.

The fossil record teaches that the same kinds of species consistently show special vulnerability to rapid extinction. Large flightless species are the most easily hunted. Often they fill the role claimed by high-order mammals on mainland, and their slow reproductive rates make them all the more susceptible to extinction.

Endemic species of insular systems are always at high risk. They are likely to have coevolved within a specific balanced ecosystem, and any alteration can have extreme repercussions. When land-based predators are absent from an island, the endemic birds have not evolved protection from them, so the sudden introduction of such predators is especially deadly. Introduced diseases, particularly when they are accompanied by a vector such as mosquitoes or domestic chickens (as is the case in post-European Hawaii), can wipe out endemic populations, utterly unprepared for such impacts. Flightlessness, endemism, insular habitats, forest-type dependence, and lack of land-based predators are flagship characteristics of vulnerable bird species, revealed clearly in the recent fossil record—knowledge that can be put to immediate use in conservation strategies.

The relevance of this record is stressed by the modern list of threatened, endangered, or extinct species. The human impacts that killed over half the endemic Hawaiian birds are *the same ones* that imperil the modern avifauna in Hawaii and on the North American continent.

Of the 1,000 bird species known to be at risk of global extinction, 90 percent are threatened primarily by forest destruction and introduced predators. At least 9 percent are endangered by overhunting, and 2 percent by the wild bird trade. Kirtland's warbler is threatened by conversion of its specific habitat. The clapper rail is endangered by earlier hunting and introduced predators. Masked bobwhite: depletion of habitat by nonnative agricultural species. Least Bell's vireo: destruction of riparian woodlands. Nihoa millerbird: introduction of rats, disease, and exotic plants. Sharp-tailed grouse: conversion of grasslands to agriculture, overhunting. Trumpeter swan: agricultural conversion. And the extinct birds once numbering in the millions or billions—the passenger pigeon, heath hen, great auk? Overhunting of these multitudes in combination with habitat destruction spelled their doom. Other methods of imperilment, such as pesticide use and lead-shot poisoning, are modern incarnations of the same ills.

The fossil record offers further commentary on cornerstone theories, such as island biogeography. In their seminal paper of 1963, MacArthur and Wilson present a model of insular zoogeography in which species equilibrium is based on the area and isolation of an island. The bigger and less isolated the island, the more species it can support. When the Hawaiian islands are examined in light of the newly understood extinctions, this theory, at least in the classic MacArthur and Wilsonian sense, doesn't seem to hold up. The island of Hawaii, with an area of 4,037 square miles, supported twenty-six species of endemic land birds—twenty-three known from the fossil record and three known historically. Molokai is only 261 square miles yet supported thirty species (twenty-one fossil, nine historical). The other islands show a similar disinterest in species-area correlations. Of course, not all the evidence is in. No one is near ready to claim that all fossil species endemic to these islands have been discovered. The work on the island of Hawaii thus far has been relatively meager, and a more complete future census may support a species-area curve. These numbers do not call us to make a final declaration regarding island biogeography. Rather, they remind us to assess *all factors* that contribute to species' vulnerability—insularity and area being just two of many.

Several scientists are overcome with caution. They argue that it is reckless to extrapolate from certain situations (like prehistoric Hawaii and fossil birds) to others (like modern Hawaii, North America, the continental tropics, and living birds). But when the forces at work line up so perfectly, it is much more reckless *not* to extrapolate. Why take precious time to relearn, to redocument what we already know?

The tropics are being burned, the cattle loosed, the ducks shot, as environmental policy makers scratch their heads, seek more data, and wonder whether the creatures will be able to take it. The fossil record answers with a resounding *no*. We don't have to wait and see what the impacts will be; we've been shown. The experiments were performed before us. The data are there for the taking. Yes, we must proceed with the census, reveal what may be lost, and accomplish everything possible to conserve it. But at the same time, let's look to the fossil record and *use* the teaching on biodiversity we already have. Overlay the future upon a *deep* comprehension of the past, and the creatures that have gone before, and we may finally practice the restraint necessary to accommodate other species.

SOURCES

Berger, A. 1971. *Hawaiian Birdlife.* Honolulu: University Press of Hawaii.

Cassels, R. 1984. Faunal extinction and prehistoric man in New Zealand and the Pacific Islands. In *Quaternary Extinctions: A Prehistoric Revolution,* ed. P. Martin and R. Klein. Tucson: University of Arizona Press.

Diamond, J. 1984. Historic extinction: A rosetta stone for understanding prehistoric extinctions. In *Quaternary Extinctions: A Prehistoric Revolution,* ed. P. Martin and R. Klein. Tucson: University of Arizona Press.

Diamond, J. 1991. Twilight of Hawaiian birds. *Nature* 353(6344): 505–6.

Ehrlich, P., D. Dobkin, and D. Wheye. 1992. *Birds in Jeopardy: The Imperiled and Extinct Birds of the United States and Canada, Including Hawaii and Puerto Rico.* Stanford, Calif.: Stanford University Press.

Furness, R., and J. Greenwood. 1993. *Birds as Monitors of Environmental Change.* London: Chapman and Hall.

MacArthur, R., and E. O. Wilson. 1963. An equilibrium theory of insular zoo-geography. *Evolution* 17: 373–87.

Martin, P. 1992. The last entire earth. *Wild Earth* 2(4): 29–32.

Martin, P., and P. Steadman. 1984. Extinction of birds in the late Pleistocene of North America. In *Quaternary Extinctions: A Prehistoric Revolution,* ed. P. Martin and R. Klein. Tucson: University of Arizona Press.

Olson, S., and H. James. 1982. Fossil birds from the Hawaiian Islands: Evidence for wholesale extinction by man before western contact. *Science* 217(4560): 633–35.

Olson, S., and H. James. 1984. The role of Polynesians in the extinction of the avifauna of the Hawaiian Islands. In *Quaternary Extinctions: A Prehistoric Revolution,* ed. P. Martin and R. Klein. Tucson: University of Arizona Press.

Olson, S., and H. James. 1991. Descriptions of 32 new species of birds from the Hawaiian Islands. *Ornithological Monographs* 45 and 46.

Pratt, D., et al. 1987. *The Birds of Hawaii and the Tropical Pacific.* Princeton, N.J.: Princeton University Press.

Rands, M., and M. Kelsey. 1994. Call to action. *American Birds* 48(1): 36–48.

Ward, P. 1994. *The End of Evolution.* New York: Bantam.

Wilson, E. O. 1992. *The Diversity of Life.* New York: Norton.

The Great Denial
PUNCTURING PRONATALIST MYTHS

Sandy Irvine *(1997)*

A remarkable feature of human population growth is the abundance of people who deny that human numbers count. Across the spectrum of public opinion, there is near unanimity that the notion of overpopulation is either a silly fantasy dreamed up by a few ecofreaks or a temporary phenomenon, affecting only a few places in the Third World, and one that will dissipate of its own accord. In the latter case, incantation of the phrase "demographic transition" is usually thought sufficient to dispel the specter.

Examples abound of the mental and moral affliction that might best be christened the Overpopulation Denial Syndrome (ODS). At the time of the first Earth Day in 1970, for example, there was considerable concern about population increase, partly due to the writings of ecologist Paul Ehrlich. Since then, the global population has shot up by 1.6 billion people (a 43 percent increase), yet on Earth Day 1990 there was virtual silence on the subject.

The 1992 Earth Summit largely ignored population problems. Friends of the Earth, Greenpeace, and most mainstream environmental organizations hardly address the issue. The political parties, "green" ones included, are silent. None of the green lifestyle guides mention overpopulation, even though giving birth to children is the most significant environmental choice any couple makes.

Beyond silence or ambivalence lie the antiabortion groups, the progrowth economists, the right-wing "libertarians," and the like, who militantly deny the problem. The right-wing economist Julian Simon, with his view that humans are the ultimate resource, argues that in the longer run, "additional people lead to less pollution." And there are religious baby boomers. The opposition of the Catholic Church (or, rather, powerful groupings within it) to "artificial" birth control is well known, but other religions—including the Mormons, Orthodox Zionists, Rastafarians, and Muslims—share its commitment to procreation.

Unfortunately, these folk are not alone in their delusions. The scientist and former U.S. presidential candidate Barry Commoner argues that "it is a totally spurious idea to claim that rising population anywhere in the world is responsible for the deteriorating environment" (*Utne Reader,* January 1988). Many social ecologists, ecofeminists, and liberation ecologists now focus on "reproductive rights," arguing that a woman should have complete freedom to choose how many children she has (rather than concentrating upon, say, the provision of free contraception and sex education). The left-wing world development magazine *New Internationalist* even argues that "with population due to stabilize at *merely* twice the current numbers, there would appear to be little cause for concern" (October 1987, emphasis added). Third World charities like Oxfam vociferously denounce those who dare to suggest that population growth might be a factor in the rising level of human misery across Africa, Asia, and Latin America.

Many ecofeminists share this stance. The Women's Environment Network in the United Kingdom circulated a pamphlet that discusses the "myth of overpopulation." Some go further. Farida Akher's *Depopulating Bangladesh* even suggests that there is a sinister plot by family planners to depopulate the country. Ynestra King similarly claims that "overpopulation is a hoax by wealthy, privileged white males" (*Utne Reader,* January 1988). *Whose Common Future?,* a special issue of the leading green journal *The Ecologist* published in 1992, implied that overpopulation was a myth promulgated by technocrats (needless to say, white and male ones).

Add to the ranks of the pronatalists the many governments

around the world that actively promote population growth. In 1988, for example, the Quebec government offered a $500 premium for the first child, $1,000 for the second, and $4,500 thereafter; there was a 6 percent increase in the number of babies born in 1989. In Zimbabwe, which experienced one of the highest population growth rates in the world after independence, the government's health minister attacked family planning as a "white colonialist plot" to limit black power.

Sometimes population growth takes the form of a demographic race, as in the case of Israel trying to squeeze in as many Jews as possible in order to keep pace with the rapidly growing population of Arabs within and around its borders. At other times, stabilized or even falling birth rates are perceived as a sign of national weakness, a fear that often takes the form of warnings about an aging population. Occasionally individuals or groups take up the campaign. In the Czech Republic, for example, there is an anonymously financed billboard campaign urging Czechs to produce more children. It depicts, erroneously, the composer Bach with twenty male children.

ODS sufferers cross the political spectrum: Marxists, social democrats, conservatives, and liberals share the same basic faith in industrial growth. They may quarrel bitterly about the best means— collective planning versus private enterprise, for example—but at their core lies the same vision of technoindustrial progress, and the same hostility to the thesis of overpopulation.

MISCONCEPTIONS

The delusions of ODS sufferers are sustained by a rich diversity of false assumptions and non sequiturs. These misconceptions about population problems pop up in everyday conversation, are recycled by commentators and analysts in the mass media, and make regular appearances in learned textbooks.

Some of the popular fallacies and half-truths underlying the syndrome are based on bad ecology and a failure to take the mathematics of the situation seriously. Others stem from a focus on only part of the picture—birth rates but not death rates, for example. Sometimes, blind optimism leads people to treat decreases in population growth *rates* as if they were actual decreases in population *levels*. The following ten myths are pernicious in that they do contain a measure of truth. The pronatalist lobby uses these snippets of truth to conceal or deny more important truths.

Myth 1: Affluence is the answer.

The classic myth, argued by social scientists and many others, is that the population problem will solve itself as a result of economic and social changes collectively known as the "demographic transition." This theory suggests that as people become healthier and wealthier they will parent fewer children. This, it is argued, explains the decrease in family size in Europe over the past two hundred years. Poverty begets large families, they argue. Affluence, it is said, is the best contraceptive.

No matter how popular and pervasive the theory, it is still a simplistic, one-sided view of reality, building unrealistic hopes of a demographic "happy ending." The global environment simply could not supply the volume of resources nor assimilate the attendant pollution required to generalize the level of affluence characteristic of materially richer countries. For example, if the world's population rises to 11 billion before stabilizing, as predicted, and if each person were to live like today's North Americans, almost half of our twenty-four key minerals would be exhausted within thirty-five years. Environmental degradation and pollution would rise to catastrophic levels.

The same story repeats itself at the level of individual countries. Average annual income in Ethiopia today is $120; at a 3 percent growth rate, it would take sixty years to raise it to $700 per annum, by which time there wouldn't be a crumb of fertile soil left in the country as a result of population pressure in the meantime. Contrary to the demographic transition theory, family planning is beginning to succeed in poor countries like Bangladesh, even though there has been no general rise in affluence.

Furthermore, the postwar baby boom took place during an unprecedented increase in per capita consumption, when parents could afford more children. A switch to smaller families took place later—as opportunities for easily accessible education, careers, and wealth decreased. In Britain, a decrease in family size was more pronounced among working-class than among more affluent middle-class couples in recent decades.

More generally, there are no automatic links. In Sri Lanka, average per capita income is about $400 and average family size is 2.5 children. In Libya, average per capita income is much higher—over $3,000 per annum—yet most women have more than five children. In recent decades, France has gone from nongrowing to a growing demographic situation. In Sweden, too, there are signs of a return to larger families.

Contrary to the demographic transition theory, extremely affluent individuals often parent more children than those lower on the economic ladder. Britain's Queen Elizabeth is apparently the richest woman in the world, but she and Prince Philip ignored the demographic theory and conceived four children. The late corporate raider Sir James Goldsmith was one of the world's richest men . . . and father of eight children.

Finally, in the short period of two generations, improved health and income in countries such as India and Turkey has led to faster population growth. It may level off, but in the meantime, it will have quadrupled the size of these countries' populations, and therefore quadrupled every problem they face. As Garrett Hardin and other scientists have shown, increased supply of resources tends to be converted into a larger population. In the 1950s, for example, land redistribution in Turkey (in itself a good thing) encouraged formerly landless peasants to increase significantly the size of their families. Among African Sahel pastoralists, deep-water wells drilled by donor countries in the 1950s and 1960s prompted larger herds of cattle and goats, earlier marriage (because bride-prices were paid in animals and the required number became easier to accumulate), and, thereby, higher fertility. But disaster soon followed because the basic ecological constraints of the region had not changed.

Myth 2: Affluence is the problem.

A popular way of evading or denying the population problem is to blame the world's woes on overconsumption by the richer sections of global society. It is certainly true that the small segment of the world's population in the overdeveloped industrial states consumes a grossly large slice of the world's resources, and therefore has a disproportionate impact on the global environment and economy. However, this simply demonstrates that such countries are overpopulated and, using the metaphor of cancer, even more cancerous than less profligate nations. This reality does not alter another fact, namely, that most other people aspire to the level of affluence of that minority.

Furthermore, the not-so-affluent already are creating unsustainable impacts that most figures underestimate because official statistics like the gross national product record quantifiable data, especially monetary transactions. The not-so-affluent often function on the edges of, or outside of, the formal economy; their activities go underrecorded. The biggest cause of deforestation, for example, is the cumulative impact of small-scale nibbling at forests by settlers and peasant farmers. Most data, however, report the impacts of the timber trade, dam construction, cattle ranching projects, and other aspects of the formal economy. Often myths surround these issues, especially the exaggerated "hamburger" connection to deforestation (an observation not intended to let the burger barons off the hook).

Myth 3: Country X has a high population density but it isn't starving.

Pronatalists often point to densely populated but nonetheless affluent countries like the Netherlands or Britain, and sometimes to newly rich localities such as Singapore, arguing that population density does not produce ruin. Yet the populations of such places can survive only by exploiting the resources of other lands, both as "wells" of raw materials and as "sinks" to dispose of their wastes and excess peoples. If not for the new worlds of the Americas and Australia, the population of the United Kingdom would have reached 70 million by 1900.

The density argument is in fact rather dense, overlooking the fact that the resource base drawn upon often does not coincide with the political boundaries of a given population. The British, Dutch, and other such peoples escape poverty and starvation largely because they use "ghost" acres and fisheries beyond their borders as well as draw down the natural capital (soil fertility, naturally regenerating forests, healthy fish stocks, etc.) that responsible people would leave intact for their successors. Furthermore, they have eliminated both the richness and the diversity of flora and fauna once characteristic of their lands for expanded agriculture and housing. These societies' ecological footprints, or rather bootprints, are huge, both geographically and temporally, and hugely unsustainable.

Myth 4: Malthus got it wrong, so neo-Malthusians are wrong.

The Reverend Thomas Malthus was the father of modern fears about population growth exceeding resource supply. The population-induced starvation he predicted did not happen, for he did not foresee refrigeration and other technological developments that make possible long-distance food shipments from colonized lands.

Malthus did get a number of things right, though. From his analysis of population and food resources, for example, he predicted that over the next 200 years human numbers would not grow to more than seven and a half times that of his own time, the 1800s. The actual increase was some five and a half times the population of 1800, a remarkably accurate prediction for someone widely reviled for getting his sums wrong. His real triumph, however, was to recognize that our species is just as dependent upon Earth's biogeophysical systems as any other species, an insight many people still fail to heed.

Myth 5: There are more than enough resources to go around.

Among "progressive" folk, including major pressure groups and charities, it is an article of faith that the real problem is *misallocation* of resources. The world obviously is a very unfair place, with the comparative few hogging most of the world's resources. To an extent, the proposed solution—redistribution of land, food, and other resources—can buy vital breathing space.

Yet an equitable distribution of available resources does not make the population problem disappear. Ongoing expansion, be it in human numbers or per capita consumption, must eat up the benefits from any sharing of wealth. Studies in Guatemala, for example, show that the benefits of land redistribution would disappear within a generation simply because of population growth and increased demand for land. Even in the frequently praised Indian state of Kerala, where there has been genuine social progress and the growth rate of the state's population has been cut to 1.7 percent, the population will still double on that basis in just forty-seven years. In other words, the population-resource crunch would reappear within half a century.

Part of this myth is the notion that since resource prices haven't risen as rapidly as predicted (and even have fallen in some cases), there is no need to worry about resource availability in the future. However, the environmental crisis is not simply a shortage in the near future of specific resources, though already there are growing conflicts over water rights and certain minerals in some regions. In the short term, greater efficiency and the substitution of more abundant resources for scarcer ones are likely to keep factories running.

Prices only reflect the interaction of buyers and sellers in a given market. Timber may sell for a pittance, but its low price doesn't mean that forests are abundant and healthy. Our economic system ignores the preferences of those without spending power, those yet to be born, and those physically unable to join the bidding (spotted owls are not known for their intervention in the timber market). This system also discounts many intangibles, things on which no price can be put: a stable climate, an intact ozone layer, water retention on forested slopes, the existence of species that cannot be eaten or otherwise directly used, human health, and so on. Economists may try to put "shadow" prices on such priceless assets, but normally the exercise is an absurdity. In short, trends in energy, food, and mineral prices are no sure guide to future prospects. Basic geology and ecology give better guidance. Furthermore, one day geologically finite and nonrenewable resources must run out or become too expensive to tap; we are now "mining" supplies of freshwater, fish, fertile soil, and forests to such an extent that we are likely to exhaust them long before we run short of coal.

A more formidable resource barrier is the depletion that would result from attempts to spread across all countries the lifestyles prevalent in affluent regions like western Europe. If the rest of Asia, for example, were to achieve the same ratio of cars to people as Japan (which is not high compared to America), the number of cars in the world would double. Yet the planet is already choking on present traffic levels. To give China the same number of computers per head as in the United States in 1993 would require some 315 million more machines. Yet even now, computerization is causing many serious ecological problems, such as water pollution around circuit board plants.

The fundamental ecological problem is not short-term scarcity but the degradation resulting from resource extraction, processing, manufacture, consumption, and disposal of goods and services. Our concern about coal, for example, should not be the size of untapped deposits but the consequences of continuing to burn them on anything like the current scale.

Earth's crust may contain large quantities of useful minerals. The crunch would come from attempting to tap them. Mineral processing usually consumes vast amounts of energy and water while producing equally enormous amounts of pollution. The extraction and processing of currently worked deposits is already causing great damage to soil, water, wildlife, and human health around the world, and such damage will only worsen as miners attempt to exploit less-accessible and poorer-grade sources. The production of one ton of copper from an open pit site, not a deep mine, creates over 500 tons of waste. Annual world production of gold and silver produces some 900 million tons of rock waste. The annual fueling of a typical nuclear reactor with uranium requires 100,000 tons of rock to be brought to the surface, most of which is dumped as waste tailings, where 90 percent of the original radioactivity in the rock remains. In the main, the horrific damage to nature is not the product of mismanagement but the inevitable entropic by-product of energy and material throughput in the human economy.

Myth 6: If waste were eliminated, there would be adequate resources for every-one's needs.

This is an extension of myth #5. People rightly point to the colossal waste of resources on war and preparation for war, among many other follies. If the energy and raw materials squandered on such destructive activities were diverted to socially useful things such as food production and health care, the argument goes, there would be enough for everyone's needs.

Again, there is much truth in this argument yet it contains a deadly fallacy. It thoroughly muddles the ecological and thermodynamic accounts. For example, although health spending is doubtless more beneficial to the human good than arms expenditure, building ambulances clocks up the same debts in nature's accounts as building tanks. Similarly, ecological processes do not distinguish between fertilizer spread on golf courses and that used on farmland.

It might be added that the term *needs* often goes undefined. One person's luxury is another's necessity. Different people have their eyes on that same military budget as the means to resolve the health care crisis, to fund more education, boost the arts, abolish homelessness, eradicate poverty, and so on.

Myth 7: Putting food production first can cure hunger.

A close cousin of the Redistribution Fallacy is the belief that there is more than enough food to feed everyone if only the cake were cut evenly. This argument is powerful and pervasive, with high-profile advocates such as Frances Moore Lappé. They argue that hunger could be eradicated and any danger from overpopulation dispelled if land were devoted, first and foremost, to food cultivation. Some go further and argue that much more food would be available if meat consumption were to be reduced. They correctly note that the more conversions a foodstuff undergoes (grains fed to cows, for example), the more energy is lost, en route, to the dinner table.

Again, this argument touches a responsive chord. Its influence is aided by the sight of food surpluses being burned and otherwise dumped simply to maintain market prices. Many people rightly find it obscene that good farmland is being used to satisfy the indulgences of the rich while, nearby, people starve. Countries such as Britain and the United States have neither need nor right to use "ghost acres" in the poorer countries to supply themselves with exotic fruits and vegetables, cut flowers, or downright dangerous substances like tobacco and opium.

The Food First argument is persuasive but erroneous. It wrongly takes for granted current levels of food production. High-output agriculture is fast undermining its very foundations via soil impoverishment and erosion, aquifer depletion, dependence on chemical inputs, and other unsustainable impacts with which it is inescapably linked. The needed adoption of organic and other less destructive farming methods will initially reduce yields, since fewer inputs (synthetic fertilizers, for example) must mean lower output, at least until soil fertility can be restored.

The Food First argument also ignores the likely diminishment of future food supplies due to increased pollution and ultraviolet radiation and climatic disruptions associated with global warming. With global warming, a rise in sea levels may engulf some of the world's most productive cropland.

Current, let alone projected, increases in population make even a basic diet for everyone a difficult target. The official goal of the Chinese government is to raise annual egg consumption per person from 100 to 200. Soon there will be 1.3 billion Chinese. Assuming that a hen can lay 200 eggs a year, that goal would require 1.3 billion additional birds. Feeding them would require more than the total grain output of Australia.

Moreover, land devoted to cultivation of any crop (staple or luxury) produced conventionally or organically means fewer natural forests, wetlands, and other wildlife habitats. China's Hunan Forestry Research Institute estimates, for example, that the country's annual growth rate of 28 million additional people leads to the destruction of 1 to 1.4 million hectares of forest annually. Such habitat conversion is disastrous for biodiversity, of course; but in the long run, it is also bad news for people, since wild or comparatively unmodified ecosystems are vital to a healthy Earth, the prerequisite of all human activity—agriculture included.

Myth 8: More people means more workers and more production.

This myth has taken many forms. One manifestation was Marx's Labor Theory of value. More recently, Julian Simon has revived it as the theory of People as the Ultimate Resource. The underlying fallacy remains the same, however. The simple fact of life on Earth is that humans do not create wealth. They transform what is made available by Earth's biogeochemical systems and by external solar energy. Humankind depends on green plants for the process of photosynthesis. The wastes inevitably created by human activities are not eliminated by people but are reabsorbed by those same ecological systems. There are geological, thermodynamic, and ecological limits to all stages of what we arrogantly call wealth creation and those limits are now being transgressed. More people only increase those transgressions.

This "extra hands" myth also confuses what might be true at an individual or household level, especially in the short term, with overall gains and losses, especially in the long term. A family of farmers might gain from an extra worker in the fields. However, this additional pair of hands might lead to increased forest clearance, the grazing of more cattle and goats, or intensified tillage, which, on balance, will lead to greater soil erosion as well as fewer resources for nonhuman species.

Myth 9: Technological innovation makes population growth irrelevant.

A pervasive fallacy is the assumption that science and technology have exempted humans from the influences and constraints to which other species are subject. Virtually all problems are soluble, it says, mostly by technological innovation. The nineteenth-century radical writer Friedrich Engels, for instance, did not hesitate to claim that the progress of science "is just as limitless and at least as rapid as that of population. . . . We are forever secure from the fear of overpopulation." This myth was more recently popularized by the American biologist and socialist Barry Commoner in his book *The Closing Circle*.

While some people see technology as salvation, others perceive it—or the forms it has taken—to be a source and an amplifier of our ecological problems. Think of technomonsters like nuclear power, ozone-depleting and cancer-causing chemicals such as CFCs and PCBs, or mundane technologies like cars and computers, and contemplate the vast disruptions to the natural world they have wrought.

Reformers will tout increased efficiency and appropriate technology but fail to recognize that all technologies have an environmental impact, so a rising population with the same per capita consumption must eventually cancel out the benefits of more resource-efficient and less-polluting technologies. The potential for technological reform is usually grossly exaggerated. Many studies of life-cycle, cradle-to-grave impacts of different goods—virgin/recycled, "natural"/synthetic, nonrenewable/renewable—have shown that the differences are not as great as commonly supposed. Pollution control does not make pollution go away: it just changes pollutants from one form, place, or time to another, perhaps making them safer but often at the expense of increased energy consumption. Pollution is simply the by-product of energy and material conversions and processing, so ultimately it too is related to population levels. Moreover, the impacts of a growing human population are not limited to the depletion of finite resources or the generation of pollutants. Also important is general environmental degradation (soil erosion, deforestation, wetland drainage, hydrological disruption, introduction of exotic species, and so on), for which pollution filters and the like provide no cure.

Myth 10: Reproductive rights are the most basic of freedoms.

The very mention of population policy spotlights one last myth employed by pronatalists—namely, that freedom to reproduce is the most fundamental of rights. The United Nations Universal Declaration of Human Rights assumes that the individual has an unqualified right to parent as many offspring as desired. In many countries, this has been socially underwritten, with welfare benefits not limited to, say, the first two children.

Yet rights are not abstractions, divorced from contexts and consequences. *Rights have real meaning only if the conditions in which they are exercised can be sustained.* Otherwise, they are just license to create ruin for everyone. With regard to procreation, the failure to adopt reasonable goals and policies has opened a dangerous chasm between power (to reproduce as well as to move and settle freely) and responsibility (to control family size and to avoid overcrowded areas).

The pretense to a right to reproduce without limits is an arrogant presumption. In effect, it makes unlimited claims on this and future generations of people, on other species, and on Earth's natural habitats and processes without their consent. Furthermore, an open-ended right to reproduce in a finite, interconnected world can only mean the reduction of other rights. Freedom in a finite world is not indivisible. In other words, there are many other liberties, most of which decrease as human numbers increase.

For instance, the democratic "weight" of each voter goes down as the number of voters in an electorate goes up. Or, to take a more fanciful example, if everyone in the United Kingdom exercised the "right" to go to the coast on the same hot summer day, each would enjoy ten centimeters of seaside. (Of course, they would not get there because of the traffic gridlock their numbers would cause.) The trade-off between population and liberty can be seen most clearly in cities, where all kinds of planning controls and other restrictions are necessary simply because so many people are packed together.

With extreme examples of population limitation measures such as China's one-child policy, it should be remembered that however distasteful they might be, and no matter how odious the possible side effects (female infanticide, for example), the alternative—mass starvation and social breakdown—would be far worse. It should be noted as well that if China had encouraged family planning much earlier (instead of denouncing it as an imperialist trick, as happened under Mao), there would have been no need for such drastic steps.

PROGROWTH PREJUDICE

Though it is possible to refute with reason every delusion experienced by sufferers of Overpopulation Denial Syndrome, unfortunately we are arguing with deeply held beliefs, not evidence. Assertions that Earth's life-support systems cannot sustain current (let alone projected) human population levels run counter to the core, often unspoken articles of faith of modern society. Ours is a civilization addicted to the notion that unlimited growth is both possible and desirable. As American biologist Garrett Hardin puts it, "growth, change, development, spending, [and] rapid turnover [are] viewed as goods without limits." Such ideas have been all-pervading in modern times. The futurist Herman Kahn, coauthor of the study *The Next Two Hundred Years* (1976) had no doubts that endless growth was possible and that, in 2176, people would be "numerous, rich and in control of the forces of nature."

Such notions of progress and human potential have at their heart a virulent individualism. Egotistical gratification is central in contemporary culture. Symptomatic is the rhetoric about personal choice that is invoked by all kinds of individuals and groups from the gun lobby to supermarkets that defend their sale of environmentally unfriendly products on the grounds that it is a matter of consumer choice. Correspondingly, there is a pathological hostility to anything that threatens the right to do one's own thing. No threat cuts to the quick more than the idea that individuals are subject to ecological constraints, since it affects every space of our being and none more so than reproductive preferences. The right to parent without limit—aided by technology if necessary—is deemed to be an inalienable personal right that, it is widely believed, only ecofascists could question.

A CULTURE OF DENIAL

There are other reasons why so many people refuse to countenance the ecological case, including the decay in general awareness and understanding. But perhaps the most significant reason for human blinkeredness was originally christened by Garrett Hardin as the Tragedy of the Commons (though perhaps a better name might be the Tragedy of Commonplace Decisions). People generally discount the effects of their own individual choices and actions on the common welfare: "I'm just one person. What difference does my car, computer, child, etc. make?" Most people do not actively seek to create a world overflowing with humankind. Nor is there some sinister organization, a global

Pro–People Hive, brainwashing and otherwise manipulating people into producing more offspring. Population growth is the product of myriad single, everyday actions whose result is childbirth, planned or otherwise.

Whatever the motivation, whatever the circumstances, the result is the same: more people. In the next three days, the net increase in human numbers will be enough to fill a city the size of San Francisco. Each year there's another Mexico of mouths to feed and in nine years' time another India. Yet few people see that the gestation of the macrocosm—overpopulation—takes place in the microcosm of individual procreation.

At this writing, there are roughly 5.9 billion people in the world. Some 7 to 8 percent of all humans ever born are alive today. More humans have been added to the total world population in the past forty years than in the previous 3 million years. In the year 2000, there will be over 1.5 billion women of childbearing age, the highest number in all history. And it is probable that such figures are underestimates.

It is no wonder that we are called the human race. There is overwhelming evidence that we must reverse these trends if the Earth is to retain its capacity to sustain both our lives and those of the thousands of other species now threatened with extinction. Population limitation policies will benefit women whose health is threatened, opportunities restricted, and rights violated by all the economic, social, and cultural pressures to produce more offspring. Similarly, unemployment, homelessness, traffic congestion, demands on education and welfare services, ethnic rivalries, urban sprawl, rural land use conflicts, resource depletion, pollution, wildlife destruction . . . all these problems and more would be less severe and more solvable if human numbers were not so great. To paraphrase Paul and Anne Ehrlich, whatever your cause, it will be a lost cause without, first, the stabilization and then reduction of human numbers.

SOURCES

Briggs, V. 1992. Despair behind the riots: The impediment of mass immigration to Los Angeles blacks. *Carrying Capacity Network Bulletin* 10: 3–4.

Catton, W. R. 1980. *Overshoot: The Ecological Basis of Revolutionary Change.* Urbana: University of Illinois Press.

Catton, W. R. 1993. Can irrupting man remain human? *Focus* 3(2): 19–25.

Crosby, A. 1986. *Ecological Imperialism: The Biological Expansion of Europe, 900–1900.* New York: Cambridge University Press.

Ehrlich, P., and A. H. Ehrlich. 1990. *The Population Explosion.* New York: Simon & Schuster.

Estrada, R. 1993. The impact of immigration on Hispanic-Americans. *Focus* 3(2): 26–30.

Galle, O. R., et al. 1972. Population density and pathology: What are the relations for man? *Science* 176: 23–30.

Grant, L., ed. 1992. *Elephants in the Volkswagen.* New York: W. H. Freeman.

Hardin, Garrett. 1993. *Living within Limits: Ecology, Economics, and Population Taboos.* New York: Oxford University Press.

Kyllonen, R. L. 1967. Crime rates versus population density in United States cities: A model. *General Systems* 12: 137–45.

McGraw, E. 1984. *Population Misconceptions.* London: Population Concern.

McGraw, E. 1990. *Population: The Human Race.* Detroit: Bishopsgate Press.

Wisniewski, R. L. 1980. Carrying capacity: Understanding our biological limitations. *Humboldt Journal of Social Relations* 7(2): 55–70.

Nulliparity and a Cruel Hoax Revisited

Stephanie Mills *(1997)*

A while back at my weekly women's meeting, I sat among friends. One woman, lacking child care, had brought her new baby daughter. While Mom ventilated the emotional strains she was experiencing as a single parent, baby Felicia captured every heart in the room. Most of the women could barely restrain themselves from snatching her out of the arms of whoever was cuddling her at the moment. It was a sweet, primal disturbance of our adult conversation. Then another woman, a tough-minded news hen and something of a jock, spoke of the pangs she felt putting her youngest child on the school bus for the first time and wept.

Clearly, mother love is a force of nature, easily trumping mere reason. Dave Brower used to say that you couldn't reason prejudice out of a person because it didn't get in that way. Reason is a pip-squeak, the melting tip of the iceberg of mentality. Which kind of makes me wonder why, back in 1969, I was so sure that I could and would get through my natural female life without becoming a mother.

I became a notorious nonmother when I shocked the media and my classmates at our graduation ceremonies with a commencement address titled "The Future Is a Cruel Hoax." I declared that given the seriousness of all the ecocatastrophes then gaining momentum, "the most humane thing for me to do would be to have no children at all." An amazing amount of uproar ensued, but my gesture manifestly didn't launch a mass anti–mass movement—not if all the baby-having going on around me, or the absence of overpopulation as a subject of concern in the public mind, is any indication.

While I consider myself to be a staunch feminist, the largest system about which I can care is not womankind or humankind but Earth's evolutionary processes. Because it's axiomatic that wilderness preservation, restoration, and expansion are the minimum conditions necessary for these processes to continue, my ultimate loyalty is to the wild.

Ecocentric, biocentric, animist, alone in a world of wounds—strange is the lot of those who chance into the deep-ecological mind-set, who believe that "our community" means the ecosystem, watershed, bioregion, biome, continent, planet, all our relations; that every living thing is as important as any person; that they all could get along fine without *Homo sapiens* but not us without them. It's humbling and troubling; makes one feel like a grinch and superfluous all at once.

Population is, let's face it, a horrible issue. It's quantitative, parsing the richness and pathos of human life on Earth in incomprehensibly large numbers. It's an observable reality, but because exponential growth is not a sudden event, overpopulation remains somehow below the threshold of being perceived as catastrophic. As Garrett Hardin observed, "Nobody ever dies of overpopulation."

Here in northwest lower Michigan our pretty rural landscape—never mind the howling wilderness—is dying of overpopulation. Perhaps it's progress that nobody around here is in favor of just plain growth anymore. They want the sustainable kind. I'm about the only person I ever hear wishing that people would quit having children. And because it really is an offensive thing to say, I do so only rarely.

In my community, baby-having and child-rearing automatically justify all manner of hyperconsumption, from the use of disposable diapers to acquisition of a family van, to trips to Disney World and a succession of pairs of hundred-dollar sneakers. In the utterly atomized nuclear family, "parenting" seems to have become a major job of work, for mothers, mostly, and therefore warrants such indulgence. Whereas among those unselfconscious, backward ecosystem peoples we hear that babies weren't the individual's or couple's property, privilege, or sole responsibility. There were fewer, happier, less fashionable babies (and slicks of baby poop on the cave floor, probably). I have found that not having children is a great time-saver and an easy way to shrink one's ecological footprint. In conjunction with authorhood, a notoriously unremunerative calling, nonmotherhood has kept my ecological footprint positively dainty.

In an interconnected world, the decision to bear a child isn't only a personal matter, nor does it pertain only to one's moment. Won't even the wanted, cared-for children feel betrayed to discover (assuming that such thoughts are still thinkable in the future) that previous generations ignored the problem of overpopulation and dodged the difficult choices in favor of a comfortable, conventional existence whose price included migratory songbirds, large mammals, old-growth forests, and polar ice shelves?

I bite my tongue a lot. I don't want to risk alienating my friends, or nowadays their daughters, by arguing against their childbearing, except in the obliquest ways. Regardless of which birth it is, first, second, or third, I wind up congratulating new parents, especially mothers, warmly. At that point the horse is out of the barn. New parents have plenty of crap to deal with, even without a population bomber's disapproval, and children need and deserve to feel welcome once they're here.

As I push my grocery cart down supermarket aisles of sugar-frosted fiber puffs, overlit thoroughfares gridlocked with parents often rudely and sometimes abusively attempting to appease or curb the advertising-inculcated desires of their TV-transmogrified kids, I find myself wishing that it were somehow possible to get my fellow Americans to be at least as thoughtful and caring about these children they've already had as they are about their cars.

In my youth I came across a women's magazine interview with illustrious nonmom Katharine Hepburn. In it Hepburn said she didn't think she could be as good as she wanted to be at being an actress and a mother both, so she felt she had to choose between them. Fortunately for film fans, she went with acting. It struck me as eminently reasonable—that one should assess oneself and one's society realistically, then make a considered decision about the likeliest way to spend one's life.

Thus when women of my cohort and younger bewail the difficulty of combining motherhood and a career, or how hopeless it is to get their husbands (if said husbands are still around) to take on some responsibility for doing the wash or schlepping the kids around, I have to bite my tongue pritnear off. I'm sure that parenthood is exhausting. I agree totally that in contemporary circumstances the gender-based division of labor grossly exploits women. But I have to wonder whether these women imagined that the revolution would be accomplished before the end of their pregnancy.

People refuse to believe that the rules apply to us, that human beings are subject to biological constraints. The reasons for this exceptionalism are various—theological, ideological, technotopian. Me, I'm a Rules Girl. And minus human exceptionalism, things are looking grim.

As the most hard-nosed population biologists have been patiently pointing out all along, if we do not address overpopulation by using birth control, nature will deal with it by overriding death control. Given global climate change, sprawling megacities, declining nutrition, assaults on our immune systems, drug-resistant pathogens, and, with GATT (the General Agreement on Tariffs and Trade, an instrument of economic globalization), the prospects of no impediments to the worldwide movement of agricultural commodities and their hitchhiking pests, to say nothing of the possibility of rogue bugs bolting from germ warfare or genetic engineering labs, an awful lot of epidemics may be in store. The current opinion seems to be that death itself should be curable and whenever it befalls, it's a tragedy. When the myth that modern medicine has conquered or should be able to cure infectious disease is shattered, we will have a lot of philosophical maturing to do.

"Fear of individual death and grief," wrote Gregory Bateson, "propose[s] that it would be 'good' to eliminate epidemic disease and only after 100 years of preventive medicine do we discover that the population is overgrown" ("Time Is Out of Joint" in *Mind and Nature: A Necessary Unity*). These days, as forensic anthropology attempts to probe our deep past, some say that the growth of human population has steadily driven the series of technological changes—extinction of Pleistocene megafauna, thus hunting and gathering, then agriculture, and civilization, industrialization, and imperialism—now approaching apogee. Thus checking epidemic disease is only the most recent factor in the long, lurching history of our species' expansion. However, Bateson's insight that "fear of individual death and grief" is a driving force of our disproportion with the rest of life illuminates the core dilemma of overpopulation. Among individual human beings, birth brings joy and death brings sorrow. Forgoing children and suffering natural death will always be very tough to sell, given the abstract, almost absent nature of the rewards for such an ethic.

I've got a friend in her seventies who's dying of cancer. She's been relentlessly introspective, inquisitive, and iconoclastic for the decade of our friendship and is facing her demise right in character. When I asked her, What is the meaning of life?, her answer was, more or less: It's no big deal. She intends no argument for living carelessly, but it's an interesting summation of a life of self-examination, spiritual exploration, artistic creativity, philanthropy, and humanism. Not nihilism, but liberation into a detached, nonanthropocentric relation to the cosmos. Fine for her, but what about those of us left to mourn her?

It's going to take some pretty heavy philosophizing to get the human race to consciously check its will to love and will to live.

If a lot more women—say 90 percent—would follow my sterling example of nulliparity it would unravel the biological family, seed-syllable of human culture, and make for a wrenching, possibly disastrous discontinuity for our kind. Yet the need to contain, restrain, and minimize our species vis-à-vis more-than-human-nature is extreme. Earth's in a highly unnatural state of affairs. Can we be unnatural enough to regain our just proportion to all the rest of life? Which is the greater distortion of human essence—not to reproduce, or to live in a completely anthropogenic environment, every terrain dominated and depleted by the human species?

Deep down inside, population is nothing if not a women's issue. Personally, I wish that billions of women would just say no to motherhood and set up Amazon republics instead. All men have to do then is take their matters into their own hands. Of course it would be marvelous if ecocentric men would organize "snip-ins"—mass vasectomy festivals. To reinforce and reward this behavior, urologists could tattoo a beauty mark on the vasectomee's face above the beard line once he's flunked the sperm test. Kind of an antithesis to the semiotics of the wedding ring.

Once birth control and abortion are universally and freely available and the various pronatalist policies tucked away in the tax code have been abolished, but artfully, so that children don't wind up deprived as a result, propaganda might be the one acceptable means of civic action available to deal with overpopulation: an all-out attempt to change public opinion about reproductive behavior. And I'm not talking about a "stop at two" or even "one is plenty" campaign, but "Don't Do It!" There needs to be a steep decline in human numbers. Our last chance for it to be volitional rather than apocalyptic is for the vast majority of people now on Earth not to reproduce.

The trouble with propaganda for nonparenthood is that it has tended to be tacky and materialistic, dissing children and gushing about all the fun you can have (read money to spend) if you're not buying magnetic alphabets for your refrigerator door. Economic calculus has yet to vanquish the drive for procreation. For just about everyone but the Amish, children are a major expense, noncontributors to the household economy. Still *Homo economicus* keeps on making babies. I would like to think that this means that our hearts are still flesh, even if everything else about us is bent by economism.

Of course, if the idea of persuading people not to reproduce is too heartless and objectionable, another way to attack the problem would be to promote, even insist on BreathAirianism. BreathAirianism is drawing your sustenance from breath alone. Although to date its most prominent practitioners have been unmasked as fakers, not fakirs, given to gobbling candy bars off-camera, genuine BreathAirianism might be a way to dodge the birth control bullet. OK—no more gloomy talk about overpopulation. Have all the children you want, just nobody eat anything. Or go outside.

Philanthropy and National Parks
AN AMERICAN TRADITION

Robin W. Winks *(1998)*

There are 385 units of the National Park System of the United States, and it is likely that some portion of every one is the result of private philanthropy. Whether the nucleus of an entire national park (as at Virgin Islands National Park on St. John) or the contents of a major interpretive center (as at Pecos National Historical Park) were a gift to the nation by a private individual or individuals, the art of giving to create or expand the parks, and through them benefit the American people and American wildlife, was well developed and widely practiced until after World War II. This is not so much the case now, and one wonders why. It may also be that there is a resurgent interest in wildlands philanthropy these days, though largely from foundations rather than individuals. While public support and funding for protection of natural areas will continue to be fundamental, private conservation efforts are a necessary complement; without philanthropy, the national parks will not thrive.

The general public tends to believe that national parks consist of lands purchased by the United States government in places where a federal agency—the National Park Service—set out consciously to preserve a landscape, to protect a natural resource, to commemorate a historical event. This is far from the truth, even though some parks have been created in just this way. Parks are the product of a political process, and that process often gets its start from the dream of one person, or a small group of people, who put their minds, their energies, their time, and often their money into making a park happen.

Many people know the story of how John D. Rockefeller Jr. quietly bought up much of the ranching land in Jackson Hole, Wyoming, and then gave it to the National Park Service to form the glorious forefront to the present Grand Teton National Park. Fewer realize that large parts of the lands along the Blue Ridge Parkway or in Great Smoky Mountains National Park are the result of private gifts. Fewer still recognize that key collections at interpretive centers grew from timely donations of either money or the collections themselves. Even fewer, perhaps, understand that the gift of time—of countless hours writing to members of Congress, helping to build shelters and maintain trails, organizing meetings of park supporters—is a significant act of philanthropy of untold value.

There should be a systematic study of the role of philanthropy for the parks. We should know more about why individual giving has declined, and how foundations and corporate bodies have contributed to the shape of the National Park System. We need to recognize more fully that while the parks belong to the people, they often are also the products of the people.

Is it foolish to imagine a meeting between the five richest individuals in the United States, each wealthy beyond imagination, in which each pledges $200 million to protect and preserve, to help set right, our decaying and underfunded National Park System? Philanthropy is built on dreams, of those who give and those who receive; of course, it is also built on tax codes and hardheaded judgments about the future. Surely, though, we can rediscover the importance of philanthropy to the health of the nation's national parks and encourage, more systematically and imaginatively than we do now, private giving to support them. Indeed, what better choice could any philanthropist make than to invest in this intellectually rich and elegant embodiment of how our nation perceives and celebrates its goals, its achievements, and its natural and cultural heritage?

BEAR NECESSITIES
GRIZZLIES, WILDERNESS, AND THE SCIENCE
OF EXTINCTION

LOUISA WILLCOX *(1998)*

The survival of the grizzly and the wolf in the U.S. Northern Rockies
is no accident. Without extensive wildlands—public and private—and
relatively low numbers of people, large carnivores such as grizzlies and
wolves would be discussed here as they are in most of their former
range: in the past tense. Since the mid-1970s the Endangered Species
Act (ESA) has also buttressed the survival of grizzlies and wolves by
prohibiting their killing, trapping, and harassment. As scientists learn
more about how and why sensitive species such as the grizzly bear become extirpated, it becomes increasingly clear that the need for secure
habitat is fundamental, and the scientific arguments for an expanded
wilderness system deepen. So too does the case for a much more comprehensive program of ecosystem protection, for even if every acre
of potential wilderness were protected in the Northern Rockies, the
grizzly populations here could still "wink out" due to conflicts on adjacent public and private lands.

   This article will focus on what science tells us about the needs
of the grizzly—the most telling barometer of the health of Northern
Rockies ecosystems—and will revisit the essential role of wilderness in
grizzly recovery. It will also highlight how the Wilderness Act of 1964,
which created our National Wilderness Preservation System, is limited
in the complex arena of endangered species recovery. Other complementary tools will be necessary to ensure a sound future for this icon
of the American West and the wildland ecosystems that it represents.

Although the scientific data and literature on *Ursus arctos horribilis* stand as tall as a grizzly on hind legs, the relevant findings boil down to two simple concepts: bears need protection from people who would harass and kill them, and they need secure habitat to forage, den, and reproduce successfully. It is important to note that grizzlies come into the world with formidable biological strikes against them: a low reproductive rate (the slowest in North America after the musk ox), small litter sizes (two per litter is average), and a palate similar to ours (with a memory and nose far keener), which can bring bears into conflicts with humans in the course of seeking human food. Furthermore, grizzly cubs require a long rearing period with mom (two to three years), which is essential for a bear to learn how to live within a particular ecological landscape. And whereas male bears often disperse great distances, females typically do not, setting up home territories next to or within the range of their mothers. Thus, unlike wolves, bears cannot easily recolonize formerly occupied ecosystems hundreds of miles away.

Additionally, the bear has some major public relations challenges to overcome: although exceedingly few people have been hurt or killed by a grizzly, fear runs deep. (For example, out of the 47 million people who have visited Yellowstone National Park in the past twenty-five years, .00001 percent were injured by bears.) In contrast to encounters with other wildlife (even other carnivores), human conflicts—and even high rates of human contact—with grizzlies regularly result in dead bears.

With so many strikes against them, grizzlies (like some inner-city youth) tend to die young and not of natural causes. Areas where bears survive in the lower forty-eight states are characterized by expansive wild country and few people—places where grizzlies can avoid frequent human contact. A recent study of historical data on grizzly extirpations shows that the bear's persistence correlates with western mountainous areas covering roughly 4 million or more acres of wild lands, configured geographically in a round rather than elongated shape. With less habitat than that, grizzly populations have tended to disappear.

Within grizzly territory, habitat quality varies dramatically: the best places for bears, such as valley bottoms and riparian areas, are where we humans typically have chosen to settle. The more foods are spread out geographically (by natural or human causes), the bigger the table needs to be in order for the grizzly to win the caloric race against winter. Furthermore, nature's meals are not on the same table from year to year. In Yellowstone, for example, where the amount of key high-fat foods such as whitebark pine nuts and army cutworm moths fluctuates enormously, grizzlies respond by redistributing themselves from year to year. This natural variability in foods and their scattered distribution helps to explain why the home range sizes of Yellowstone grizzly bears are the largest in the lower forty-eight states (an average of 900 square miles for males and 350 square miles for females).

This also helps to explain why in years when several essential food supplies crash, grizzly bear mortality rates skyrocket. For example, when whitebark pine and cutworm moths went bust in 1995, seventeen bears (out of a total population of a few hundred animals) died at human hands as they sought foods at lower elevations, in closer proximity to people. These facts underscore the importance of developing a system of land protection that provides secure habitat and foraging alternatives when key food sources fail.

Several studies have attempted to quantify grizzly security needs. In the South Fork of the Flathead National Forest near Glacier National Park, researchers Rick Mace and Tim Manley showed that a female grizzly needs nearly 70 percent of her home range in security condition (that is, "wilderness" or "roadless with no motorized vehicle use"). Similar studies in Yellowstone show slightly higher needs for secure habitat—most likely due to the drier, more open nature of the country as well as greater variability of natural foods. Furthermore, studies by members of the Interagency Grizzly Bear Study Team (IGBST) in Yellowstone indicate that a grizzly bear needs roughly 5,000 to 7,000 acres of secure foraging habitat, and that these areas need to be linked across the landscape to enable a bear to get from one to another without a high probability of bumping into people or human developments.

In addition to showing the need for core security habitat, these and other studies in Canada, Alaska, and northern Montana have demonstrated the link between roads and grizzly mortality levels. Several studies have quantified the probability of people and bears colliding (and bears dying) with an increased number of roads and motorized vehicle use. Using different methodologies, studies in Yellowstone and the South Fork of the Flathead have pointed to the need for total open road densities below one mile per square mile in order for females to survive. Refining the analysis to account for topographic variability and forest cover, the IGBST found that for bear habitat to be secure, road densities should be as low as .26 mile per square mile in the flat, overcut plateau area of the Targhee National Forest, where ten miles of clear-cuts define the border of Yellowstone National Park.

These studies have underpinned efforts to improve road management for grizzly recovery on the Flathead, Gallatin, Targhee, and other national forests in the region. It should be noted that these studies would not have been used effectively or completely by land managing agencies were it not for litigation under the Endangered Species Act brought by Earthjustice Legal Defense Fund on behalf of conservation organizations.

Studies considering road impacts on elk and wolves show similar results, but the grizzly is more sensitive to roads than any other species studied in the Northern Rockies. (Wolverines are perhaps even more sensitive to roads and human presence but have been little studied.)

Thus the road closure and obliteration and restoration efforts brought about through grizzly conservation work have greatly benefited other wildlife, including fish—and the health of the ecosystem as a whole.

It is clear that the more wild habitat in an ecosystem, and the fewer roads and people, the better are the prospects for grizzly bears (and other sensitive species) to survive and successfully reproduce. The scientific evidence reinforces conservation efforts for the expansion of wilderness areas and wildlands networks such as would be created by passage of the Northern Rockies Ecosystem Protection Act.

But this is not the end of the story.

WILDERNESS: ONE TOOL IN THE CHEST

Protecting remaining roadless areas as wilderness is vital to the Great Bear. This will not be enough, however. Grizzly bear research has also pointed out the limitations of wilderness as a tool for bear conservation.

1. Designation of areas as wilderness does not address threats to bears within wilderness, particularly sheepherders and, in some areas, elk hunters and recreationists.

Although grizzlies and domestic sheep are a lethal mix, wilderness designation does nothing to restrict livestock grazing, recreation, or hunting—or human behavior generally—even if they are detrimental to protection of imperiled species. Viewing sheep as an irresistible delicacy, a grizzly in sheep country rarely escapes herders' guns. Conflicts with elk hunters can have similar results, as grizzlies learn to track gunshots in search of gut piles. Since 1975, more than fifty bears have died as a result of conflicts with sheepherders and elk hunters.

Efforts to remove sheep allotments in grizzly country have been successful on the Gallatin and Targhee National Forests; however, domestic sheep grazing (in designated wilderness in the Wind River Mountains, for example) will continue to limit the expansion of grizzly bears into areas needed for recovery. Elk hunter conflicts are far worse in the Greater Yellowstone area than in any other lower-forty-eight grizzly ecosystem—even in some designated wilderness lands and lands under special management for wilderness values.

Although administrative protection of the Yellowstone back-country as a de facto wilderness did not prompt the Park Service to prohibit overnight camping in a number of critical bear areas, the grizzly's biological needs did. The Park Service's decision in the mid 1980s to implement a policy that does not allow overnight use in certain areas used heavily by grizzlies is considered by many experts to be a primary reason why the animal has survived in that ecosystem to this day. This decision was based on biological considerations and not on wilderness values per se.

2. Wilderness designation does nothing to limit human uses and development on adjacent public lands.

In the wake of the unsuccessful 1972 Parker case, which argued for "buffer zones" near Colorado's Eagle's Nest Wilderness, the term *buffer zone* has become a dirty word, and the notion of using the Wilderness Act to limit development on adjacent public lands has been abandoned like a bear den in the spring. Still, the location of key foods and habitat on lands adjacent to existing wilderness means that certain protections (such as road restrictions) must be instituted—even though these lands may not be suited for wilderness designation. The failure to do so on the Targhee National Forest abutting 2.1 million acres of wildland in Yellowstone Park resulted in massive road building and clear-cutting from the late 1960s to 1993, which in turn caused extirpation of resident grizzly bears in two bear management units on the forest (a bear management unit roughly corresponds to a female bear's home range). The core habitat protected inside Yellowstone Park was not enough to compensate for the severe impacts and prevent the loss of grizzlies on a portion of the Targhee.

In 1993 conservationists successfully sued the Targhee National Forest under the Endangered Species Act, forcing an eleven-year moratorium on clear-cutting and a road closure and obliteration program designed to restore habitat for bears, elk, and other species. It should be noted that the Wilderness Act could not have forced such restoration efforts, which were vital to making the park wilderness ecologically "whole" again.

3. Wilderness designation is limited to public lands.

In recent years scientists have noted the increasingly important role of habitat on private lands for grizzly recovery. Bear scientists and population biologists have stated repeatedly that the continued isolation of several hundred animals, such as in Yellowstone, will lead to a high risk of extinction in the long term.

Questions about how to expand grizzly bear populations within ecosystems and how to link ecosystems together (and ultimately to Canadian populations) have been addressed by several studies, including one recently completed by biologists Lance Craighead and Rich Walker. Craighead and Walker found that the best potential linkages between Yellowstone and Glacier ecosystems would be composed largely of private lands. This study underscores the need for expanding the role of land trusts involved in volunteer easement protection for private lands, as well as economic incentives for private land protection and planning at the county level. With human population growth proceeding at a runaway pace in the Northern Rockies—especially around Yellowstone and Glacier—these studies point to the urgent need for identifying and protecting key private lands within and between ecosystems. Without maintenance of important private lands as functional habitat, the grizzly bear might not survive.

4. Wilderness designation is limited to the United States only, and has no influence over the management of adjacent lands in Canada.

Four of the five remaining grizzly bear ecosystems in the lower forty-eight states straddle the Canadian border. Despite evidence of severe habitat loss and high grizzly mortality north of the forty-ninth parallel, the U.S. Fish and Wildlife Service unwisely continues to rely on an influx of Canadian bears to bolster grizzly recovery. Unfortunately, wilderness designation on U.S. lands that abut the forty-ninth parallel does nothing to influence Canadian land-use policy. In addition, Canada has no Wilderness Act, no Endangered Species Act, and no road standards that apply to grizzly bear habitat—even though many of the original studies on roads and grizzlies were conducted there. As Canadian grizzly expert Stephen Herrero says, "Don't count on Alberta saving the grizzly bears for America—it's likely to be the other way around."

5. The Wilderness Act does not account for distant and indirect impacts on habitat quality even within wilderness areas.

Habitat quality for grizzlies and other species is greatly influenced by forces outside wilderness boundaries. For example, the introduction of white pine blister rust disease, a Eurasian exotic, virtually wiped out whitebark pine from the Glacier and Selway-Bitterroot ecosystems. The disease is spreading in the Yellowstone ecosystem as well, with 11 percent of the whitebark pine study transects now infected by blister rust. Trees are dying in the Beartooth Mountains, the southeast part of Yellowstone Park, and northern portions of the Tetons, lowering the quality of habitat inside wilderness.

Moreover, climate experts predict that rising global temperatures could prevent whitebark pines from growing in the higher-elevation areas where they now occur. Should this happen, the grizzly would have to redistribute itself to lower elevations in closer proximity to humans—a recipe for high mortality of bears and occasional injury to people. In addition, there is uncertainty about the location and security of the army cutworm moth's wintering farmland habitat. In the current debate about wilderness, such uncertainties and their implications in terms of habitat quality are almost never considered.

TIME FOR NEW BEAR CONSERVATION STRATEGIES

Clearly, the science calls upon us to expand land protection using designated wilderness and a variety of other appropriate tools. And we have made some significant headway: Wilderness legislation passed in 1984 for Wyoming gave protection to several hundred thousand acres of current and potential grizzly habitat, including important lower-elevation areas in the Shoshone National Forest. The ESA litigation described earlier has forced the Forest Service to incorporate better science into road management policy and has spurred restoration activities on several national forests. Effective public campaigns created the political will necessary to stop oil and gas leasing on several hundred thousand acres of important habitat on the Rocky Mountain Front near Glacier National Park and to prevent the development of a proposed gold mine near Yellowstone Park. Furthermore, legislation to consolidate public lands on the Gallatin National Forest will make it easier to manage grizzly bear habitat as a coherent whole and to designate this area as wilderness. Also, recent funding granted under the Land and Water Conservation Fund has made it possible to purchase critical parcels such as portions of the Church Universal and Triumphant's Royal Teton Ranch near Yellowstone Park's northern boundary.

Ultimately, though, a more comprehensive approach to protecting whole ecosystems will be necessary, using mechanisms not yet invented. Increasingly, scientists are calling for integrating existing data on single species into a broader multispecies context. They are asking for risk assessments to be included in the analysis of population viability management activities on imperiled species, and they are calling for broadening our understanding of cumulative human impacts by looking at larger scales and greater time horizons than we have previously considered. How can we as conservation activists help with this process?

Our first duty is to protect the toolmakers. Scientists who work with species particularly sensitive to human impacts and who maintain a moral compass aimed at species protection tend to be at risk of losing their jobs (especially if they work for land management agencies). Sensitive species such as the grizzly bear, which predictably are extirpated if mortality or habitat destruction is excessive, require caution and restraint on the part of humans—traits that often rub against the pro-development ethos of the prevailing culture. In his book *Science under Siege,* Todd Wilkinson describes clearly and compellingly the stories of numerous endangered species biologists who stood up for principle and sound science in the protection of imperiled creatures. If there is hope for a broader ecosystems approach, it starts with the survival of these "scientists under siege."

Second, we need to get relevant scientific publications off the shelf and into the public discourse. Too often, science—especially science that argues for limiting land use—is left to collect dust. To make the situation worse, forest managers are not rewarded for continuing their education about ecological processes and species' needs. If concerned members of the public do not shoulder the responsibility, who will?

In conjunction with this, we need to ensure that the relevant science is translated for a broader audience. Because of the internal rules and protocols of scientific inquiry, many important published works are not easy for lay audiences to understand. We need to encourage and even provide training for our science allies so they can make their findings widely understood.

Finally, we need to figure out how better to match the recommendations emerging from the science arena with the strategies necessary to implement them. Economic incentives, legislation, litigation, public education, and community organizing are but a few of the tools available to us. International laws, such as the Boundary Waters Treaty Act and the North American Free Trade Act, corporate campaigns and market initiatives, and the electoral process are all underused instruments of change.

In addition, we need to take a hard look inside ourselves and our society and ask why humans are still the primary cause of death of predators such as grizzlies. After thousands of years of relatively peaceful coexistence with an animal we have called "guide" and "teacher," why in the past few hundred years have we driven grizzly bears to the brink of extinction, and why does this trend continue? What can we do to transform how we view bears and behave in bear country? Tackling these issues of human behavior and values is ultimately as critical as protecting wildlands for an animal that needs space and tolerance from the dominant species on the landscape—*Homo sapiens.*

In sum, protecting lands as wilderness, administratively or legislatively, is an essential first step—without which the grizzly would not stand a chance in the face of rapid development. However, we must also remember that grizzlies could go extinct even if every remaining acre of wildland in the Northern Rockies were protected as wilderness.

A bolder vision that links wilderness areas, invents other tools, and taps new energy and talent for the job is our ultimate challenge. Otherwise, in a few hundred years, the grizzly could be another species discussed in the lower forty-eight states in the past tense. More than half a century after Aldo Leopold considered the great bear's dimming prospects in *A Sand County Almanac,* his words are more apt than ever: "Relegating the grizzly to Alaska is like relegating happiness to heaven: the problem is you may never get there." In short, we need to make our heaven, with grizzlies, here and now.

Rewilding for Evolution

Connie Barlow *(1999)*

*"Wilderness," as Dave Foreman has said, "is the arena of evolution."
Saving it, and making space for the wildlife with which we share this
continent, is a prospect that transcends the ephemeral.*

—Tom Butler (*Wild Earth*, Summer 1998)

*Let me add here that, as brilliant and visionary as Soulé, Noss, and I may
be, we are not coming up with something new under the sun. Listen: . . .
"Only those able to see the pageant of evolution can be expected to value
its theater, the wilderness, or its outstanding achievement, the grizzly."
These words are fifty years old, they are part of the canon of the "received
wilderness idea," and they are exactly what the Wildlands Project is about
today: Ecosystem representation. Cores. Corridors. Carnivores. Aldo
Leopold wrote them.*

—Dave Foreman (*Wild Earth*, Fall 1998)

*I am convinced that we cannot hope to protect native biodiversity and
restore landscape evolutionary processes as long as the West is managed
primarily as a feedlot for domestic animals.*

—George Wuerthner (*Wild Earth*, fall 1998)

*I can still cherish the thought of large, unmanipulated wilderness on this
continent where the processes of evolution can go on more or less as they
have for millennia . . . where evolution can continue on its own terms.*

—Donald Worster (*Wild Earth*, fall 1997)

As this series of quotations demonstrates, the evolutionary value of wilderness is widely recognized in the pages of *Wild Earth*. Within a year, at least four contributors made this point, and one traced the lineage of the idea back to Aldo Leopold. Nevertheless, wide recognition is not the same as depth of treatment. The evolutionary value of wilderness has been, rather, a turnip tossed into the pot. A bit of turnip adds a nice bite to a soup; but who wants to make turnip soup?

I do.

I believe the evolutionary value of wilderness could become one of the strongest arguments in its favor. Evolutionary value would thus join biodiversity preservation and ecological self-regulation as supports for rewilding.

Why rewilding? Why should vast expanses of self-willed terrain be protected and recovered? An evolutionary perspective provides this answer: *Rewilding must be undertaken because, next to outright species extinctions, the most abhorrent outcome—the greatest crime against creation—humankind might effect would be for surviving lineages to skew their future evolution substantially in response to us.*

Arthropods and vertebrates, angiosperms and bryophytes—all these and more, right now, and whether or not we so intend, are building and shedding genes to cope with our highways, our pesticides, our herbicides, our waste dumps. Lineage upon lineage is shaping fitness—however subtly—to survive in a world in which the human presence is pervasive. Even well-intentioned and scientifically based management decisions in the most excellent of biodiversity reserves designed to preserve this planet's evolutionary *heritage* are an inescapable manifestation of humanity's unchecked reach into evolutionary *futures.*

Sadly, the human impact on evolutionary futures is substantial even in the wildest areas under federal land management today. Designated wilderness areas in many parts of the United States are open to livestock grazing. And even where large carnivores do not face the challenge of figuring out that the easiest four-legged creatures to catch (domestic sheep and cattle) are not, in fact, on the menu, they have to cope with contradictory signals from two-legged creatures who trespass into their territories. Backpackers should be easy to hunt; nevertheless, if a large carnivore experiments in this direction, the innovator will be tracked down and killed. Intermittent exposure to the magical powers of humans to kill or wound at a distance does seem to preclude that kind of experimentation in the wilderness region I am most familiar with—the Gila Wilderness in southwestern New Mexico. There bears and lions are hunted for sport. In this, the first of all designated wilderness areas, the evolutionary futures of wild beasts are thus profoundly influenced by human demands for meat and recreation.

Accordingly, philosopher Baird Callicott has contended that if conservationists begin to speak of the evolutionary value of rewilding when we push for a remnant of America to be held off-limits to the impacts of settlement, logging, and mining, then for consistency's sake we ought to go the full route and urge the elimination of grazing, hunting, and what he calls "wilderness voyeurism and tourism" too. Rewilding for evolution, in its purest form, would thus challenge common assumptions about compatible human uses of wilderness. At the very least, such discussion would make arguments for rewilding based on biodiversity preservation and ecological integrity appear modest indeed. At its best, this kind of discussion would serve to remind us all that whatever each of us may feel about the propriety of intentional genetic manipulation conducted in laboratories, that pales next to the reality of the evolutionary consequences that our species is forcing upon life everywhere outside the scientist's lab.

Conservationists need not argue that human hegemony over the future evolution of life on Earth is somehow unnatural. The most natural thing for any form of life to do is to pursue its biotic potential: to reproduce as fast as it can and to invade any habitat in which a toehold can be gained. Nevertheless, because today's biological holocaust owes to a single species, we can argue that such hegemony is unprecedented in the history of life. Indeed, this sixth major mass extinction may be the first time that life of any sort is to blame for deep cutbacks in biodiversity across the globe. Previous mass extinctions may all have been caused by volcanoes or meteors.

Natural or no, unprecedented or no, we shudder at the thought of human hegemony over future evolution. We shudder because we know in our souls that this behavior is not right. This is not the way we wish to be human. This is not our ideal for participation in the Earth Community.

To acknowledge the evolutionary value of wilderness would thus be both a strength and a burden for the rewilding movement. Evolutionary valuation of wilderness carries a strong ethical, even religious, appeal, but it questions the wisdom of allowing traditional human uses of wilderness to continue in the deepest cores of our wildest landscapes. It would also complicate "management" decisions. Consider: in rewilding a landscape that has already lost a great proportion of its endemic richness, should reintroductions be attempted? If an endemic subspecies is now extinct, should another subspecies be introduced— both as a substitute for the *heritage* of richness lost and as a chance for endemism to once again work its way into evolution's *future?* Similarly, if a keystone species is extinct, should an ecological proxy—perhaps from another continent and of another genus—be introduced?

As students of evolution, we know that much of the wildlife in North America derived from stocks that not long ago, geologically speaking, were alien invaders. Porcupines and possums originated in South America, but they waddled across the newly formed Isthmus of Panama some 3 million years ago and have long since earned their ecological citizenship in the north. Grizzlies and elk crossed over from Asia near the end of the Ice Age. (As did humans.)

Paul Martin, Pleistocene ecologist and early proponent of the Overkill theory of end-Pleistocene extinctions, encourages us to adopt a broader time perspective in our vision for rewilding. To Martin's way of thinking, a goal to restore a representative and sizable chunk of North America to the "pre-Columbian" conditions that prevailed 500 years ago is shortsighted. Rather, we should be aiming to restore conditions toward as much of America's *pre-Holocene* richness as humanly possible. That pre-Holocene richness was marked by the magnificent megafauna of the late Pleistocene.

In "Bring Back the Elephants!" Martin and coauthor David Burney remind us that our modern extinction crisis was under way well before humans figured out how to plow the prairie. North America lost its mammoths, mastodons, giant ground sloths, glyptodonts, horses, camels, shrub oxen, and a number of species of the genus *Bison* some 13,000 years ago. The extinction of most of this continent's great Pleistocene herbivores was attended by the loss of many of their coevolved carnivores and large scavengers, too: the dire wolf, sabertooth cat, giant short-faced bear, American cheetah, and American lion. All this happened a geological blink of the eye ago. Should we perhaps aim to rewild toward end-Pleistocene standards? Is it even possible?

Proxies for some of these beasts (notably, elephants for mammoths) *do* remain elsewhere in the world. Should we, as Martin and Burney urge, bring back the elephants?

Mammoths, mastodons, and the smaller gomphotheres were prominent (and, the authors argue, keystone) members of the Pleistocene menagerie on this continent. Coming from Old World lineages, the forebears of all these creatures were at one time alien invaders in this part of the world. But evolution got to work and brought forth the endemics. If we ourselves do not bring elephants back and offer them a second chance for an evolving, deepening citizenship, then Order Proboscidea will never again produce American endemics; the evolution of Order Proboscidea in the New World will be over.

Paul Martin and David Burney's proposal thus opens up a pack rat's nest of questions, delving into ecological ethics as well as ecological science. Here I wish only to encourage that the evolutionary implications also be brought to the table. We should consider, too, that a back-to-the-Pleistocene standard for rewilding, at least in one test area, would help transcend the current controversy over how extensively American Indian cultures manipulated the landscape. Because humans were not part of American ecosystems until just before the great mammals went extinct, there should be no question that wilderness areas that emulate the late Pleistocene should be places where humankind "is a visitor who does not remain." The indigenous-management argument simply does not arise in this context.

Another imperative to bring back the elephant and to offer this lineage "untrammeled" wilderness derives from the strong scientific evidence that we humans are centrally implicated in its loss. According to the Overkill theory, before the first humans became fully native to this continent, we overhunted the great, naive beasts that had evolved no behavioral defenses against our projectiles. It can thus be argued that we are ethically obliged to do whatever we can to begin to right that wrong, our once and continuing crime against creation.

Why, then, wilderness? Because wilderness is the arena of evolution—especially for the megafauna. Large herbivores and carnivores cannot be expected to survive, much less evolve, in tame little woodlots, no matter how pure the waters and how sweet the air. Great beasts will not emerge from the furrows of farm fields, no matter how organic and sustainable the agricultural practices. The human imprint on future evolution will be felt, too, wherever landscapes are intensively managed, no matter how scientifically informed and ethically enlightened the managers. For the Cenozoic era, the Age of Mammals, to continue its tens of millions of years of stunning experimentation in large, hot-blooded beasts, Earth needs wilderness.

Bring Back the Elephants!

Paul S. Martin and David A. Burney *(1999)*

Extinction of large continental vertebrates at the end of the Pleistocene (late Quaternary) has long been apparent to paleontologists (Martin and Wright 1967). Recently the consequences of this phenomenon have attracted the attention of conservationists and visionaries. "This land is the mastodon's land; while *Home on the Range* commemorates buffalo, deer, and pronghorn it misses the mammoths, glyptodonts, and camels. There was a wild America considerably wilder than any brought to us on TV. Our late Pleistocene legacy means we can imagine more, not fewer, *kinds* of large animals on public lands" (Martin 1992).

A decade ago, Michael Soulé predicted that "the reintroduction of these large animals will be controversial, but I would not be surprised to read someday that cheetahs are helping to control deer and that mesquite is being 'overbrowsed' by rhinoceroses." Soulé's presidential address at the third annual meeting of the Society for Conservation Biology was intended to prod conservationists to peer into the future of their discipline, and to acknowledge that such taxa as lions, camels, elephants, horses, and spectacled bears once native to North America disappeared relatively recently (Soulé 1990; Owen-Smith 1989).

THE ULTIMATE IN REWILDING

In the fall 1998 issue of *Wild Earth,* Michael Soulé and Reed Noss proposed *rewilding* as the foundation of a continental conservation strategy. Central to this proposition is the recovery of existing top predators such as grizzlies, cougars, and wolves to large parts of their native ranges. Here we consider the ultimate in rewilding. While the diversity of America's charismatic megafauna was severely impoverished in the late Pleistocene, we can turn to Africa and India for surrogates for restoration. We suggest that the project begin by restarting the evolution of the most influential of the missing species, the extinct animals most likely to have exerted the greatest influence on their natural environment. Based on what is known of living megaherbivores in Africa and Asia, and based on the fossil record of the New World, there is one clear choice, animals as potent as fire in their dynamic influence on ecosystems. If we want the "super-keystone species" (Shoshani and Tassy 1996), second only to our own in their capability for altering habitats and faunas (Buss 1990; Sukumar 1994), we should start with the restoration of living proboscideans—with African and Asian elephants.

We fully expect that the proposal of free-ranging elephants in the Americas will initially shock and confound many conservationists and naturalists. What could be more foreign in the New World than free-ranging elephants? Isn't this idea heretical for those of us inclined toward deep reverence for the wild?

It all turns on what one regards as wild. For example, the gomphotheres, a family of Neotropical elephants that prospered in the Americas for well over 10 million years (Shoshani and Tassy 1996), vanished at the end of the Pleistocene around 13,000 years ago, along with mammoths and mastodons. All deserve consideration as a natural part of Wild America. With such a rich fossil record and such a late American extinction, it is natural to consider restarting New World evolution of the Proboscidea with whatever taxa of elephants are left.

We are keenly aware that living African *(Loxodonta africana)* and Asian *(Elephas maximus)* elephants are not conspecific with fossil *Mammuthus* (mammoths) or other native Proboscidea of the New World. But all are in the same family and some taxonomists have considered *Elephas* and *Mammuthus* to be quite close, even congeneric;

thus, an Asian elephant living today in Thailand is more closely related to the extinct mammoths of North America than to its African cousin. African and Asian elephants are the only members of the Order Proboscidea that were not lost in the megafaunal crisis of the late Pleistocene. Thanks to a surging human population and to poaching for ivory, elephant numbers crashed in the twentieth century, and elephants are now at risk in many parts of their historic range. Recent estimates of numbers of African elephants are 550,000 to 650,000 (Douglas-Hamilton and Michelmore 1996). Numbers of surviving wild Asian *Elephas* are less by an order of magnitude, estimated between 37,500 and 54,600 animals (Sukumar and Santiapillai 1996).

Unlike explosively reproducing aliens of the New World such as kudzu, Africanized bees, or zebra mussels, animals that reproduce as slowly as elephants, with an intrinsic rate of increase of about 5 percent per year, should be controllable. To avoid unacceptable methods of regulation (for twenty years park rangers shot 300 to 800 elephants annually in the Kruger National Park, Republic of South Africa), Jay Kirkpatrick of ZooMontana and his collaborators (1999) have perfected a technique for limiting elephant populations by darting females with a long-lasting birth-control compound. Elephant forays beyond the perimeter of a reserve can be deterred, as in Amboseli National Park in Kenya, by an electrified wire. For a New World elephant park suitable for wide-ranging family units, we suggest a part of the lower Colorado River or the Rio Grande. Like most of North America, both regions were once ranged by mammoths. Both river systems are heavily invaded by alien *Tamarix,* riparian trees widely regarded as undesirable and a potential target for removal by elephants. The river banks support alien Bermuda grass *(Cynodon dactylon),* an African species eaten by elephants (Moss 1988). Other potential sites for elephant introductions would be anthropogenic savannas in Central or South America—once home to gomphotheres—now pasturing livestock.

In planning New World restorations, conservationists have endowed the large mammals of historic time with the exclusive status of hall-marks, or flagships, overlooking the missing large mammals of the late Pleistocene. The animals that the first explorers and settlers saw and wrote about became incorporated in ideas of what constituted American wildness. The viewpoint imposed by a "Columbian Curtain" is unrealistic in evolutionary time. The historic fauna lacks the largest and most representative animals of the continent. Among the more common fossils of the late Pleistocene, which was dominated by equids, camelids, bovids, and especially bones, teeth, or tooth plates of pro-boscideans, only bison is represented (Graham and Lundelius 1994).

The opportunity is at hand to explore the evolutionary view. During the cold war the U.S. Fish and Wildlife Service took the first step in intercontinental restoration by shipping American musk oxen to Siberia to reestablish breeding herds in the northern part of a conti-nent where musk oxen lived until around 3,000 years ago. Recently Sergi Zimov has started a Pleistocene Park in Siberia and plans to add woodland bison from Athabasca, Canada, to his mix of Siberian ponies and musk oxen. Zimov expects that under heavy use, unpalatable plants such as mosses and ericads will be torn up, trampled, and manured, to be replaced by more productive steppe tundra of subarctic grasses, a community that vanished with the extinction of mammoths (Stone 1998). His experiment merits watching. However, Asia and Africa have much more to offer the New World than vice versa.

As a result of the late Pleistocene extinctions we live in a con-tinent of ghosts, their prehistoric presence hinted at by sweet-tasting bean pods of mesquite *(Prosopis),* honey locusts *(Gleditsia),* and monkey ear *(Enterolobium).* Such fruits are the bait evolved to attract native large animals that served as seed dispersers (Janzen and Martin 1982). Foraging behavior of introduced livestock can help us understand how thorns, repellent oils, terpenes, tannins, and other secondary compounds might have protected plants from being overeaten by extinct megaherbivores.

When megafaunal extinction struck this continent in the late Pleistocene, at least seven species of proboscideans—the entire Order Proboscidea in the New World—vanished. Unlike erratic background extinctions that sputter along randomly through the aeons, often in step with evolutionary replacements, the late Pleistocene extinctions were catastrophic and there were no replacements. Given their evident success over the past 15 million years and the late hour of their New World extinction, a mere 13,000 years ago or so, we suggest that bringing back the Proboscidea is by no means as witless as it might seem at first. It is not the same as introducing goats or pigs onto an oceanic island whose native plants lost long ago whatever defenses they once had to protect themselves against onslaught by the tongues and teeth of large herbivores.

In evolutionary time, the floodplains, grasslands, and savannas of North America harbored a stunning variety of large animals—some forty-one species in western North America alone, over three times as many as were present historically when Lewis and Clark detected bison, elk, pronghorn, brown (grizzly) bears, and ten others. The losses included native mammals in size classes to match the largest found in Africa and Asia (Stuart 1991). Since unrelated groups of organisms, including marine invertebrates, did not vanish, as at the end of the Cretaceous 65 million years ago, the end of the Pleistocene was not a time of mass extinction. Instead, what happened in America was an extinction of the massive (plus their parasites and commensals; see Schmidt et al. 1992).

With time the distinction may vanish. Recently the blighting of coral reefs and the destruction of tropical forest biota, for example, suggest that the late Pleistocene extinctions are no more than the overture to a full-blown mass extinction under way right now, potentially capable of overtaking the Cretaceous in magnitude of loss, and, unlike the mass extinction at the end of the Cretaceous, undeniably of our own making.

JEFFERSON AND LIVING BEHEMOTHS

Two and a half centuries ago the fossils of the late Pleistocene fascinated Ben Franklin, the Quaker naturalist John Bartram, and Thomas Jefferson. Jefferson philosophized against the idea of extinction and thought the fossil bones of mastodons and ground sloths meant that behemoths were still alive. According to Jefferson, the Indians knew of them. Big bones of proboscideans had been found in Big Bone Lick in Kentucky. In the early 1800s the public flocked to see the first skeleton of a mastodon exhibited in the new nation's first museum of natural science and art, located in Philadelphia. Charles Wilson Peale, owner of the museum, purchased the rights and excavated a mastodon in Orange County, New York. Adding the mastodon to his other natural history displays, Peale charged twenty-five cents at the front door and an additional fifty cents to enter the room with the mastodon skeleton (Sellers 1980). Some of the public excitement reflected a lingering debate about whether the animals were actually extinct.

While the Indians as well as European explorers encountered the fossil bones or teeth of large extinct animals, no solid evidence of living American proboscidea emerged. What we know of the American mastodons, the Columbian mammoths, the imperial mammoths, the woolly mammoths of the boreal and subarctic regions, the dwarf mammoths of Santa Rosa and other islands off the California coast, and the gomphotheres of the tropics comes strictly from fossils and the fossil record.

Bones of the Ice Age megafauna turn up in lake sediments, spring deposits, flood plain alluvium, frozen ground, ancient dune deposits, and caves. Over one hundred fossil mammoth localities are known from Arizona alone, and there are almost two hundred localities for mammoths and mastodons in Michigan. On the Atlantic Coast the great molars of mammoths and mastodons appear in the haul of trawlers fishing the shallow bottom of the continental shelf, and mastodon remains have been dredged from the Harlem River Canal in Manhattan. The permafrost of the unglaciated subarctic in Alaska and Siberia is richer in mammoth remains than most temperate regions, probably as a result of better preservation of fossils rather than larger populations of mammoths living in the subarctic. Occasionally both the frozen ground and the driest of desert caves yield not only bones but also dung, hair, hide, horns, hooves, and the desiccated tissues of extinct animals, including mammoths. Thanks to many radiocarbon dates, it appears that North America's proboscideans and many other genera of large mammals made their exit 11,000 radiocarbon years ago (Martin 1990; Stuart 1991), which geochemists calibrate to about 13,000 calendar years.

What caused such a loss, so late in the Pleistocene? Could it have been an asteroid hit, a circumstance that many believe accounts for heavy extinction, including the loss of dinosaurs at the end of the Cretaceous? Evidently not. There is no trace of an asteroid impact large enough to generate global repercussions that late in the fossil record.

Moreover, throughout the islands and continents of the planet, late Pleistocene extinctions were not synchronous, as would be expected in the case of a cosmic or climatic accident. Radiocarbon dates show that they were globally sequential, or what geologists call "time transgressive." The time transgressive pattern creates problems for models based on sudden global change, including changes in climate. While large animal extinctions impoverished North and probably South America around 13,000 years ago, they seem to have struck Australia much earlier, perhaps 50,000 years ago (Miller et al. 1999). The last population of woolly mammoths—including some dwarfs just two meters tall—vanished from Wrangel Island in the Arctic Ocean off Siberia only 3,700 years ago, surviving their North American kin by roughly 9,000 years. In imagining that mammoths might still be alive, it turns out that Thomas Jefferson was off by only four millennia!

A DEADLY SYNCOPATION

In the South Pacific over 3,000 years ago the extinctions of thousands of species or populations of flightless birds began with the spread of the Lapita culture from the southern Solomon Islands to Fiji and Tonga (Steadman 1995). Insular extinctions involving megapodes, pigeons, parrots, flightless rails, and populations of pelagic sea birds—extinctions much more severe than those recognized in historic time—swept through the South Pacific, reaching New Zealand to obliterate its giant flightless birds, the moas, beginning 1,000 years ago. By then the shadow of extinction had already reached Madagascar. The island continent lost some sixteen species of giant lemurs up to the size of a gorilla (living lemurs do not exceed ten kilograms), at least two species each of hippos and giant tortoises, and several giant flightless birds, including the elephant bird, perhaps the *roc* mentioned by Marco Polo. In dramatic contrast, over the past 40,000 years Africa and tropical Asia lost only a few large ungulate species.

It has not been possible to fit this pattern to any climatic or cosmic forcing function. Instead these prehistoric extinctions follow the ancient footsteps of our species, out of Afro-Asia and onto other continents and eventually even to remote oceanic islands, in what Ross MacPhee of the American Museum calls a "deadly syncopation" of human arrival and faunal loss. The mean size of animals lost scales to size of land mass.

To be sure, the traditional view, that climatic or environmental change must also be involved, persists. However, the idea of humans triggering late Pleistocene extinctions—perhaps by overkill—debated in Martin and Wright (1967) and Martin and Klein (1984), is gaining traction (Brown and Lomolino 1998; MacPhee 1999; Soulé and Noss 1998; Ward 1997). And the question of exactly what caused the extinctions need not deflect us from the prospect of repairing some of the damage.

In the long pull, all species are doomed to extinction, just as death is the inevitable fate of all individuals. Most species that ever lived on Earth are no more. But this is a poor excuse for turning our backs on the extraordinary loss of flagship species on our watch. By "loss on our watch" we mean not just the extinctions accompanying the past five centuries of European conquest in the New World; we mean the time scale of our species on this continent, the past 13,000 years at least. While human remains are rarely associated with extinct megafauna, dates on the Clovis culture and the extinct fauna overlap around 13,000 years ago (Stuart 1991). We have the opportunity to restart the evolution of proboscideans, along with horses, camels, and other extinct groups native in the Americas for millions or tens of millions of years. The global pattern of extinction outlined here involved many kinds of animals of tremendous interest to us, in particular warm-blooded, bright-eyed terrestrial vertebrates, mammals, and birds, including many of large size. Our strongest emotions are generated by those animals most like ourselves in intelligence and behavior. What can be done?

AMERICAN REQUIEM, AFRICAN VISIONS

For starters, it is time to mourn our dead, especially the total loss of the mammalian Order Proboscidea. In North America we need a "Mammoth Extinction Day" and in South America a "Gomphothere Extinction Day." This might take place sometime around the summer solstice. Any of the numerous fossil localities known to yield bones of Proboscidea would be suitable, such as Rancho la Brea with its magnificent Page Museum in Hancock Park in Los Angeles. An especially appropriate place for a wake would be at the Mammoth Site in Hot Springs, South Dakota, a paleoecological cathedral where 100,000 visitors a year pay a modest admission to marvel at a unique *in situ* exhibit of splendidly preserved mammoth bones in the process of being excavated from the most concentrated natural deposit of mammoths known on the continent. With the help of Earth Watch teams, Professors Larry Agenbroad and Jim Mead of Northern Arizona University have uncovered some fifty individual mammoths of two species plus bones of the giant bear, *Arctodus.*

The dimensions of the unexcavated sinkhole deposit suggest that along with other Pleistocene fossils, another fifty mammoths remain to be discovered. Most of the animals sexed to date have proved to be subadult males, suggesting that females, like African elephants, ranged in matriarchal herds led by an experienced elderly matriarch, smart enough to escape the treacherous if enticing sinkhole. The Mammoth Site publishes books on research, symposium volumes, and popular interpretations of the site and its mammoths as part of outreach to the general and scholarly public.

From the Hot Springs Mammoth Site tourists can drive to Wind Cave National Park to see a free-ranging bison herd. There ecologists study the interrelationships between short grasses, grazing, and fire. Bison are increasingly popular as a meat animal. Near Truth or Consequences, New Mexico, over 1,000 bison, as well as prairie dogs and mountain sheep, were recently established in place of cattle on the 600-square-mile Armendaris Ranch. But bison are a small part of the preextinction Wild West. Furthermore, according to the fossil record, bison entered North America only a quarter of a million years ago, well after the arrival and evolution of New World Proboscidea. Even more interesting than determining the adaptability of bison on the Armendaris (where they were unknown historically) would be to determine the adaptability of elephant family units mixed in with the bison.

Thanks to the fossil record, we are not totally ignorant of the paleoecology of extinct American Proboscidea. A remarkable chance to learn about mammoth diet has been gleaned from the dry dung deposits found in a large cave in southern Utah (Agenbroad and Mead

1996). Dung balls nine inches in diameter discovered in the 1980s by a National Park Service team of resource managers proved too big and the texture of the plant remains in the boluses too coarse to match those of the only other species they resembled, the Shasta ground sloths, whose dung is known from other caves in the region. The mean of sixteen radiocarbon dates on mammoth dung balls was 14,500 calendar years, and the plant material in the dung indicated a cooler climate than occurs in southern Utah today. The extinct mammoths ate mainly grasses, sedges, and other riparian plants, salt bush, prickly pear, and even ingested some needles of blue spruce. The cathedral-like cave they entered was more than large enough for mammoths. The animals deposited an estimated 255 cubic meters of manure. But much more about elephant ecology can only be learned from live animals.

When elephants dig for water in the dry season, the water holes they leave behind attract other species. They thin out dense stands of low trees and shrubs. Undoubtedly the extinct mammoths, mastodons, and gomphotheres did the same. In the process, elephants improve forage production for other grazers (Owen-Smith 1988; Buss 1990). The most interesting prospect for restarting the Proboscidea in America comes from what managers have discovered in Kenya's Amboseli Park just north of Kilimanjaro. According to David Western (1997):

> If elephants and cattle had their way, they would trade places. In Amboseli . . . you see herds of cattle filing into the park to graze, passing elephants headed out to browse. With elephants and cattle transforming the habitat in ways inimical to their own survival but beneficial to each other, they create an unstable interplay, advancing and retreating around each other like phantom dancers in a languid ecological minuet playing continuously over decades and centuries. Habitats oscillate in space like a humming top, driving and being driven by climate, animals, and people.

In the New World we can substitute bison for cattle to see if bison, too, will dance the languid ecological minuet with African elephants, surrogates for the extinct American Proboscidea, to the benefit of the American range!

Our proposal to establish free-ranging elephant herds in the New World is to conduct not an agricultural but an ecological experiment. We have an extraordinary opportunity to learn more about how nature works. How are fruits dispersed? What is the relationship between elephants, vegetation, and wildfire? Long smitten with the beguiling concept of a "forest primeval" (the climatic climax of Clementsian ecologists), North American conservation biologists have had to shift gears, adopting a more flexible concept of multiple stable states or discordant harmonies (Botkin 1990; Drury 1998). Over twenty years ago, conservation ecologist Graeme Caughley (1976) found no attainable natural equilibrium between elephants and forests in eastern and southern Africa. More recently, Sinclair (1995) reported that African elephants and fire reach multiple stable states. It appears that introduced elephants might have a great deal to teach us about the dynamic nature of wildness in America in evolutionary time. In the absence of elephants, inferences about the dynamics of American vegetation types could be as one-sided as those made in the absence of fire.

CONCLUSIONS

The demise of Proboscidea in North America represents not only the loss of ecological relationships and evolutionary possibilities, but also a foreclosure on entire realms of scientific inquiry. Clearly American ecologists suffer blind spots if the largest and most potent megaherbivores native to the continent are missing. What might we learn from reintroducing them? David Western's vision of a timeless minuet between grazers and browsing elephants in Amboseli fuels thoughts of how to attempt an American experiment. Here elephants need not dance with grazing cattle. We have bison. People, bison, and elephants once coexisted in America. We see this in the Clovis sites excavated by the Arizona State Museum along the San Pedro River in southeastern

Arizona. Clovis points, a shaft straightener of mammoth bone, stone blades, knives, and lithic debris are associated with the bones of mammoths, bison, and other extinct megafauna. People, mammoths, and bison co-occurred briefly around 13,000 years ago, judging by many radiocarbon dates on charcoal from hearths (Taylor et al. 1996). The early Americans speared and processed Proboscidea. We suspect they spent many days watching them very closely, as closely as Cynthia Moss or David Western or the Masai watch African elephants today in Amboseli National Park at the foot of Kilimanjaro. While we doubt she was thinking of the New World, Cynthia Moss's words (1988) are compelling:

> I have realized that more than anything else, more than scientific discoveries or acceptance, what I care about and what I will fight for is the conservation, for as long as possible, not of just a certain number of elephants, but of the whole way of life of elephants. My priority, my love, my life are the Amboseli elephants, but I also want to ensure that there are elephants in other places that are able to exist in all the complexity and joy that elephants are capable of.

From mammoths and mastodons the Clovis foragers would have learned much about edible wild plants, where they grew, their season of fruiting, and their palatability. In the New World we suspect it was the extinct megafauna that introduced the first Americans to the sweet bean pods (or *péchita,* an Indian name becoming part of borderland Spanish) of the mesquites, a valuable food plant for people living off the land. From the large mammals of the New World the newcomers learned the right season to rip apart dagger-leafed agaves for their sugary hearts, a rich source of calories. Surely the early Americans followed the game trails of the last New World elephants through the tropics, in the process learning about palm fruits and other fruits as attractive to people as to Proboscidea.

Now African *Loxodonta,* or Asian *Elephas,* or both, can show us some of the coevolutionary secrets of America when it was truly wild. Beyond Pleistocene parks we need Pleistocene proving grounds, places to fathom as well as to celebrate our lost wildness. Above all, the time has come to consider restarting elephant evolution by enabling elephants to reinvent their ecology on the continent that once constituted an important part of their global range. What is at stake is complexity, joy, and the whole way of life of elephants.

LITERATURE CITED

Agenbroad, L., and J. I. Mead. 1996. Distribution and palaeoecology of central and western North American *Mammuthus*. In *The Proboscidea: Evolution and Palaeoecology of Elephants and Their Relatives,* ed. J. Shoshani and P. Tassy. New York: Oxford University Press.

Botkin, D. B. 1990. *Discordant Harmonies: A New Ecology for the Twenty-First Century.* New York: Oxford University Press.

Brown, J., and M. Lomolino. 1998. *Biogeography,* 2d ed. Sunderland, Mass.: Sinauer Associates.

Buss, I. O. 1990. *Elephant Life: Fifteen Years of High Population Density.* Ames: Iowa State University Press.

Caughley, G. 1976. The elephant problem—an alternative hypothesis. *East African Wildlife Journal* 14: 265–83.

Douglas-Hamilton, I., and F. Michelmore. 1996. *Loxodonta africana:* Range and distribution, past and present. In *The Proboscidea: Evolution and Palaeoecology of Elephants and Their Relatives,* ed. J. Shoshani and P. Tassy. New York: Oxford University Press.

Drury, W. H. 1998. *Chance and Change: Ecology for Conservationists.* Berkeley: University of California Press.

Graham, R. W., and E. L. Lundelius. 1994. *Faunmap: A Database Documenting Late Quaternary Distributions of Mammal Species in the United States.* Springfield: Illinois State Museum Scientific Papers 30 (1,2).

Janzen, D. H., and P. S. Martin. 1982. Neotropical anachronisms: The fruits the gomphotheres ate. *Science* 215(4528): 19–27.

Fayrer-Hosken, R., D. Grobler, C. Raath, J. J. Van Altena, H. Bertschinger, and J. F. Kirkpatrick. 1999. Immunocontraception of African elephants. *Nature* 407: 149.

MacPhee, R. D. E., ed. 1999. *Extinctions in Near Time: Causes, Contexts, and Consequences.* New York: Kluwer Academic/Plenum Publishers.

Martin, P. S. 1990. 40,000 years of extinctions on the "planet of doom." *Palaeogeography, Palaeoclimatology, Palaeoecology* 82: 187–201.

Martin, P. S. 1992. The last entire earth. *Wild Earth* 2(4): 29–31.

Martin, P. S., and R. Klein, eds. 1984. *Quaternary Extinctions: A Prehistoric Revolution.* Tucson: University of Arizona Press.

Martin, P. S., and C. Szuter. 1999. War zones and game sinks in Lewis and Clark's West. *Conservation Biology* 13(1): 36–45.

Martin, P. S., and H. E. Wright, eds. 1967. *Pleistocene Extinctions: The Search for a Cause.* New Haven, Conn.: Yale University Press.

Miller, G. H., J. W. Magee, B. T. Johnson, M. L. Folgel, N. A. Spooner, N. T. McCulloch, and L. K. Nyliffe. 1999. Pleistocene extinction of *Genyornis newtoni*: Human impact on Australian megafauna. *Science* 238: 205–8.

Moss, C. 1988. *Elephant Memories: Thirteen Years in the Life of an Elephant Family.* New York: William Morrow.

Owen-Smith, R. 1988. *Megaherbivores: The Influence of Very Large Body Size on Ecology.* New York: Cambridge University Press.

Owen-Smith, R. 1989. Megafaunal extinctions: The conservation message from 11,000 years B. P. *Conservation Biology* 3(4): 405–12.

Schmidt, G. D., D. W. Duszynski, and P. S. Martin. 1992. Parasites of the extinct Shasta ground sloth, *Nothrotheriops shastensis*, in Rampart Cave, Arizona. *J. Parasitology* 78(5): 811–16.

Sellers, C. C. 1980. *Mr. Peale's Museum: Charles Wilson Peale and the First Popular Museum of Natural Science and Art.* New York: Norton.

Shoshani, J., and P. Tassy, eds. 1996. *The Proboscidea: Evolution and Palaeoecology of Elephants and Their Relatives.* New York: Oxford University Press.

Sikes, S. K. 1971. *The Natural History of the African Elephant.* London: Weidenfeld and Nicholson.

Sinclair, A. R. E. 1995. Equilibria in plant-herbivore interactions. In *Serengeti II: Dynamics, Management, and Conservation of an Ecosystem,* ed. A. R. E. Sinclair and P. Arcese. Chicago: University of Chicago Press.

Soulé, M. E. 1990. The onslaught of alien species, and other challenges in the coming decade. *Conservation Biology* 4(3): 233–39.

Soulé, M., and R. Noss. 1998. Rewilding and biodiversity: Complementary goals for continental conservation. *Wild Earth* 8(3): 18–28.

Steadman, D. W. 1995. Prehistoric extinctions of Pacific Island birds: Biodiversity meets zooarchaeology. *Science* 267: 1123–31.

Stone, R. 1998. A bold plan to re-create a long-lost Siberian ecosystem. *Science* 282: 31–34.

Stuart, A. J. 1991. Mammalian extinctions in the late Pleistocene of northern Eurasia and North America. *Biol. Rev.* 66: 453–562.

Sukumar, R. 1994. *Elephant Days and Nights.* New York: Oxford University Press.

Sukumar, R., and C. Santiapillai. 1996. *Elephas maximus:* Status and distribution. In *The Proboscidea: Evolution and Palaeoecology of Elephants and Their Relatives,* ed. J. Shoshani and P. Tassy. New York: Oxford University Press.

Taylor, R. E., C. V. Haynes, and M. Stuiver. 1996. Calibration of the late Pleistocene radiocarbon time scale: Clovis and Folsom age estimates. *Antiquity* 70: 515–25.

Ward, P. 1997. *The Call of Distant Mammoths: Why the Ice Age Mammals Disappeared.* New York: Copernicus Books/Springer-Verlag.

Western, D. 1997. *In the Dust of Kilimanjaro.* Washington, D.C.: Island Press.

And I Will Be Heard
ABOLITIONISM AND PRESERVATIONISM IN OUR TIME

Jamie Sayen *(1999)*

In 1988 the region's conservation community was unprepared when a million acres of land in northern New England formerly belonging to the timber company Diamond International were sold. Mainstream groups, more concerned about political collaboration with the timber industry than with protecting the region's battered forests, attacked and marginalized those of us who called for wilderness protection for the Diamond lands.

Several environmental groups in Maine collaborated with the timber industry to defeat a citizen-initiated referendum to ban clear-cutting in Maine's industrial forest in 1996. During this period, the Northern Forest Alliance, a consortium of more than thirty conservation organizations working in New England, supported legislation that would have given the timber industry billions of dollars in tax breaks without requiring it to reform its forestry practices.

In 1997 the Northern Forest Alliance defined "wildlands" as "a mosaic of wilderness and managed forests" (Northern Forest Alliance 1997). The Alliance has not been forthcoming when pressed on the question "How much wilderness?"

Blockbuster sales of paper company lands in northern New England have occurred regularly since 1988. In 1998–99 nearly 4 million acres in Maine alone—one-fifth of the state—were sold. Despite Maine's paucity of public land (only 5 percent of the state is in public ownership; roughly 1 percent is designated wilderness), the region's establishment conservation groups still refuse to call for wilderness

105

protection for a substantial portion of these lands. "Wilderness" seems to have disappeared from their vocabulary.

Similar stories of appeasement, compromise, accommodation, and failure to protect ecological integrity can be cited in many other regions of the United States. Social change movements face such internal conflicts when entrenched power tries to co-opt them.

Fundamental social change occurs only when its agents refuse to play the insiders' game. Consider the abolition of slavery.

The summer of 1846 was a busy time for Henry David Thoreau. It was the midpoint of his two-year stay on Walden Pond. He was hard at work on the first of eight drafts of *Walden*. On July 23 or 24, he was jailed for his refusal to pay a poll tax—his protest against the Mexican War, then being waged to extend slavery into new territory. His celebrated essay "Civil Disobedience" grew out of this experience. On August 1 he helped organize an abolitionist gathering to commemorate the anniversary of the emancipation of slaves in the West Indies.

A month later, he set out on his first trip into the Maine wilderness. Climbing Mount Katahdin, he experienced the raw indifference of nature, which was "not bound to be kind to man." Humanity, he realized, was a part of nature, not lord over it.

That summer, Thoreau's two great interests in life—the individual's relationship to society and humanity's relationship with nature—converged. His lifelong effort to answer the question "How should I live?" became a celebration of wildness. Katahdin challenged him to search for the laws, the limits, and the rhythms of nature. In a letter written in 1848, he exalted: "What Nature is to the mind, she is also to the body. As she feeds my imagination, she will feed my body" (Richardson 1986).

The laws of nature govern humans as well. Thoreau noted in his journal: "This world is not a place for him who does not discover its laws" (Richardson 1986). In his first book, *A Week on the Concord and*

Merrimack Rivers, composed during his sojourn at Walden, he wrote: "Though Nature's laws are more immutable than any despot's yet to our daily life they rarely seem rigid, but permit us to relax with license in summer weather" (Richardson 1986). Nature's laws teach us limits that liberate us from the folly of self-absorption and materialism.

If we seek to understand nature's laws, learn her limits, and let our imaginations run wild within those confines, we achieve a freedom unattainable through merely political channels. To Thoreau, "wild" meant "self-willed"—or free. "The most alive," he sang in his essay "The Wild," "is the wildest. . . . All good things are wild and free" (Anderson 1973).

But Thoreau could not be truly free while others were enslaved. The quest for inner freedom led him into the natural world. The quest for personal freedom made him an abolitionist, a conductor on the Underground Railroad, and an ardent defender of John Brown.

Thoreau recognized that slavery and abuse of nature grew out of the same "ethical myopia" (Nash 1989) that has characterized much of American history. The economic ethic that countenanced slavery turned our forests, rivers, and wildlife into commodities. In America's quest for material prosperity, black humans and wild ecosystems were simply resources to be appropriated for economic advantage.

Affluence in America has been underwritten by the degradation of people and wild nature (Nash 1989). Puritans sold Native Americans into slavery during and after King Philip's War in 1675–76. Slave labor cleared away the wilderness of the South. Southern affluence—at least for the plantation owners—was made possible by the use of slaves.

To Thoreau and the abolitionists, slavery was not an economic issue: it was a moral crisis. Institutionalized slavery denied the moral standing of black humans. Southern apologists for slavery as well as some of its critics, including Thomas Jefferson, denied that blacks were fully human, entitled to the inalienable rights Jefferson celebrated in the Declaration of Independence. Slaves were property; slavery was a system of force that protected the "property rights" of slave owners. If we listen carefully today, we will hear very similar arguments from timberland owners, polluting industries, and land developers regarding the moral standing of nonhuman nature. In both instances, economic self-interest defines the limits of moral standing; slavery and ecological degradation have been defended as necessary for economic survival.

In 1830 the issue of slavery was viewed as a matter for individual states to address, much the way forest management practices are today. Massachusetts had abolished slavery in the 1780s, and most northern states had done so during the early years of the new republic. In the South, slavery was a source of great anguish among many slave owners. Jefferson wanted to liberate his slaves, but could not afford to. Others viewed it as a necessary evil. Most opponents to slavery supported schemes for the gradual emancipation of slaves or the recolonization of freed blacks to Africa. These reformers were unwilling to confront the slave owners, or to assert the right of the federal government to abolish slavery, fearful the South would secede from the Union.

But the economics of slavery, like the economics of industrial forestry, transcended regional boundaries; the market forces in play were global. The colonial-era slave trade sent English calico and linen, wrought iron, brass, and gunpowder to West Africa in exchange for slaves who were transported to the Indies and the Americas. Cotton, sugar, and tobacco from the colonies were sent to England. The nineteenth-century New England textile industry relied on slave-grown cotton transported in Yankee ships.

In 1830 only one-third of southern households owned slaves, but three-quarters of the slaves were on plantations that owned more than twenty slaves. By 1860 only a quarter of southern households owned slaves, and the wealthiest plantations owned the large majority. The South's economic elite controlled a vast accumulation of human "capital" and exercised great power over the non-slave-owning whites through economic domination and by fostering a culture of xenophobia and racism.

In 1831 William Lloyd Garrison, an obscure twenty-five-year-old printer, began publication of *The Liberator,* an antislavery paper that he would publish for thirty-five years. He had recently served time in a Baltimore jail for publishing an attack on a Massachusetts shipowner for engaging in the illegal slave trade. He threw down the gauntlet in his inaugural editorial on January 1, 1831: "I am in earnest—I will not equivocate—I will not excuse—I will not retreat a single inch—AND I WILL BE HEARD."

Slave owners had long lived in dread of an insurrection. A bloody revolt had occurred in Haiti three decades earlier. Late in 1831, Nat Turner led a slave revolt in Virginia. Although Turner was betrayed before he could mount the full-scale revolt he had planned, his rebellion mortified the South. In the aftermath, the South suppressed further debate over slavery. Without such debate, southerners lived in a fantasy world that caused them to believe they could win the Civil War and survive on a one-crop economy based on slavery.

Garrison understood the role of free and open debate in exposing untruth and injustice. In 1830 he realized that the greatest obstacle to the eradication of slavery was the conspiracy of silence on the subject. Southerners naturally did not want to examine it too carefully, and northerners were unwilling to risk the Union by encouraging divisive debate. Garrison believed that people in free states had a "righteous duty" to break that silence, to articulate the cause of the slaves. "Let us begin to talk," he wrote, "and depend upon it, something noble will be done—and not till then" (Mayer 1998). In breaking the genteel silence on slavery, Garrison and the other radical abolitionists were able to frame the terms of the debate. It was a moral issue, not merely an economic or political question, or a matter of charity. It was simply *wrong* to deny political rights to other human beings.

Garrison's editorials were intentionally confrontational. He baited the slavers. He used the slavers' rhetoric against them, liberally quoting southern hotheads in the pages of *The Liberator.* He attacked the gradualists and colonizers as appeasers of evil. He quoted an English Quaker, Elizabeth Heyrich, who said gradualism was the "very masterpiece of satanic policy." When critics charged that immediate emancipation was inexpedient, Garrison shot back: "The question of expedience has nothing to do with that of right" (Mayer 1998). Many reformers desired to abolish the evils of slavery without challenging the legitimacy of the institution itself. Garrison scorned such accommodationism.

The agitation of the early radical abolitionists in the 1830s contributed to the South's slide deeper into tyranny. South Carolina's Senator John Calhoun moved to silence debate over slavery in Congress. By 1836 Congress had imposed a gag rule on antislavery petitions. The political parties—the Jacksonian Democrats and the Whigs (led by slave owner Henry Clay)—had no interest in debating slavery because it would antagonize their southern supporters and undermine their efforts to build a national coalition to win the presidency. The problem of slavery would be solved by denial. Critics of industrial forestry and preservationists unable to get a friendly word for wilderness out of today's politicians understand this head-in-the-sand approach.

In response to Garrisonian abolitionism, the South began to assert that slavery was morally right, even humane. As the years wore on, the South grew more demanding on the national political front, pushing for the annexation of Texas, the War with Mexico, the Fugitive Slave Law, and the expansion of slavery into Kansas, Nebraska, and other territories. As the abolitionists intensified their attacks upon the slavers, the southern defense of slavery and states' rights became increasingly irrational and violent, culminating in the assault of a Massachusetts senator by a South Carolina congressman on the floor of the U.S. Senate in 1856.

Antislavery interests lost the vote to admit Texas to statehood in 1845; despite the defeat, Garrison celebrated the power of open debate to advance a moral revolution when authority and comfortable elites suppressed independent thought. "We have too little, instead of too much dissent among us," he concluded (Mayer 1998).

While the South turned to censorship (and placed a bounty on Garrison's head), well-to-do northern whites, who fancied themselves potential abolition supporters, advised him to soften his pronouncements before they would contribute to *The Liberator.* Accommodationists worried that Garrison's attacks would make the fate of slaves worse and undermine their efforts to engage the South in meaningful dialogue. Garrison turned a deaf ear. Efforts to censor him provoked this retort: "Tell me not that an evil is cured by covering it up . . . that if nothing be said, more will be done" (Mayer 1998).

Agitation was the great political counterweight to the national conspiracy of silence on slavery from 1836 through the presidential election of 1856. The orator and abolitionist Wendell Phillips declared in 1852: "Only by unintermitted agitation can a people be kept sufficiently awake not to let liberty be smothered in material prosperity. . . . Republics exist only on the tenure of being constantly agitated." Joshua Giddings, another antislavery leader, declared: "Agitation is necessary to purify the political atmosphere of this nation" (Reynolds 1995). Former slave Frederick Douglass stated bluntly: "Power concedes nothing without a demand."

Open debate within the abolitionist movement generated constant friction about fundamental goals and tactics. In the late 1830s the movement split over the issue of returning liberated slaves to Africa. America was deeply racist, and many abolitionists viewed blacks as inferiors who could never live in harmony with whites in America. They proposed gradual emancipation and deportation to Africa. Moderate abolitionists, who viewed themselves as much more politically realistic than the Garrisonians, supported this plan.

Garrison snorted that these people supported the "gradual abolition of wickedness" (Mayer 1998).

Around 1840 another split developed in the ranks of the abolitionists. As support of the abolitionists had grown and the power of the American Anti-Slavery Society had increased, some of its more wealthy and politically well connected members decided it was time to make abolitionism an electoral issue. They formed the Liberty Party and ran presidential candidates every four years, garnering a minuscule percentage of the popular vote, not unlike today's Green Party.

Garrison argued that moral education, not political activity, remained the most urgent job. While the radicals sought to raise the ante with their attacks on the institutions—including the U.S. Constitution—that supported slavery, the political wing sought to soften the message to appeal to more moderate voters and to muzzle Garrison and other loose cannons in the radical wing.

The underlying conflict, common to all social change movements, was a matter of expediency versus principle—reform at the margins versus fundamental change. Mainstream reformers traditionally have believed in a political solution to a specific problem. They believe we can lobby Congress and effect an end to slavery, or clear-cutting, or inappropriate land development. Political outsiders, grassroots activists, and the Garrisonian wing of the abolitionist movement reject the status quo. They believe that the system itself is the problem. Merely abolishing slavery would not change other exploitative political and economic institutions. Radical abolitionists also supported the rights of women; many were pacifists; and most recognized that merely freeing the slaves, without accompanying educational, economic, and land reforms, would perpetuate the injustice suffered by black Americans.

Garrison's opposition to the Liberty Party was also pragmatic, even though the party's woolly-headed promoters viewed themselves as the truly practical abolitionists. They believed they could abolish slavery through congressional action without provoking secession.

Garrison believed it was essential for a small social change group to work on the people—not the politicians—first. He agreed with his friend George Thompson, the English abolitionist: "The people must emancipate the slaves for the government never will." Political change would only happen after moral change had transformed the political landscape. The job of the abolitionists was to effect that moral transformation (Mayer 1998).

History has shown that Garrison's radical, moral stance was more pragmatic than the positions of moderate opponents of slavery. He rejected compromise: "If we demand anything short of justice . . . if we ask for a part, we shall get nothing." In 1854 he declared: "Freedom is of God, and Slavery is of the Devil. . . . I will not try to make as good a bargain for the Lord as the Devil will let me . . . and be thankful that I can do so much" (Mayer 1998).

He had unwavering faith that a small minority can effect revolutionary change if it remains true to its ideals. When Garrison was told in 1844 that the abolitionist movement was too small to make a revolution, he retorted: "We are enough to begin one, and once begun it can never be turned back." In fact, he believed that the American Anti-Slavery Society was most effective as a small, not a mass, organization. Large powerful groups had never championed great reforms. Small groups could act as catalysts for moral revolutions (Mayer 1998).

Half a century later, the great Russian novelist Leo Tolstoy wrote admiringly of Garrison's insistence on a moral campaign: "Garrison understood . . . that the only irrefutable argument against slavery is the denial of the right of any man over the liberty of another under any conditions whatsoever." Most proponents and opponents of slavery argued over the evils of slavery and the dangers of emancipation, Tolstoy wrote, but Garrison understood that slavery was "only a particular instance of universal coercion." Accordingly, Garrison articulated a "general principle with which it is impossible not to agree—the principle that under no pretext has any man the right to dominate, i.e., to use coercion over his fellows" (Tolstoy 1967).

The slavery crisis came to a head when California applied for statehood in 1849 after the Gold Rush. If California was admitted as a nonslave state, it would tip the balance of power in the U.S. Senate away from the slave states. The hard-liners of the South, as usual, threatened secession. An aged Henry Clay and a youthful Illinois senator, Stephen Douglas, cobbled together the notorious Compromise of 1850 that admitted California as a nonslave state. The South received a series of concessions: slavery would remain in the District of Columbia; Congress would deny that it had power to regulate interstate slave trade; the remainder of the territory taken from Mexico would be open to slavery; and the federal government would forcefully return fugitive slaves to their southern "owners." The Fugitive Slave Act swelled the ranks of abolitionists and split the North and South. Architects of the 1850 compromise deluded themselves into thinking they had saved the Union. Garrison accused Henry Clay of moral cowardice for striking a position "halfway between right and wrong" (Mayer 1998).

In 1857 the Supreme Court ruled in the Dred Scott case that Congress had no right to exclude slavery from the territories, that blacks had no constitutional rights of citizenship, and that the property rights of slave owners must be respected at all costs.

In 1859 John Brown raided a federal arsenal in Harpers Ferry, Virginia, in a doomed attempt to launch a slave insurrection. Although he was captured and condemned to death, his raid electrified the nation. Most northerners initially condemned his violence, but Thoreau, who had met Brown earlier that year, immediately rose to his defense in a public lecture, "A Plea for John Brown." "The government puts forth its strength on the side of injustice," Thoreau charged. The day after Brown was hanged, Thoreau helped one of Brown's soldiers escape to Canada. Brown's raid and the reaction of the North unified the South on the issue of secession.

Southern elites, grown more and more extremist in defense of slavery, the cotton economy, and the southern way of life, had gained control over the federal government after the 1850 election, in part due to the collapse of the Whig Party. At the same time, the economic power of northern elites was eclipsing the one-crop economy of the South. Northern economic interests that wanted economic growth and expansion, free land, free labor, free markets, and high tariffs collided with a southern elite that opposed all these programs. The slavery issue eventually united northern economic elites with abolitionists to defeat the accommodationist Democrats and elect Abraham Lincoln as president.

Lincoln was obsessed with the preservation of self-government, not emancipation. He viewed the Civil War as an "insurrection," not a war. He did not recognize the right of states to secede. The states had made an indissoluble compact when their representatives had signed the Declaration of Independence. Secession in response to a national crisis was not an option.

The southern leadership asserted its right to revolution, claiming the South was the great defender of liberty, the true heir of the Revolution. Nonsense, replied Lincoln. Secession was no revolution; it was a counterrevolution—a repudiation of the ideals of the Declaration of Independence. "It may seem strange," Lincoln said, "that any men should dare to ask a just God's assistance in wringing their bread from the sweat of other men's faces." The politician Lincoln understood the moral dimension of the crisis. In the summer of 1861 he declared: "The right of revolution is never a legal right. . . . At most, it is but a moral right, when exercised for a morally justifiable cause. When exercised without such a cause, revolution is no right, but simply a wicked exercise of physical power" (McPherson 1991).

Lincoln was slow to free the slaves, fearing that emancipation would cause the border states of Kentucky and Maryland to secede. He initially believed that the Constitution, enacted by a vote of the whole people, prevented him from liberating the slaves, just as it forbade unilateral secession by the South. An act by the whole people—amending the Constitution—was required (Wills 1992).

When he finally freed the slaves, he justified his action by citing the constitutional requirement that the president maintain the government. Emancipation had become a military necessity to crush the insurrection, restore the union, and save the nation. Abolitionist pressure on Lincoln had pushed him toward that decision. Wendell Phillips remarked that if Lincoln had grown in moral stature, "it is because we watered him" (Wills 1992; Zinn 1990).

When Lincoln issued the Emancipation Proclamation in 1863, he stated: "In giving freedom to the slave we assure freedom to the free." The South had forgotten that our freedom depends upon the freedom of others. In 1856 a Richmond, Virginia, paper had declared: "Freedom is not possible without slavery."

Lincoln and the abolitionists based their case for a moral politics on the Declaration of Independence. Garry Wills writes that, to Lincoln, the Declaration was "the statement of a permanent ideal" whereas the Constitution, with its accommodation of slavery, was "an early and provisional embodiment of that ideal, to be tested against it, kept in motion toward it." The framers of the Constitution, Lincoln believed, rejected slavery in principle, but tolerated it *only by necessity.* It was the task of succeeding generations to complete the unfinished business of the founders (Wills 1992).

In November 1863 Lincoln used his brief Gettysburg Address to redefine the meaning of the Declaration of Independence. He demonstrated that the Declaration has different meanings to different generations. The founders had professed equality; they had not achieved it because, at the time, they could not. To Lincoln, the Civil War had been necessary to complete the unfinished business of the American Revolution—a second American Revolution. No longer could America countenance the disparity between the noble sentiments of the Declaration and the ugly reality of slavery. Henceforth, all men would, at least in theory, be equal before the law. Lincoln's reinterpretation of the Declaration challenges succeeding generations to examine it afresh. Today we must study it in the context of global ecological limits.

Lincoln made still more explicit the connection between morals and politics in his second inaugural address in March 1865: The Civil War was a great punishment inflicted upon the whole nation for the sin of slavery and must become, in Garry Wills's words, a "repenting war" (Wills 1992). Healing the nation required reconciliation, not vindictiveness; however, healing first required purging the nation of the sin of slavery.

War introduces new forms of corruption into society. Four years of civil war hardened the naive soldiers, most of whom had left home for the first time in their lives. It also wrought ecological destruction. Forests were cleared near battle sites and army camps for fuel, shelter, and rail transportation. Following the war, the final push to subdue the wilderness of the West began.

Because America and its political leaders had not been mature enough to resolve the slavery crisis peaceably, resolution of the crisis was violent and incomplete. Following the war and Lincoln's assassination, America ignored its moral obligations to the emancipated slaves. It refused to institute necessary political and economic reforms. Instead America fell into one of the most corrupt and disgraceful periods of its history.

Land reform, in particular, was critical; the freed slaves could not adequately exercise their political freedom without land. Failure to redistribute the vast land holdings of the planter aristocracy to the freed slaves condemned southern blacks to generations of poverty. Slavery had been abolished, but the inequality of the antebellum order remained.

The Reconstruction era, like the final decades of the twentieth century, concentrated economic and political power in the hands of the elites as never before. The modern corporate economy emerged from this period, which Mark Twain branded the "Gilded Age."

One of the bitterest ironies of that era involves the Fourteenth Amendment. Historian Pauline Maier writes that the Fourteenth Amendment was part of an effort "to read into the Constitution principles in the Declaration of Independence" (Maier 1997). Section 1 of the Fourteenth Amendment protects the "life, liberty and property" of all citizens. It assures all persons "equal protection of the laws."

In the hands of the Supreme Court of the 1880s, however, it became a vehicle for extending the rights (but not the responsibilities) of corporations. Corporate lawyers argued successfully that the "persons" protected by the Fourteenth Amendment included corporations and that the amendment was actually designed to prohibit governmental regulation of private enterprise—the ultimate fantasy of laissez-faire economics (Burns 1985). The Court reasoned that contracts and many other economic activities were forms of property protected by the amendment. In 1886 the Court concluded that corporations were persons whose rights must be protected by the government.

The Court was a good deal less enthusiastic about extending those rights to freed slaves. Instead, the Court generally used the property clause against efforts to improve working conditions, labor organizing, or the extension of civil rights. In 1896, in *Plessy v. Ferguson,* the Court cited the Fourteenth Amendment's equal protection clause to uphold southern segregation as long as it was "separate but equal." Between 1890 and 1910, the Court cited the Fourteenth Amendment nineteen times to uphold the rights of black Americans. In these two decades, it applied the amendment 288 times in defense of corporate rights. The Fourteenth Amendment had granted political rights to citizens but had not assured the economic rights of all (Burns and Burns 1991).

Fundamental reform of society is as necessary to the survival of a healthy culture as natural disturbance is to the health of ecosystems. Circumstances change, and the healthy society will adapt. The unhealthy one will resist until it is too late to effect peaceful change.

Proponents of fundamental reforms are invariably vilified by mainstream society. Entrenched elites who benefit from inequities will resist change. Most humans desire security and peace, not social tension. Reformers, such as nineteenth-century abolitionists and today's preservationists, are outsiders whose message must be radical, shrill, and antagonistic in order to be heard. The reformer must act as an Archimedean counterweight to mass apathy on moral issues utilizing a very long—radical—lever to move the apathetic mass. Our political system has never willingly considered moral questions. Once the reforms have been adopted and future generations look back, horrified that there ever could have been slavery—or industrial forestry—the reforms, if not the reformers, are lionized.

Nevertheless, the marginalized cadre of radical abolitionists succeeded where their more accommodating, appeasing, politically oriented contemporaries failed. *Complete emancipation* resolved the slavery crisis—not the Missouri Compromise, the Compromise of 1850, recolonization schemes, efforts at electoral politics of the Liberty Party, or strategies to contain the spread of slavery while leaving it untouched where it already existed.

Political compromise cannot resolve a moral crisis. Only a moral approach can effect needed change. There can be no middle ground between good and evil. At best, political incrementalism can delay the day of reckoning, but always at a cost. Appropriate political change occurs only after an uncompromising moral campaign has brought the issue to a head.

Garrison and his allies also succeeded because of personal qualities. Henry Mayer suggests that Garrison possessed "an absolute unswerving confidence in his principles, a belief in the power of ideas advocated with the relentless urgency of an independent press, and a faith in the moral and religious transformation of both a people and its politics." Speaking the truth, Garrison reflected late in life, means that "there is no need for despair" (Mayer 1998).

His charm, his gentleness, his playful sense of humor, and his tender devotion to family and friends disarmed those who expected that the public firebrand was consumed by hatred and anger. His biographer writes: "It is clear to me now that he became an agitator as much out of love as hate" (Mayer 1998).

Today's conservation movement may learn several valuable lessons from Garrison and the abolitionists. If we hope to protect evolutionary integrity and avoid violence, we must agitate and educate. We must have a clear moral vision and convey it to the public clearly. We must refuse to enter into political compromise when the issues are moral and ecological. And, as Garrison's thirty-five-year career as editor of *The Liberator* teaches, we must persist.

There are eerie similarities between the antebellum South and the Northern Forest region today. Most slaves and land were then owned by a small number of wealthy, frequently absentee, white planters; absentee corporations or speculators own most of the timberland in the Northern Appalachians today. The backbone of both economies was a single crop—cotton then, timber today. The cotton-growing states exported 95 percent of the crop for manufacture into cloth in Europe and New England. The South imported two-thirds of its clothing. Residents of northern New England communities are familiar with the sight of raw-log trucks heading into Canada, and trucks carrying milled lumber returning to New England. In the 1850s the slaveocracy put its energy into expanding slavery to the tropics and territories, not diversifying the home economy. In the Northern Appalachians, the paper companies have invested in modern mills in the southeastern United States and in the third world, preferring to allow the aged mills of the northeastern states to deteriorate now that the industry has largely completed the liquidation of the forests that supply these mills.

The nineteenth-century South was a demoralized society characterized by great poverty among the poor whites as well as the slaves. For decades, southern politics defended slavery and constructed legal protections for it, instead of addressing issues of economic backwardness and political inequality.

The South's political immaturity prevented discussion, debate, or negotiation over the issue. Slavery destroyed democracy in the South. Those of us who have fought against the ecological slavery imposed on the forests of northern New England by the large timber corporations have encountered a similar situation—a stunted economy and a warped politics that cannot forgive criticism and dissent.

Defenders of both economies use similar language: slavery was necessary for economic survival; so are clear-cuts, herbicides, raw log exports, and cheap Canadian logging labor today. For decades southern politicians blackmailed the North with threats of secession. The demagogues of the timber industry rely on job blackmail to fight any progress toward forest-practices reform and creation of publicly owned wildlands. Curiously, where industrial foresters strip an area of all trees, plant a monoculture, and follow with intensive herbicide spraying, they call the land—a plantation.

There are a number of other similarities between nineteenth-century slavery and twentieth-century industrial forestry. In both cases, the conflict is over the control and exploitation of other living beings. Arguments over property rights are central. Timberlands are viewed as property today, just as slaves were then. Slavers and clear-cutters alike assert states' rights and denounce efforts to involve the federal government. Reform efforts are thwarted by dividing the opposition, and by duping the moderate reformers into marginalizing radicals and supporting compromises that fail to address the problem. A focus on tangential issues, such as slavery in the territories then (instead of abolition of slavery everywhere), and conservation easements and green certification today (instead of wilderness protection and the abolition of industrial forestry practices), distracts energy from the core moral and ecological issues.

Abolitionism was then and preservationism is now a moral—not merely political—concern. Radical land reform is essential to solving both problems. Here, Reconstruction offers a depressing historical lesson. Reconstruction failed the emancipated slaves because it refused to emancipate the land from the wealthy landowners. Without land, the freed slaves were forced into sharecropping. To protect ecological integrity today, we must also institute sweeping, but reasonable, land reforms.

Ownership of land should in no way entitle the landowner to degrade the ecological integrity of the land. This is an absolute—not a relative—ethic. Absentee land ownership is a form of land slavery that must be abolished. No individual ought to own more land than her family can responsibly manage, and the family must reside on or nearby that land. The only exception to this should be for landowners who place a forever wild covenant on the land and manage it strictly for ecological and evolutionary values. The disgraceful condition of industrial forestland is sufficient to disqualify corporations from owning land.

The land does not belong to us; we belong to it. Public ownership of lands currently enslaved by absentee masters is an essential step toward preserving ecological and evolutionary integrity across the landscape.

Garrison's genius lay in his understanding that he and his colleagues could never defeat the political power of the slave owners and their allies and accomplices in the political arena. He never considered playing by their rules: fighting the slavers' game by their rules could never succeed. He based his moral campaign on the New Testament and the

Declaration of Independence. He believed in the power of democracy and free speech to incite a moral revolution that would sweep away the political opposition the abolitionists could never have defeated head-on.

He understood that politics is all about compromise, and that moral issues are not susceptible to compromise. If slavery is wrong, it cannot be improved by reforms; it must be abolished. Liberty, Jefferson wrote, is an inalienable right.

I once asked Lois Marie Gibbs, the leader of the Love Canal community fight against dioxins in the 1970s and 1980s, how her grassroots antitoxics allies got on with the large mainstream environmental groups in Washington, D.C. She replied that relations were not good: "They're into control; we're into prevention." While the politically savvy insiders were negotiating with the Environmental Protection Agency, Congress, and the polluting industries to limit the discharge of toxins into the environment, mothers, workers, and other victims of that pollution were fighting to prevent *any* discharge of toxic substances into their communities. Setting controls on the amount of pollution industries are permitted to spew forth sustains business as usual; prohibiting toxic discharges requires global corporations to reinvent themselves.

In the Northern Appalachians, this rift in the conservation community also exists. The large environmental groups work together under the umbrella of the Northern Forest Alliance. They promote small political reforms, studies, and collaborative initiatives with the timber industry. They have distanced themselves from the grassroots groups that call for an end to clear-cutting and the creation of large wilderness reserves. Maine Audubon Society informed the region's conservation groups in July 1998 that it would oppose calls for designating a significant chunk of wilderness out of the 3 million acres of paper industry lands that were then on the market in Maine. In the ensuing months, the Alliance avoided public defense of wilderness.

Only a campaign of moral suasion can rescue the natural and human communities of the Northern Appalachians, or of any region, from the clutches of the industrial global economy. If exploitation of humans is wrong, as the abolitionists argued, then the continued exploitation of humans *and* wild nature must be even more wrong. Moreover, preservationists who would extend the realm of ethical concern to the land have not just moral law but also natural law on our side. We live in a world of real limits that the global economy ignores. Why should an absentee multinational corporation care if the forests of Maine are degraded for the next fifty or one hundred or five hundred years? It can turn its attention to the southeastern United States and the tropics. What does it care if it leaves behind a shattered economy that has lost its options for decades to come because the region's citizens, politicians, and environmental advocates acquiesced to the tyranny of the ecological slavers?

The argument for wilderness preservation and environmental protection, ultimately, is over the limits of physical and ecological reality. Those who willfully ignore limits are ecologically wicked. Accommodating wickedness is sinful. Sustaining a campaign of moral and ecological education cannot fail. Failure to act now condemns future generations to a bleak existence.

Imagining a future of healthy natural and human communities is the first step to realizing them. "If you have built castles in the air," Thoreau exhorts us, "your work will not be lost; that is where they should be. Now put the foundations under them."

We need more radical abolitionists in the preservationist movement. Their work will make the world of politics safe enough to bring forth an ecological Lincoln or two.

LITERATURE CITED

Anderson, C. R., ed. 1973. *Thoreau's Vision: The Major Essays.* Englewood Cliffs, N.J.: Prentice-Hall.

Burns, J. MacGregor. 1985. *The Workshop of Democracy: From the Emancipation Proclamation to the Era of the New Deal.* New York: Vintage.

Burns, J. MacGregor, and S. Burns. 1991. *A People's Charter: The Pursuit of Rights in America.* New York: Vintage.

Maier, P. 1997. *American Scripture: Making the Declaration of Independence.* New York: Knopf.

Mayer, H. 1998. *All on Fire: William Lloyd Garrison and the Abolition of Slavery.* New York: St. Martin's Press.

McPherson, J. M. 1991. *Abraham Lincoln and the Second American Revolution.* New York: Oxford University Press.

Nash, R. 1989. *The Rights of Nature: A History of Environmental Ethics.* Madison: University of Wisconsin Press.

Northern Forest Alliance. 1997. *Wildlands: A Conservation Strategy for the Northern Forest.* Montpelier, Vt.

Reynolds, D. S. 1995. *Walt Whitman's America: A Cultural Biography.* New York: Vintage.

Richardson, R. D. Jr. 1986. *Henry David Thoreau: A Life of the Mind.* Berkeley: University of California Press.

Tolstoy, L. *Tolstoy on Civil Disobedience and Non-Violence.* New York: Mentor, 1967.

Wills, G. 1992. *Lincoln at Gettysburg: The Words That Remade America.* New York: Simon & Schuster.

Zinn, H. 1990. *A People's History of the United States.* New York: Harper & Row.

WILD THINKING

LANGUAGE AND EXPERIENCE

I consistently confuse the marsh frog
with the purple pitcher plant.
Maybe it's because each alike makes
a smooth spine of the light, a rounded
knot of forbearance from mud.

And which is blackbird? which prairie thistle?
They both latch on, glean, mind their futures
with numerous sharp nails and beaks.

Falling rain and water fleas are obviously
synonyms, both meaning *countless
curling pocks of pond motion*.
And aren't seeding cottonwood laces
and orb weavers clearly the same—clever
opportunists with silk?

I call field stars and field crickets
one and the other, because they're both
scattered in thousands of notches
throughout the night. And today I mistook
a blue creekside of lupine for *generosity*,
the way it held nothing back. O reed
canary grasses and grace—someone tell me
the difference again.

Write this down: my voice and a leaf
of aspen winding in the wind—we find the sun
from many spinning sides.

> —PATTIANN ROGERS

Island Civilization
A Vision for Planet Earth in the Year 2992

Roderick Frazier Nash *(1991)*

It is no news today that Planet Earth is not well. The problem, in a nutshell, is that one species out of thirty-odd million is growing in both its numbers and its impact on the environment to levels that are unsustainable on the finite spaceship that carries the only life of which we are aware through the cosmos. In the larger community, the global ecosystem, *Homo sapiens* is no longer a good neighbor. Our ability to coexist responsibly with other life forms began to disappear about 15,000 years ago, when we turned from hunting and gathering to herding and agriculture. Since then, through technological civilization we have carried environmental modification to dangerous extremes. Now there are signs that in our tendency toward uncontrolled growth, humans are a kind of cancer in the Earth organism. Like cancer cells, we destroy normal systems. Like cancer, we are very good at growth. We both do well in frontierlike contexts where expansion is a virtue. But ultimately, and ironically, we fail from our own success. It is well to remember that at the moment of a cancer's greatest achievement, its host organism is near death, *but so is the cancer.* Humans too will go down with the ecological ship unless we cultivate the capacity for self-restraint.

We are presently in the midst of the most powerful environmental movement in history. There is talk in the 1990s of a green decade and a coming green century. And we are starting to do some things reasonably well. Recycling, nonpolluting production, and energy efficiency are more than slogans. But most of today's environmentalists lack vision. I mean long-term vision: a conception of what we want civilization to be like in a thousand years. Without it, we have no compass to guide us through what will certainly be rough ecological seas ahead. Lacking long-term vision, we are like a skier whose focus is fifty feet down the hill. The short-term performance (contemporary conservation) may be impressive. But up ahead there is a cliff (the thresholds of irreversible change in the planet's life-support systems), and the myopic skier runs the risk of carving perfect turns right into the abyss! We need bifocal vision. We must operate in the day-to-day and year-to-year arena, but at the same time, we must keep an eye on the big, long-range picture. We are now playing God. For better or for worse, but probably for worse, the future of the planet is in our often clumsy hands.

The vision I am about to advance will be controversial because I am addressing the big, tough issues that entail subordination of human interests to the interests of the biotic whole. Even biocentrists and deep ecologists will disagree with parts of my proposal. But before the fur flies, let me urge the importance of futuristic thinking in general. If you don't like some or all of my dream of Island Civilization, create your own. The essential thing is that we occasionally lift our eyes from everyday details to the far horizons of planetary possibility. Where do we want our species, and nature in general, to be in a millennium? Without such goals there can be no direction. And without direction we drift into an increasingly frightening environmental abyss.

I will begin with four hopes or objectives that I entertain for the future of the human endeavor on Earth. The adjustments I then propose are designed to assist realization of them. First, I hope our presence on this planet can be sustained for many thousands of years. I do not share the misanthropy of the most radical deep ecologists whose extreme biocentrism persuades them that the best course for *Homo sapiens* is species suicide. Neither am I among the futurists who expect that Earth will no longer be our principal habitat in a thousand years.

Regardless of whether expansion into space works or not, it seems to me that we are morally obligated to care for our first home. To abandon a ravaged Earth for greener planetary pastures would be, at minimum, the height of ingratitude.

Second, I believe in the existence rights of all species and of normal ecosystematic processes. I further believe that these rights trump the rights of humans to increase their numbers, their affluence, and their claim to habitat. I hope that the avalanche of species extinctions occurring presently can be curtailed and that environmental ethics will guide future people-planet relationships. The moral community should eventually be identical with the ecological one. I anticipate natural rights expanding to embrace the rights of nature. I hope that in a thousand years not only all human beings, but also four-footed beings and rooted beings and flying beings and microbiotic beings will all join together in an expanded ecological brotherhood. Building on Martin Luther King Jr.'s 1963 rhetoric, I say let freedom ring not only from but *for* Stone Mountain in Georgia and also for oceans, rivers, and forests everywhere.

Third, I hope that a meaningful amount of wilderness will remain on this planet forever. I do not applaud a totally humanized, homogenized environment, no matter how beneficent or benign. Wilderness preservation is essential, not merely for human recreation, but as a gesture of planetary modesty on the part of a species that desperately needs to be reminded that it is a member and not the master of the ecosystem. Aldo Leopold understood this in the 1940s when he warned that the first law of successful tinkering is to save all the parts. The second law, we could now add, is to save the instructions, and these are contained in healthy wild ecosystems.

Finally (and here I expect to part company with respected colleagues on the more radical frontiers of environmentalism), I hope for full development of the human intellectual and technological potential. The sticker "Back to the Pleistocene" does not appear on my bumper. I regard many characteristics of modern civilization as worthy of protection and extension. What's wrong with symphonies, universities, and modern medical technology? Computers, television, and nuclear power are marvelous tools—if we only knew how to use them responsibly. And in a thousand years what wonders might exist?

Technology, you see, is not the basic problem. Machines only express human values. Change these values and you can alter the most basic pollution of all: mind pollution. And, since we are in control here, profound change is theoretically possible. The trick, as Henry David Thoreau recognized a century and a half ago, is "to secure all the advantages" of civilization "without suffering any of the disadvantages." Moreover, don't a reasonable number of humans have as much right to fulfill their evolutionary potential as any other form of life? *The essential proviso is that in doing so they don't compromise, or eliminate, the chances of other species to do the same.*

My thousand-year vision starts with the assumption that on a finite planet, shared with other species, only limited numbers of humans can enjoy unlimited opportunities. Restraint, in other words, is the key to progress. Less is indeed more. The first essential limitation must be in our numbers. We are now 5.3 billion and growing—fast. Demographers think that between 1 billion and 2 billion humans, living carefully and efficiently, is a sustainable population. So, in 2992, I call for about 1.5 billion human beings maximizing their potential while respecting the potentials of other beings. Wouldn't this be preferable to 14 billion or 40 billion barely clinging to a pathetic existence on a biologically impoverished planet?

The other major application of restraint that my proposal demands concerns living space. From the point of view of other species, one of the worst characteristics of contemporary human civilization is its tendency to sprawl. In the past five hundred years in the temperate latitudes, we have witnessed a frightening explosion of the human-modified environment. In Europe and large parts of Asia, Africa, and

North America we approach saturation. Unchecked, this expansion could affect every part of the planet. Remember, we are facing in the next thousand years an extrapolation of technical abilities beyond our wildest imaginings. Domed cities covering the poles and undersea subdivisions are very conceivable. Instead of this explosion, I call for *implosion*.

My dream for the next millennium envisions most of the 1.5 billion human beings living in five hundred concentrated habitats. Integrated into each one would be the means of food and material production and energy generation. In the vast spaces between these human habitats would be the habitats of other species. Most of the planet in 2992 should be returned to a wilderness condition. Instead of dominating the globe, humankind and its works should occupy small niches in a continuous wild ecosystem. Instead of islands of wildness in a matrix of civilization, as presently exists, we would have *Island Civilization*.

I use "habitats" rather than "cities" to imply that these future human environments will be unlike anything with which we are familiar. Accommodating about 3 million people each, they could be a mile high, both above and below ground or, perhaps, the surface of the sea. The technology of 2992 would permit habitats to exist anywhere on the planet. Civilization could be expected to expand on the poles, but it would shrink radically in the temperate latitudes. To more fully understand what I have in mind, consider that legally designated wilderness areas amount in 1992 to about 2 percent of the contiguous forty-eight American states. In 2992 the ratio would be reversed; Island Civilization would need no more than 2 percent of American soil. This is a much bigger "Outside" than even Dave Foreman has envisioned. It needs some explanation.

First, bear in mind that in a thousand years the 1.5 billion people on Earth will be using technology that is inconceivable today. For example, there will be no need to cut trees in 2992; wood will have been outmoded as a building and printing material (along with, perhaps, newspapers and books). With energy, water, materials, and foodstuffs produced inside or close by the habitats, dams and aqueducts are gone and with them all long-distance pipelines, cables, and transmission wires. Freeways and railroads no longer exist. All transportation in 2992 is in the air and, more likely, instantaneous. Science fiction, you say? Well, consider what was thought in the 1890s about a moon landing. I think that if humans can keep the planet habitable, they have unlimited technological potentials. Turn our best minds loose on the technical challenges of Island Civilization (rather than repairing the old, unsustainable paths) and it is not necessary to go back to the Pleistocene for a model of low-impact living.

What would living in Island Civilization be like? In addressing this important consideration it is necessary to put aside the termite-mound apartment house image. I am confident that architects of the future, building on the ideas of visionaries like Paolo Soleri, will be capable of designing very dense but very appealing single-structure habitats. Of course there will be sacrifices. What will be gone completely in the imploded habitat of 2992 is the "American Dream": single-family homes on half-acre lots widely separated from business and cultural centers and linked with networks of roads into a nearly continuous fabric of civilization.

But while I have in mind an *intensely* urban culture, I envision far more possibilities for contact with high-quality wilderness than exist at present. Just a few miles from the civilized islands will be where the wild things are: bears and wolves and elephants and tigers but also the full complement of the more humble species whose presence defines biodiversity and ecological health. Those who venture into this paradoxically wilder wilderness of a higher-technological culture must take it on its own terms. This will mean restraint in how people get into and what they take into wilderness. It will mean training and licensing in responsible wilderness etiquette. Backcountry skills would be commonplace in 2992 because every able-bodied citizen would have attended the University of the Wilderness. This educational interlude would be required between secondary schooling and college or career at the age of about twenty. I am not talking here about two-week Outward Bound courses but about several years of subsistence hunting and gathering completely out of contact with the civilized islands. Here is where we do go back to the Pleistocene! Young people, organized in tribal groups, follow the caribou through the mountain passes and fish for the salmon whose runs have been restored to the free-flowing rivers. They learn the ancient and primitive skills and, more importantly, the land wisdom and reverence of indigenous peoples.

Could someone live off the land a thousand years from now? You bet, considering that the numbers of eighteen- to twenty-one-year-olds doing so would be approximately equal to human population in the Pleistocene, and also considering that ecological integrity (especially healthy populations of edible animals) would have been restored. For example, in 2992, the Great Plains of the United States would, according to my scenario, consist of three human habitats occupying a few dozen square miles and 100,000 square miles of wild prairie. The buffalo would be back, along with the wolf and the grizzly. Humans could take their place along with the other predators. Southern California would have its several human habitats, but on the hundreds of miles of wild shoreline, foraging opportunities would be as good as they were for the ancient Chumash. Also as good as ever would be the chance to acquire an environmental ethic that underlies the ecological responsibility of Island Civilization.

How to make the dream of Island Civilization come true is beyond the scope of this outline proposal. Suffice it to observe that if the reform route proves ineffective, the radical option of force or revolution will make increasing sense, particularly to a population shocked and frightened by the early-warning signs of ecological catastrophe.

Violence, after all, has figured frequently in human history as a way to change paradigms. One thinks of the American Revolution and the Civil War. The abolitionist movement led in the 1860s to a violent solution to the problem of slavery in the United States. Environmentalism could similarly rationalize the use of force for the liberation of nature. Or, as some are starting to argue, the violence may come from nature, striking back and purging itself of the threatening human cancer. But whether by choice, coercion, or catastrophe, there *will* be an end to the present unsustainable levels of growth and devastation. It may be closer than we think. The twenty-first century could well be the last one with the option to correct the course of civilization in a mood of deliberation.

I am a historian, and from my perspective humankind now stands at a crossroads not merely of human history but of the entire evolutionary process. Life has evolved from stardust over billions of years until one species has developed the capacity to disrupt the whole biological miracle. But amidst the fear to which this thought leads, there is one comfort. We are not threatened, like the ecosystem of the dinosaurs, by a death star. *We are the death star.* We could also be the star of ecological salvation. This is simply the greatest challenge life on Earth has ever faced. Will the vision of Island Civilization help?

A Minority View
REJOINDER TO "ISLAND CIVILIZATION"

JOHN DAVIS *(1991)*

I cannot resist an editor's rejoinder to the foregoing. First, though, let me stress the importance of Professor Nash's article, whatever the merits or demerits of his specific suggestions. Rod Nash has made a profound suggestion: People need to begin to plan in accordance with the needs of life forms—all life forms—a thousand and more years hence.

I agree with about 98 percent of his vision but find the other 2 percent troubling. I offer the following objections to "Island Civilization" with the utmost respect for Professor Nash—one of the premier historians and environmental ethicists today. No one else associated with *Wild Earth* should be held accountable for what follows. These objections emanate from the perspective of a walking anachronism.

1. To speak of Earth as a "spaceship" or "ecological ship" is to heave insults at the only biologically diverse orb we know. This may seem a minor point, but the metaphors we use strongly influence the way we think about and relate to the natural world.

2. As Jerry Mander argues in his brilliant book *In the Absence of the Sacred,* it's time we disabuse ourselves of the notion that technology is neutral. Technologies developed in the past 15,000 years have almost invariably led to exploitation of nature, centralized power structures, and biological impoverishment. History does not lend itself to the view that post–Paleolithic technologies are likely to be used in a benign and sustainable fashion. As our ancestors developed tools and precursors to technology, they should have rested content with earthen

139

cookware, spears (perhaps), and—most important—fire. We could have spent happy millennia contemplating, telling stories about, weaving myths around, and perfecting appropriate uses of the tremendous power we know as fire.

3. Professor Nash used three too many zeros in his recommended population: 1.5 billion would almost certainly be incompatible with a full flowering of biodiversity; 1.5 million is plenty. Some will say the idea that we can peacefully reduce our population to 1.5 million is laughable. Not so. If, starting now, we all simply refrain from giving birth, we can reduce our numbers by three orders of magnitude in less than one hundred years. (Admittedly, implementing a birth moratorium will be problematic.) Moreover, 1.5 million far exceeds what most conservation biologists consider a minimum viable population for a large mammal. If human migration corridors (paths along what once were highways, for example) were maintained, a global human population of under 1 million could easily preserve its genetic diversity.

4. We may now be "playing God," but we shouldn't be. Conservationists should oppose such hubris at every turn. The thought of biological evolution being directed by a bunch of bumbling naked apes—some of whom wear thick glasses and pointy shoes—is, at best, distasteful.

5. Islands of civilization would almost inevitably cause extinctions, thus violating the existence rights of other beings. If we take seriously the idea of intrinsic, inalienable rights for all life forms, we cannot justly consign any sizable portion of the biosphere to human domination. Every area has unique life forms. Biologists are continually raising their estimates of the number of species on the planet (as well as the number going extinct every day). Recent studies suggest that even the ocean floor (which Nash says might someday be inhabited by humans) has indescribably great biodiversity. As scientists do more intensive studies of ocean sediments, forest soils, stream bottoms, caves, and other relatively unknown environments, they may well find

such high and localized diversity of organisms that we will be forced to concede that any thoroughly humanized landscape will extinguish singular life forms—each with as much right to exist as *Homo sapiens.*

6. Island civilization would perpetuate our alienation from nature. If we spend most of our lives in humanized environments, and especially if we don't experience the Big Outside until the age of eighteen, we will not gain Earth wisdom or knowledge of place. We'll be bleary-eyed dweebs.

7. Unless we accept the old Judeo-Christian idea of *creatio ex nihilo* (creation from nothing, an ability historically attributed only to God and capitalists), it's hard to see how large concentrations of people could sustain themselves without exploiting outside regions. Humans cannot persistently flout the laws of nature, in particular the second law of thermodynamics (entropy).

8. Again, humans will remain essentially at odds with nature as long as they employ high technology and live in artificial environments, as long as they refuse to be regular members of the biotic community. Moreover, as long as we are at odds with nature, we will remain like a cancer. It seems wildly improbable that a living organism can long play host to 500 benign tumors. Sooner or later, a tumor will turn malignant. Metastasis will follow; and before long, we'll be back to 1991.

To conclude these rough and hasty objections: Roderick Nash has done us a great service by making us look ahead, and has given us an enticing glimpse of a possible world a thousand years hence. I suggest, however, that a small part of his vision needs radical modification. We are indeed like skiers headed blindly toward an abyss. Let us, then, stop, shed these plastic appendages, climb back up the mountain while we still remember the way, and glissade gracefully down the side from whence we came . . . back to the Pleistocene.

Conservation Is Good Work

WENDELL BERRY *(1992)*

There are, as nearly as I can make out, three kinds of conservation currently operating. The first is the preservation of places that are grandly wild or "scenic" or in some other way spectacular. The second is what is called "conservation of natural resources"—that is, of the things of nature that we intend to use: soil, water, timber, and minerals. The third is what you might call industrial troubleshooting: the attempt to limit or stop or remedy the most flagrant abuses of the industrial system. All three kinds of conservation are inadequate, both separately and together.

Right at the heart of American conservation, from the beginning, has been the preservation of spectacular places. The typical American park is in a place that is "breathtakingly" beautiful or wonderful and of little apparent economic value. Mountains, canyons, deserts, spectacular landforms, geysers, waterfalls—these are the stuff of parks. There is, significantly, no prairie national park. Wilderness preserves, as Dave Foreman points out, tend to include much "rock and ice" and little marketable timber. Farmable land, in general, has tempted nobody to make a park. Wes Jackson has commented with some anxiety on the people who charge blindly across Kansas and eastern Colorado, headed for the mountains west of Denver. These are nature lovers and sightseers, but they are utterly oblivious of or bored by the rich natural and human history of the Plains. The point of Wes Jackson's anxiety is that the love of nature that limits itself to the love of places that are "scenic" is implicitly dangerous. It is dangerous because it tends to exclude unscenic places from nature and from the respect that we sometimes accord to nature. This is why so much of the landscape that is productively used is also abused; it is used solely according to standards dictated by the financial system and not at all according to standards dictated by the nature of the place. Moreover, as we are beginning to see, it is going to be extremely difficult to make enough parks to preserve vulnerable species and the health of ecosystems or large watersheds.

"Natural resources," the part of nature that we are going to use, is the part outside the parks and preserves (which, of course, we also use). But "conservation of natural resources" is now in confusion because it is a concept that has received much lip service but not much thought or practice. Part of the confusion is caused by thinking of "natural resources" as belonging to one category when, in fact, they belong to two: surface resources, like soils and forests, which can be preserved in use; and underground resources, like coal or oil, which cannot be. The one way to conserve the minable fuels and materials that use inevitably exhausts is to limit use. At present, we have no intention of limiting such use, and so we cannot say that we are at all interested in the conservation of exhaustible resources. Surface or renewable resources, on the other hand, can be preserved in use so that their yield is indefinitely sustainable.

Sustainability is a hopeful concept not only because it is a present necessity but because it has a history. We know, for example, that some agricultural soils have been preserved in continuous use for several thousand years. We know, moreover, that it is possible to improve soil in use. And it is clear that a forest can be used in such a way that it remains a forest, with its biological communities intact and its soil undamaged, while producing a yield of timber. But the methods by which exhaustible resources are extracted and used have set the pattern also for the use of sustainable resources, with the result that now soils and forests are not merely being used but are being used up, exactly as coal seams are used up.

Since the sustainable use of renewable resources depends on the existence of settled, small local economies and communities capable of preserving the local knowledge necessary for good farming and forestry, it is obvious that there is no simple, easy, or quick answer to the problem of the exhaustion of sustainable resources. We probably are not going to be able to conserve natural resources so long as our extraction and use of the goods of nature are wasteful and improperly scaled, or so long as these resources are owned or controlled by absentees, or so long as the standard of extraction and use is profitability rather than the health of natural and human communities.

Because we are living in an era of ecological crisis, it is understandable that much of our attention, anxiety, and energy is focused on exceptional cases, the outrages and extreme abuses of the industrial economy: global warming, the global assault on the last remnants of wilderness, the extinction of species, oil spills, chemical spills, Love Canal, Bhopal, Chernobyl, the burning oil fields of Kuwait. But a conservation effort that concentrates only on the extremes of industrial abuse tends to suggest that the only abuses are the extreme ones when, in fact, the earth is probably suffering more from many small abuses than from a few large ones. By treating the spectacular abuses as exceptional, the powers that be would like to keep us from seeing that the industrial system (capitalist or communist or socialist) is in itself and by necessity of all of its assumptions extremely dangerous and damaging and that it exists to support an extremely dangerous and damaging way of life. The large abuses exist within and because of a pattern of smaller abuses.

Much of the Sacramento River is now dead because a carload of agricultural poison was spilled into it. The powers that be would like us to believe that this colossal "accident" was an exception in a general pattern of safe use. Diluted and used according to the instructions on the label, they will tell us, the product that was spilled is harmless. They neglect to acknowledge any of the implications that surround the accident: that if this product is to be used in dilution almost everywhere, it will have to be manufactured, stored, and transported in concentration somewhere; that even in "harmless" dilution, such chemicals are getting into the water, the air, the rain, and into the bodies of animals and people; that when such a product is distributed to the general public, it will inevitably be spilled in its concentrated form in large or small quantities and that such "accidents" are anticipated, discounted as "acceptable risk," and charged to nature and society by the powers that be; that such chemicals are needed, in the first place, because the scale, the methods, and the economy of American agriculture are all monstrously out of kilter; that such chemicals are used to replace the work and intelligence of people; and that such a deformed agriculture is made necessary, in the first place, by the public's demand for a diet that is at once cheap and luxurious—too cheap to support adequate agricultural communities or good agricultural methods or good maintenance of agricultural land and yet so goofily self-indulgent as to demand, in every season, out-of-season foods produced by earth-destroying machines and chemicals.

We tend to forget, too, in our just and necessary outrage at the government-led attack on public lands and the last large tracts of wilderness, that for the very same reasons and to the profit of the very same people, thousands of woodlots are being abusively and wastefully logged.

Here, then, are three kinds of conservation, all of them urgently necessary and all of them failing. Conservationists have won enough victories to give them heart and hope and a kind of accreditation, but they know better than anybody how immense and how baffling their task has become. For all their efforts, our soils and waters, forests and grasslands are being used up. Kinds of creatures, kinds of human life, good natural and human possibilities are being destroyed. Nothing now exists anywhere on earth that is not under threat of human destruction. Poisons are everywhere. Junk is everywhere.

These dangers are large and public, and they inevitably cause us to think of changing public policy. This is good, so far as it goes. There should be no relenting in our efforts to influence politics and politicians. But in the name of honesty and sanity we must recognize the limits of politics. It is, after all, much easier to improve a policy than it is to improve the community the policy attempts to affect. And it is also probable that some changes required by conservation cannot be politically made and that some necessary changes will have to be made by the governed without the help or approval of the government.

I must admit here that my experience over more than twenty years as part of an effort to influence agricultural policy has not been encouraging. Our arguments directed at the government and the universities by now remind me of the ant crawling up the buttocks of the elephant with love on his mind. We have not made much impression. My conclusion, I imagine, is the same as the ant's, for these great projects, once undertaken, are hard to abandon: we have got to get more radical.

However destructive may be the policies of the government and the methods and products of the corporations, the root of the problem is always to be found in private life. We must learn to see that every problem that concerns us as conservationists always leads straight to the question of how we live. The world is being destroyed, no doubt about it, by the greed of the rich and powerful. It is also being destroyed by popular demand. There are not enough rich and powerful people to consume the whole world; for that, the rich and powerful need the help of countless ordinary people. We acquiesce in the wastefulness and destructiveness of the national and global economics by acquiescing in the wastefulness and destructiveness of our own households and communities. If conservation is to have a hope of succeeding, then conservationists, while continuing their effort to change public life, are going to have to begin the effort to change private life as well.

The problems we are worried about are caused not just by other people but by ourselves. And this realization should lead directly to two more. The first is that solving these problems is not work merely for so-called environmental organizations and agencies but also for individuals, families, and local communities. We are used to hearing about turning off unused lights, putting a brick in the toilet tank, using water-saving shower heads, setting the thermostat low, sharing rides, and so forth—pretty dull stuff. But I'm talking about actual jobs of work that are interesting because they require intelligence and because they are accomplished in response to interesting questions: What are the principles of household economy, and how can they be applied under present circumstances? What are the principles of a neighbor-hood or a local economy, and how can they be applied under present circumstances? What do people already possess in their minds and bodies, in their families and neighborhoods, in their dwellings and in their local landscape, that can replace what is now being supplied by our consumptive and predatory so-called economy? What can we sup-ply to ourselves cheaply or for nothing that we are now paying dearly for? To answer such questions requires more intelligence and involves more pleasure than all the technological breakthroughs of the last two hundred years.

Second, the realization that we ourselves, in our daily economic life, are causing the problems we are trying to solve ought to show us the inadequacy of the language we are using to talk about our connec-tion to the world. The idea that we live in something called "the envi-ronment," for instance, is utterly preposterous. This word came into use because of the pretentiousness of learned experts who were em-barrassed by the religious associations of "Creation" and who thought "world" too mundane. But "environment" means that which surrounds or encircles us; it means a world separate from ourselves, outside us. The real state of things, of course, is far more complex and intimate and interesting than that. The world that environs us, that is around us, is also within us. We are made of it; we eat, drink, and breathe it; it is bone of our bone and flesh of our flesh. It is also a Creation, a holy mystery, made for and to some extent by creatures, some but by no means all of whom are humans. This world, this Creation, belongs in a limited sense to us, for we may rightfully require certain things of it—the things necessary to keep us fully alive as the kind of creature we are—but we also belong to it, and it makes certain rightful claims on us: that we care properly for it, that we leave it undiminished not just to our children but to all the creatures who will live in it after us. None of this intimacy and responsibility is conveyed by the word *environment*.

That word is a typical product of the old dualism that is at the root of most of our ecological destructiveness. So, of course, is "biocentrism." If life is at the center, what is at the periphery? And for that matter, *where* is the periphery? "Deep ecology," another bifurcating term, implies that there is, a couple of layers up, a shallow ecology that is not so good—or that an ecosystem is a sort of layer cake with the icing on the bottom. Not only is this language incapable of giving a true description of our relation to the world; it is also academic, artificial, and pretentious. It is the sort of language used by a visiting expert who does not want the local people to ask any questions. (I am myself an anthropobiotheointerpenetrist and a gastrointeroenvironmentalist, but I am careful to say so only in the company of other experts.)

No settled family or community has ever called its home place an "environment." None has ever called its feeling for its home place "biocentric" or "anthropocentric." None has ever thought of its connection to its home place as "ecological," deep or shallow. The concepts and insights of the ecologists are of great usefulness in our predicament, and we can hardly escape the need to speak of "ecology" and "ecosystems." But the terms themselves are culturally sterile. They come from the juiceless, abstract intellectuality of the universities which was invented to disconnect, displace, and disembody the mind. The real names of the environment are the names of rivers and river valleys; creeks, ridges, and mountains; towns and cities; lakes, woodlands, lanes, roads, creatures, and people.

And the real name of our connection to this everywhere different and differently named earth is "work." We are connected by work
even to the places where we don't work, for all places are connected; it
is clear by now that we cannot exempt one place from our ruin of another. The name of our *proper* connection to the earth is "good work,"
for good work involves much giving of honor. It honors the source of
its materials; it honors the place where it is done; it honors the art by
which it is done; it honors the thing that it makes and the user of the
made thing. Good work is always modestly scaled, for it cannot ignore
either the nature of individual places or the differences between places,
and it always involves a sort of religious humility, for not everything is
known. Good work can be defined only in particularity, for it must be
defined a little differently for every one of the places and every one of
the workers on the earth.

The name of our present society's connection to the earth is
"bad work"—work that is only generally and crudely defined, that
enacts a dependence that is ill understood, that enacts no affection and
gives no honor. Every one of us is to some extent guilty of this bad
work. This guilt does not mean that we must indulge in a lot of breast-
beating and confession; it means only that there is much good work
to be done by every one of us and that we must begin to do it. All of
us are responsible for bad work, not so much because we do it ourselves (though we all do it) as because we have it done for us by other
people.

Here we are bound to see our difficulty as almost overwhelming. What
proxies have we issued, and to whom, to use the earth in our behalf?
How, in this global economy, are we to render anything like an accurate geographical account of our personal economies? How do we
take our lives from this earth that we are so anxious to protect and
restore to health?

Most of us get almost all the things we need by buying them;

most of us know only vaguely, if at all, where those things come from; and most of us know not at all what damage is involved in their production. We are almost entirely dependent on an economy of which we are almost entirely ignorant. The provenance, for example, not only of the food we buy at the store but of the chemicals, fuels, metals, and other materials necessary to grow, harvest, transport, process, and package that food is almost necessarily a mystery to us. To know the full economic history of a head of supermarket cauliflower would require an immense job of research. To be so completely and so ignorantly dependent on the present abusive food economy certainly defines us as earth abusers. It also defines us as potential victims.

Living as we now do in almost complete dependence on a global economy, we are put inevitably into a position of ignorance and irresponsibility. No one can know the whole globe. We can connect ourselves to the globe as a whole only by means of a global economy that, without knowing the earth, plunders it for us. The global economy (like the national economy before it) operates on the superstition that the deficiencies or needs or wishes of one place may safely be met by the ruination of another place. To build houses here, we clear-cut the forests there. To have air-conditioning here, we strip-mine the mountains there. To drive our cars here, we sink our oil wells there. It is an absentee economy. Most people aren't using or destroying what they can see. If we cannot see our garbage or the grave we have dug with our energy proxies, then we assume that all is well. The issues of carrying capacity and population remain abstract and not very threatening to most people for the same reason. If this nation or region cannot feed its population, then food can be imported from other nations or regions. All the critical questions affecting our use of the earth are left to be answered by "the market" or the law of supply and demand, which proposes no limit on either supply or demand. An economy without limits is an economy without discipline.

Conservationists of all kinds would agree, I think, that no discipline, public or private, is implied by the industrial economy and that none is practiced by it. The implicit wish of the industrial economy is that producers might be wasteful, shoddy, and irresponsible and that consumers might be gullible, extravagant, and irresponsible. To fulfill this wish, the industrial economy employs an immense corps of hireling politicians, publicists, lobbyists, admen, and adwomen. The consequent ruin is notorious: we have been talking about it for generations; it brought conservation into being. And conservationists have learned very well how to address this ruin as a public problem. There is now no end to the meetings and publications in which the horrifying statistics are recited, usually with the conclusion that pressure should be put on the government to do something. Often, this pressure has been applied and the government has done something. But the government has not done enough and may never do enough. It is likely that the government *cannot* do enough.

The government's disinclination to do more than it does is explained, of course, by the government's bought-and-paid-for servitude to interests that do not want it to do more. But there may also be a limit of another kind: a government that could do enough, assuming it had the will, would almost certainly be a government radically and unpleasantly different from the one prescribed by our Constitution. A government undertaking to protect all of nature that is now abused or threatened would have to take total control of the country. Police and bureaucrats—and opportunities for malfeasance—would be everywhere. To wish only for a public or a political solution to the problem of conservation may be to wish for a solution as bad as the problem and still be unable to solve it.

The way out of this dilemma is to understand the ruin of nature as a problem that is both public and private. The failure of public discipline in matters of economy is only the other face of the failure of private discipline. If we have worked at the issues of public policy so long and so exclusively as to bring political limits into sight, then let us turn—not instead but also—to issues of private economy and see how far we can go in that direction. It is a direction that may take us further and produce more satisfactory and lasting results than the direction of policy.

The dilemma of private economic responsibility, as I have said, is that we have allowed our suppliers to enlarge our economic boundaries so far that we cannot be responsible for our effects on the world. The only remedy for this that I can see is to draw in our economic boundaries, shorten our supply lines, so as to permit us literally to know where we are economically. The closer we live to the ground that we live from, the more we will know about our economic life; the more we know about our economic life, the more able we will be to take responsibility for it. The way to bring discipline into one's personal or household or community economy is limit one's economic geography.

This obviously opens up an agenda almost as daunting as the political agenda. The difference—a consoling one—is that when we try to influence policy, only large jobs must be done; whereas when we seek to reform private economies, the work is necessarily modest, and it can be started by anybody anywhere. What is required is the formation of local economic strategies—and eventually of local economies— by which to resist abuses of natural and human communities by the larger economy. And, of course, in talking about the formation of local economies capable of using an earthly place without ruining it, we are talking about the reformation of people; we are talking about reviving good work as an economic force.

If we think of this task of rebuilding local economies as one large task that must be done in a hurry, then we will again be overwhelmed and will want the government to do it. If, on the other hand, we define the task as beginning the reformation of our private or household economies, then the way is plain. What we must do is use well the considerable power we have as consumers: the power of choice. We can choose to buy or not to buy, and we can choose what to buy. The standard by which we choose must be the health of the community—and by that we must mean the *whole* community: ourselves, the place where we live, and all the humans and other creatures who live there with us. In a healthy community, people will be richer in their neighbors, in neighborhood, in the health and pleasure of neighborhood, than in their bank accounts. It is better, therefore, even if the cost is greater, to buy near at hand than to buy at a distance. It is better to buy from a small, privately owned local store than from a chain store. It is better to buy a good product than a bad one. Do not buy anything you don't need. Do as much as you can for yourself. If you cannot do something for yourself, see if you have a neighbor who can do it for you. Do everything you can to see that your money stays as long as possible in the local community. If you have money to invest, try to invest it locally, both to help the local community and to keep from helping the larger economy that is destroying local communities. Begin to ask yourself how your money could be put at minimal interest into the hands of a young person who wants to start a farm, a store, a shop, or a small business that the community needs. This agenda can be followed by individuals and single families. If it is followed by people in groups—churches, conservation organizations, neighborhood associations, groups of small farmers, and the like—the possibilities multiply and the effects will be larger.

The economic system that most affects the health of the world and that may be most subject to consumer influence is that of food. And the issue of food provides an excellent example of what I am talking about. If you want to reform your own food economy, you can make a start without anybody's permission or help. If you have a place to do it, grow some food for yourself. Growing some of your own food gives you pleasure, exercise, knowledge, sales resistance, and standards. Your own food, if you grow it the right way, will taste good and so will cause you to wish to buy food that tastes good. So far as you can, buy food that is locally grown. Tell your grocer that you are interested in locally grown food. If you can't find locally grown food in stores, then see if you can deal directly with a local farmer. The value of this, for conservationists, is that when consumers are acquainted and friendly with their producers, they can influence production. They can know the land on which their food is produced. They can refuse to buy food that is produced with dangerous chemicals or by other destructive practices. As these connections develop, local agriculture will diversify, become more healthy and more stable, employ more people. As local demand increases and becomes more knowledgeable, small food-processing industries will enter the local economy. Everything that is done by the standard of community health will make new possibilities for good work—that is, for the responsible use of the world.

The forest economy is not so obviously subject to consumer influence, but such influence is sorely needed. Both the forests themselves and their human communities suffer for the want of local forest economies—properly scaled wood-products industries that would be the basis of stable communities and would provide local incentives for the good use of the forest. People who see that they must depend on the forest for generations, in a complex local forest economy, will want the forest to last and be healthy; they will *not* want to see all the marketable timber ripped out of it as fast as possible. Both forest and farm communities would benefit from technologies that could be locally supplied and maintained. Draft horses, for example, are better than large machines, both for the woods and for the local economy.

The economy of recreation has hardly been touched as an issue of local economy and conservation, though conservationists and consumers alike have much to gain from making it such an issue. At present, there is an almost complete disconnection between the economic use of privately owned farm and forest land and its use for recreation. Such land is now much used by urban people for hunting and fishing, but mainly without benefit to the landowners, who therefore receive no incentive from this use to preserve wildlife habitat or to take the best care of their woodlands and stream margins. They need to receive such incentives. It is not beyond reason that public funds might be given to private landowners to preserve and enhance the recreational value—that is, the wildness—of their land. But since governments are unlikely to do this soon, the incentives need to be provided by consumer and conservation groups working in cooperation with farm groups. The rule of the food economy ought to apply to the recreation economy: find your pleasure and your rest as near home as possible. In Kentucky, for example, we have hundreds of miles of woodland stretching continuously along the sides of our creek and river valleys. Why should conservation and outdoor groups not pay an appropriate price to farmers to maintain hiking trails and campsites and preserve the forests in such places? The money that would carry a family to a vacation in a distant national park could thus be kept at home and used to help the local economy and protect the local countryside.

The point of all this is the use of local buying power, local gumption, and local affection to see that the best care is taken of the local land. This sort of effort would bridge the gap, now so destructive, between the conservationists and the small farmers and ranchers, and that would be one of its great political benefits. But the fundamental benefit would be to the world and ourselves. We would begin to protect the world not just by conserving it but also by living in it.

NIGHT AND FOG
THE BACKLASH AGAINST THE ENDANGERED SPECIES ACT

R. WILLS FLOWERS *(1992)*

"The struggle against the great beasts is ended, but it is being inexorably carried on against the tiny creatures."

—ADOLPH HITLER

Of all the ongoing commemorations and fifty-year anniversaries of World War II events, the most bizarre has been unfolding during 1992. In 1942 and half a century later, two government committees met with very similar agendas. The 1942 committee became known as the Wannsee Conference, which was convened to organize Hitler's Final Solution and give it a patina of legality; the 1992 Endangered Species Committee gave Interior Secretary Manuel Lujan and the timber industry a similar license to deal with the "spotted owl problem." Both cases illustrate governments fixated on the idea that lesser, nonhuman creatures had become "obstacles to progress" and required removal. When the Endangered Species Act (ESA) comes up for renewal following fall elections, Congress could, by weakening or killing the act, complete the process begun by the "God Squad" and make the United States the second country in history to give legal sanction to extermination as legitimate social policy. Why has the Endangered Species Act, which has been seen as a proud and uniquely American contribution to ethical development, run into so much trouble?

In recent years, complaining about endangered species has become the last socially acceptable form of publicly airing racist proclivities. The same media that take the moral high ground with regard to hate-mongering against human minorities see no contradiction in passing on the same sort of ranting against nonhumans. "Speciesism," despite its rather dry academic sound, is a brand of racism: the appeals to base emotions, the whipping up of hatred, the scapegoating are done the same way, whether the chosen victims are Jews, Orientals, Africans, or spotted owls. It is perhaps a measure of the interconnectedness of all life that racist attitudes and rhetoric can be readily transferred back and forth between unpopular human minorities and inconvenient non-human species.

As most people involved in human rights issues would agree, the truly insidious racism comes cloaked in guises of logic and science. Also, historically, difficult economic times lead to racism of all kinds. With the current recession (due in no small part to past orgies of growthmania) the developers and their political allies, long chafing under current environmental laws, are looking forward to a return to the pre-ESA days when wiping out plants and animals was no big deal.

The January 1992 issue of the *Atlantic Monthly* ran a "Playing God" spread of three articles that together give an excellent preview of the coming charge by the developers against the Endangered Species Act. "The Butterfly Problem" (Mann and Plummer 1992) and "The Case for Human Beings" (Palmer 1992), two triumphs of moral obtuseness and ethical obfuscation, sound notes we will no doubt be hearing with increasing frequency and volume: saving species is not necessary if it costs money, and species have been going extinct for aeons anyway, so don't worry, be happy.

Palmer, in a fine display of what David Ehrenfeld (1981) calls the "arrogance of humanism," professes himself concerned with the image of *Homo sapiens* "as a vast, featureless mob of yahoos mindlessly trampling this planet's most ancient and delicate harmonies." Most of us would say that image is rather accurate and, interestingly, Palmer himself raises no substantive contradictions. His preference is to retreat into the now-familiar, self-congratulatory New Age fantasizing about ourselves as "special planetary geniuses," "the crown of creation," and the like. Mann and Plummer use an incident in Oregon, where a developer came up against an endangered butterfly while trying to build yet another golf course, to air a long litany of complaints against the Endangered Species Act: it is complicated and political, and its mandate is far beyond its present capabilities. And it interferes with making money.

What both articles carefully avoid is the central issue: endangered species get that way because humans are killing them and destroying their habitat. Obscuring this point has become a common debating trick of the extermination lobby, evidently with some effect: even some biologists (who should know better) talk confusedly of "the debate about preservation and management versus letting nature take its course" (Morowitz 1991). The "playing God" metaphor invoked by the *Atlantic* is similarly devious (not to mention blasphemous); we are not "planetary geniuses" deciding whether or not to interfere in some tragedy caused by "nature." If metaphors are in order, a more recent one fits: the Lebensraum politics of half a century ago when a pack of hack politicians convinced a cultured, literate nation that their economic problems could be solved by taking over "underused" land populated by lesser beings who were obstructing progress for the "special Aryan geniuses." World War II and its aftermath resulted in formal legal recognition that genocide is legally indefensible. To claim that deliberate extermination is evil only when it is applied to human gene pools is itself a racist argument.

THE NEW FINAL SOLUTIONISM

The negative reaction of developers to the Endangered Species Act is predictable. Less understandable is the almost torpid response of many biologists and even many conservationists. Perhaps they are daunted by the prospect of thousands of snail darter–style battles. The term "triage" is now often used in discussions on endangered species. People on both sides of the issue like this word: it can let developers off a lot of legal hooks (one for each species deemed "too far gone" to save); it can let environmentalists pick and choose their battles with an eye to good publicity and, of course, winning. By using the triage analogy, they evade moral responsibility: the triage officer in a hospital is not the one causing the injuries. In the real world, some of the very interests that push a species to the brink of extinction get to shape the "compromises" that are supposed to save that species.

However, developers have taken a measure of the times and have decided that they need not settle for halfway measures; they seek a "flexible" Endangered Species Act that can be bent whenever a developer or land speculator might lose money. The attacks by developers, "wise-usies" (including the "Moonies" who subsidize them), the Bush administration and other right-wing politicians, and obnoxious talk-radio gurus form what we may call the New Final Solutionism. Like the first Final Solution, present-day Final Solutionism seeks the legal power to eliminate entire genetic stocks of beings that the dominant power structure deems "inconvenient." And like the original, the New Final Solutionism masks its true agenda with a fog of scientific and economic buzz-concepts. Even the propaganda the developers are using is recycled from fifty years ago: one of the bills offered with the intent to subvert the ESA is called the Human Protection Act, as if we have to be protected from all those threatening hordes of almost extinct species. Those with a sense of history should note that as prelude to the Final Solution, the Nazis devoted considerable effort to cultivating the perception that the German people were in desperate need of "protection" from Jews, Slavs, Gypsies, trade unionists, Seventh-Day Adventists, and so on.

"The banality of evil" was Hannah Arendt's famous line describing the first Holocaust; one could apply the same to the politics of the present biodiversity holocaust. While the developers scheme and maneuver for their "flexible ESA," they are also busy slithering through legal loopholes in the existing Endangered Species Act to get on with the business of eliminating inconvenient life-forms. When court rulings in the 1970s forced the government to protect species whether they were large and cute or not, the Endangered Species Committee was created under pressure from a mixture of developers and Republicans such as former senator Howard Baker. The committee became known as the God Squad, but their mission can scarcely be called divine. They were created to find excuses, and a legalistic gloss, for the extermination of species whose existence crimps the money-making of this or that special interest. Given the nature of their mission, "God" seems rather inappropriate in a nickname for the Endangered Species Committee. My suggestion would be Night and Fog Squad, named for the Night and Fog Decree of the Third Reich—one of the decrees that gave legal cover for the killing taking place at Auschwitz, Treblinka, and elsewhere. Considering its unsavory political genesis, it is perhaps surprising that the "exemption" for the spotted owl is only one of two granted by our modern Night and Fog Squad. Administration spin doctors quickly pointed to the 2,684 acres still off-limits and Lujan's "alternative plan" [also known, for no sane reason, as the "preservation plan"], which supposedly will keep the owl going for another hundred years. The other unique species of the Pacific Northwest old growth never even made it into the political dialogue (though salmon have belatedly been given some attention). Typical of political decisions, the Endangered Species Committee action on the owl is a "compromise" that guarantees extinction but not right away, so that current office holders and bureaucrats will not be held responsible for the consequences of their actions. Here again, comparisons between Hitlerism and Lujanism force themselves to our attention. As any competent analysis of the timber industry shows, the spotted owl is no more responsible for loggers' job losses than an "international Jewish conspiracy" was for the inability of the German army to stand up to American doughboys in World War I. But Bush and Lujan have their scapegoat, which serves the double purpose of diverting loggers' attention from antijobs policies in their own industry, and of taking a whack at environmentalists, a group that the Right evidently needs as an enemy now that Communism has gone bust.

As the "owl vs. jobs" debate and all the other controversies surrounding the Endangered Species Act grind on, many conservationists talk of "protecting habitat" as a better alternative to the present law of protecting species. This looks attractive—until you start thinking like a lawyer. What, legally, is a "habitat"? How would you define and limit a habitat or ecosystem in ways that would be comprehensible to the legal profession? Given the lack of agreement even among ecologists (remember the debate about whether climax communities are real?), there seems little reason to think anyone could draft a habitat protection law that would stand the legal buffeting that the Endangered Species Act has so far weathered. The *Atlantic's* "God" issue carried a third article about the "habitat alternative" and its great hope: gap analysis (Winckler 1992). As a tool of conservation biology, gap analysis could be very helpful (although it is not so very new: Ian McHarg years ago promoted an almost identical technique for rational urban development). It could also be a cover for yet more moral cop-outs: Winckler sees the strongest virtue of gap analysis as its ability to locate "species-rich land least encumbered by controversy." Yet a proper "habitat protection act" could be far more controversial than the ESA. As Noss (1991) has shown, only 2 percent of recognized ecosystem types in the United States may be adequately protected. Given that conservation biologists by and large agree that "adequate protection" means protecting large areas (like 1 million hectares), one can imagine the howling and bellowing from the wise-usies, Lujanistas, Quayle-udes, and their ilk once they got wind of such a plan.

"WHEN THEY CAME FOR THE BUTTERFLY, I DID NOT OBJECT"

Racism is as often thoughtless as it is malicious. I suspect most practitioners and boosters of the New Final Solutionism, from Manuel Lujan and Dan Quayle's Council on Competitiveness to the loggers with their "Eat an Owl / Wipe with a Woodpecker" bumper stickers, would be genuinely upset to be confronted with the fifty-year-old pedigree of their ideology. Insensitivity and selfishness come especially easily in economic hard times, when the "circle of expanding ethical concern" (Nash 1989) has a habit of contracting. The backlash against endangered species can be seen as part of such a general contraction, where women, inner-city dwellers, and most ethnic minorities also find themselves being pushed outside the circle. The Nazi experience shows just how dangerous life outside that circle can be.

To some extent, the Endangered Species Act is analogous to the laws enacted by postwar Germany and Japan and recent civil rights legislation in our own country to atone for and prevent recurrence of past crimes of racism. With its current regulations and legal interpretations, the Endangered Species Act is also the closest thing we have to legal recognition of the concept that all life has value. Accordingly, any repeal or watering down of the ESA would also be a recantation of that concept of respecting all life and a return to tacit legal acceptance of genocide. Even dyed-in-the-wool humanists should be uncomfortable with that. As John Rodman wrote in his essay "The Liberation of Nature?" (1977), "the insane vision of an Aryan Europe purged of Jewish influence is intimately bound up with the equally insane vision of a humanized planet on which all other species have been either enslaved or liquidated."

In his book *The Rights of Nature,* Roderick Nash (1989) has drawn detailed parallels between pre–Civil War abolitionists and today's radical environmentalists. There are similar connections between the Emancipation Proclamation and the Endangered Species Act. Both were enacted with very limited aims, but in both cases it soon became apparent that the act had broken new ethical ground that would cause fundamental changes in society. And today's backlash against the Endangered Species Act echoes an earlier backlash—in the North—against the Emancipation Proclamation. At the end of 1862, there was widespread disillusionment and discontent in the North and a strong sentiment to end the war and accept slavery or a divided nation. Freeing the slaves was costing more money and blood than many voters thought worthwhile. Against this backdrop, President Lincoln sent his State of the Union message to Congress. His defense of the moral necessity of the Proclamation applies with equal force today: by legalizing the right to life of every species, we further protect the right to life of all races and cultures of humans. "We—even we here—hold the power and bear the responsibility. . . . In giving freedom to the slave, we assure freedom to the free—honorable alike in what we give and what we preserve. We shall nobly save or meanly lose the last, best hope of earth."

LITERATURE CITED

Ehrenfeld, D. 1981. *The Arrogance of Humanism.* New York: Oxford University Press.

Mann, C. C., and M. L. Plummer. 1992. The butterfly problem. *Atlantic Monthly* 269(1): 47–70.

Morowitz, H. J. 1991. Balancing species preservation and economic considerations. *Science* 253: 752–54.

Nash, R. 1989. *The Rights of Nature: A History of Environmental Ethics.* Madison: University of Wisconsin Press.

Noss, R. 1991. What can wilderness do for biodiversity? *Wild Earth* 1(2): 51–56.

Palmer, T. 1992. The case for human beings. *Atlantic Monthly* 269(1): 83–89.

Rodman, J. 1977. The liberation of nature? *Inquiry* 20: 83–145.

Tolland, J. 1976. *Adolf Hitler.* Garden City, N.Y.: Doubleday.

Winckler, S. 1992. Stopgap measures. *Atlantic Monthly* 269(1): 74–81.

ECOPORN AND THE MANIPULATION
OF DESIRE

José Knighton *(1993)*

Along the eastern horizon, the swollen orange edge of the sun finally burns into view after staining the December morning for an hour with a wash of mauve, maroon, and crimson. I howl to my distant companion, out of sight along the rim of a ghostly world just being unveiled by highlights. He, I'm sure, is well aware of our world's enlightenment, peering through the window of his large-format camera, adjusting the bellows above its cumbersome tripod. But I howl anyway for the pure joy of it.

The towering Wingate cliffs are first to be splashed with frost-dispelling fire—Island in the Sky above us, Ekker and Elaterite Buttes to the west and the ribbon of the Orange Cliffs beyond. Bands of mist with echoing shadows condense across their faces, rising from the bewildering, convoluted ridges of the Maze. The meandering tangle of canyons beyond and below my perch on the undercut White Rim is as convoluted as the surface of the brain, and their depths as ineffable. An interlocking sandstone sprawl fills the arc of horizon beyond the Green River down to its confluence with the Colorado, to Cataract Canyon, the Needles' distant prongs of light, Horse Mountain, the Seven Sisters, Cathedral Butte, the blue bulk of the Abajo Mountains. Backlit luminescent mist rises from frosted meadows beyond the Colorado. The other Wingate rim of the world, Hart's Point to Hatch Point and the Needles Overlook, drapes long shadows below the now-full disk of sun.

A picture is worth a thousand words. From my precipitous peninsula I can just discern a dark fleck along the bay of overhanging cliffs where Todd is stationed to catch a fragment of fantastic morning fusion. He frames the glowing monument of Ekker Butte with its hoop of uncanny mist. In his foreground a shadowed, absurdly overbalanced hulk of White Rim looms on a tapering pedestal flake that could peel and collapse under the weight of a chittering junco. One picture will capture a minor fraction of an immense, yet intimate, moment of magical Canyonlands sunrise, a meager instant of the shifting tide at the warm end of the spectrum across a thousand canyons, cliffs, spires, buttes, and indescribable sculpted forms. But captured it will be.

One picture . . . and I could babble a million words in feeble approximation. In an hour, full daylight will again cast normality across Canyonlands. The odd mist will burn off. Hard white light will fill the deep shadows. A miraculous dawn will become a savored memory. But Todd's camera, barring any major lapses in technology and technique, will have trapped a sacred moment like a rabbit in a snare. And its reproductions will be as permanent as a taxidermied jackalope.

My petty resentment is showing, my mean-spirited stinginess. I want to embrace this moment that we struggled for, rose before a frozen dawn for, thawed an ice-filled coffeepot for, slept through a too-long, frost-rimed December night for. I want to hoard the immeasurable, transitory glory that we share with no other visible humans. Someday, potentially, Todd's fragment of this brilliant dawn could be reexperienced by someone warm and comfortable in an easy chair, leafing through a magazine or glancing at a calendar. But there is more to my concern than petty resentment, something that has stirred a disconcerting apprehension.

My friend Bruce, a photographer of significant discipline and taste, and I stood around a table of this year's barrage of nature calendars criticizing the undeniable allure of their contents. I made a flippant and spontaneous comment about this year's crop of "ecoporn."

Bruce, although he had been critical of nearly every posed bit of land-scape, gave me a sudden look of what was at once dumbfoundment, horror, and recognition. Our shared laughter dissolved the tension and irony of my statement.

Unfortunately, once they are coined, metaphors, portentous or vacuous, tend to circulate. I found myself compelled to analyze this one mainly to dispel what I felt was a superficial illusion that perti-nence arose merely from the pinup style of calendars.

Pornography, even in a liberal atmosphere, is a heavy accusation. Even the tame Hefneresque version is insidious because it manipulates desire, taints it with consumerism, and misdirects passion away from reality toward an inanimate object. Worst of all, it mutates a living, breathing human being into an inanimate object in the eye of the beholder.

The model, chosen for her (or his) approximation of a stereo-typed ideal, is posed in the intimate setting of a bedroom or shower. Selectively provocative lighting simulates dawn or evening glow through a shuttered window. A suggestive atmosphere manipulated by rose-colored filters or Vaseline lens reveals those physical attributes most alluring to the viewer, attributes otherwise available only after achieving an intimate relationship. The vital, animate sexual persona becomes an object of desire—cheesecake. Even if no response or pas-sion is aroused in the viewer (a frequent but questionable claim), a physical persona of surpassing beauty has been grotesquely trivialized by being removed from essence and context.

After drawing parallels to the preceding analysis of pornographic imagery, I have to include much landscape photography as effectively pornographic. Landscape photographers resort to the methodology of creating a pornographic image, and the result is equally manipulative and exploiting.

The stereotyped ideal, the towering peak or other monumental landform, is posed in a setting of intimacy from the scenic viewpoint.

Perspective and foreground further reveal familiarity. Selectively provocative lighting—dawn, alpenglow, and stormlight—is preferred. A suggestive atmosphere manipulated by rose-colored, diffusing, or polarizing filters reveals those physical attributes most alluring to the viewer, attributes otherwise available only after achieving an intimate relationship. All the same techniques are used to enhance the captured reality, to beef up the bosom of the Grand Tetons.

This could all be perceived as a coincidence of photographic method were it not that, as with cheesecake and beefcake, the intention of most landscape photography is to appeal to, even seduce, the beholder with an image removed from its physical context, amplified into a commodity by technique. Neutral reality is objectified to evoke a subjective response for commercial gain, to sell calendars and magazine subscriptions or to connive contributions.

This accusation does not deny the artistry of landscape photographers. Nor does it necessarily invoke an Islamic edict against representationism. In fact, the manipulation of the viewer's (or participant's) response is an intrinsic aspect of art. It does, however, reveal a certain kinship between David Muench and David Hamilton, between Ansel Adams and Helmut Newton. The commercialization of art may be an unavoidable consequence of capitalism. This flaw, though, is not the sin in the heart of greater and lesser landscape photographers. Nor is its counterpart the focus of outrage from the women's rights movement toward pornographic imagery.

That outrage is aimed squarely at the exploitation of the female body, and the psychic damage to individuals (both model and voyeur) and society caused by the pervasion of pornography. In this context, the parallels of cheesecake and landscape are most incriminating. The catchword for the women's rights movement's counterassault against pornography is "exploitation." The dehumanization of women (image as object) is the most evident and undeniable negative aspect of pornography.

The psychic damage, however, is more subtle and pervasive. Cheesecake images generate a cumulative, aesthetic ideal of the female body in the cultural unconscious. All women are then evaluated by an unrealistic standard, one that even the models would fall short of without being carefully posed and augmented by technique. Women who fail to match this prejudicial standard are then devalued as homely, flat-chested, or overweight, even though they may in fact be more productive or creative individuals than those who might pass as centerfolds. One need not subscribe to *Playboy* magazine to be influenced by the *Playboy* standard. It pervades our commercial culture. Especially in advertising, we are continually assailed by the same female (and male) contrived ideal. Our social fabric is warped by distorted perception.

It can be argued that since the primary complaint against pornography is the trivialization of women as sex objects, then landscape photography is not pornographic because landforms *are* objects and the content of these images is not sexual. What this argument truly reveals, however, is the depth of our cultural malaise.

The Grand Tetons and the Grand Canyon, both stereotyped objects of idealized, romanticized desire in our cultural psyche, are in fact living environments more vital than any single human being. The glamorization of these particular protrusions and cleavages, primarily by landscape photographers, into erogenous zones of our collective imagination has damaged both them and us. They have been damaged by our cumulative attention. We make pilgrimage to the objects we have admired on calendars and trample the habitats of other species or exterminate them for their inconvenience to our viewing pleasure. In the process, our perceptions have been blunted and perverted, just like those of the readers of *Playboy*.

We also devalue homely, flat-chested, overweight landscapes. The empty plains, the overgrown woods, the mosquito-ridden sloughs are more productive habitats than most scenic viewpoints in national parks, but few people care about, or for, them. We are collectively seduced by the rectangular stormlight portrait of the bosom of the Grand Tetons, with its crafted illusion of intimacy totally detached from the context of the high plains where herds of antelope trapped by grazing allotment fences on public lands starve to death in windrows to be buried by drifting snow.

Although a general aesthetic response may be innate, the specifics of beauty are not facts. Our attention has been captured and coerced by a conspiracy of consumerism. It would be unfair to attack landscape photographers for catering to our tastes. We are all guilty of not being aware of manipulation and its effects.

It is not guilt, however, that I wish to solicit with this cultural introspection. I do not mean to add yet another brick to our collective burden of environmental remorse. It is already more than we can heft. Neither do I wish to disparage the dedicated professionals in this field who are sincerely concerned about our greater home. What I intend is to invoke awareness, to reveal how easily our passions are manipulated to our detriment. Without the intervention of conscious perception, our passive attention is little more than a gullible victim of petty consumer tyranny. Without vigilant and discerning senses, artist and observer are both equally abused.

We need to see the kinship between the image of Antelope Canyon's convoluted narrows bathed in reflected light being used to pimp Kodak film and the image of lathered curves of ambiguous flesh being used in a Zest commercial. We also need to recognize less evident implications of this same aesthetic hydra.

Eliot Porter's landscape photography directs the intimate and inherently manipulative techniques away from glamorous vistas to reveal the magnificence of the mundane. His detailed portraits of nature's glorious chaos cater less to our naturalistic prurience. Because of his stature as an artist, he is a significant influence on younger photographers. But his stylistic connections to contemporary ecoporn are still quite evident.

The book *Secrets from the Center of the World* exhibits an eye for a startlingly altered and refreshing perception. Steven Strom's photographs reveal secrets of the obvious that have been concealed by the prevalent, dissembling intimacy of ecoporn. Textures of undulant landforms are painted with sparse desert plant communities. Relationships are exposed. Landscape icons are shunned. It wasn't until I began struggling with the issue of ecoporn that the exceptional nature of these photographs was manifest. They are taken, for the most part, at midday! No blush of alpenglow here.

Now the appeal of these homely southwestern landscapes seems to presage my own delinquent concern. There is no seductive illusion of intimacy or accessibility. They are images of a stark and harsh land where the inhabitants have struggled for accommodation. The mind readily extends these images beyond their limiting formats. They are not captured, trapped images removed from context. They are context.

I find hope in these brazen noonday impressions, hope that is stifled in the seductive shadows of more glamorous landscape images. I find hope that such unselfconscious images could find a niche in our marketplace. I find hope that men and women might recognize each other beyond phony cheesecake and beefcake stereotypes. I find hope that we may recognize the living Earth beyond postcard modernism. I find hope for attentiveness and discernment. I find hope that I may not always resent sharing a hard-won and spectacular dawn with someone casually leafing through a magazine or glancing at a calendar.

A Critique of and an Alternative to the Wilderness Idea

J. Baird Callicott *(1994)*

I gave a talk at a symposium in Bozeman, Montana, celebrating the thirtieth anniversary of the 1964 Wilderness Act. I was preceded at the podium by a well-spoken, Amherst College–educated cattleman, Chase Hibbard, who described himself as the token redneck at this gathering of the wilderness faithful. He proclaimed his love of things wild and free and his dedication to steward the lands, private and public, grazed by his stock. He urged us all to find consensus and strike a balance between wilderness preservation and economic necessity.

When it was my turn to speak, I began by saying that if Mr. Hibbard was the token redneck, I was fixing to be the skunk at this garden party—a little simile I borrowed (without attribution) from a piece by Dave Foreman in *Wild Earth*. Thus at once I endeared myself to the audience—people can't hate a self-proclaimed skunk—and put them on notice that I might have something unsettling to say. There are two debates about the value of wilderness, I went on to note. One we just heard about, that between wilderness preservation and "jobs." (And, I pointed out, *profits,* doubtless the most important consideration to Mr. Hibbard, who doesn't work for wages, but one he never mentioned in his speech.) The other debate—*within* the community of conservationists, not between conservationists and cowboys—is about the value of the wilderness ideal to the conservation of biological diversity.

As a dedicated conservationist and environmentalist, I think we must reexamine the *received* wilderness idea, that is, the idea that wilderness is, as the Wilderness Act states, "an area where the earth and its community of life are untrammeled by man, where man is a visitor who does not remain." I want to emphasize that my intent in doing so is not to discredit the *areas* designated "wilderness," and thus make them more vulnerable to development pressures. On the contrary, we need to multiply and expand such areas. Here I criticize rather the *concept* of wilderness, that is, how we conceive of the areas that we call wilderness. I do so hoping to strengthen conservation efforts by helping to ground conservation policy in a sound environmental philosophy.

After the existence of an "environmental crisis" was widely acknowledged the late 1960s, the benchmark of environmental quality was the wilderness ideal of pristine, untouched nature. Accordingly, the new breed of environmentalists believed that the best way to preserve nature, if not the only way, was to exclude all human economic activities from representative ecosystems and designate them as wilderness preserves. In them, some old-growth forests could remain standing, wild animals could have a little habitat, and so on. In effect, we attempted to achieve environmental preservation by zoning the planet into areas where environmentally destructive human economic activities—like livestock grazing, mining, logging, agriculture, mechanized recreation, manufacturing, and real estate development—would be permitted and areas where such activities would be excluded. Several recent and not so recent realizations are subverting this simple philosophy of nature conservation through wilderness preservation.

First, at the practical level, the original rationale for wilderness preservation was not articulated in terms of biological conservation by turn-of-the-century environmentalists like John Muir. Instead, they emphasized the way wilderness satisfies human aesthetic, psychological, and spiritual needs. Wilderness, in short, was originally regarded as a psychospiritual *resource*. Often the most haunting, beautiful, silent, and solitary places are too remote, rugged, barren, or arid to be farmed or logged or even mined. Hence, an early criterion for identifying suitable areas for national parks, such as Yellowstone and Yosemite, long before the Wilderness Act of 1964 and public acknowledgment of the environmental crisis, was their *uselessness* for practically any other purpose. Consequently, as Dave Foreman puts it with his characteristic bluntness, much designated wilderness is "rock and ice," great for "scenery and solitude" but not so great for biological conservation.

Second, at the political level, the wilderness preservation philosophy of nature conservation is defensive and ultimately represents a losing strategy. The development-permitted zones greatly exceed the development-excluded zones in number and size. More acreage of the contiguous United States is under pavement than is under protection in wilderness areas. Less than 5 percent of the lower forty-eight states is in a designated or de facto wilderness condition. As the human population and economy grow, the pressure on these ragtag wild areas becomes ever greater. In temperate North America, wilderness reserves, national parks, and conservancy districts have become small islands in a rising tide of cities, suburbs, farms, ranches, interstates, and clear-cuts. And they are all seriously compromised by human recreation and by exotic species colonization. Big wilderness has receded to the subarctic and arctic latitudes. Even these remote hinterlands are threatened by logging, hydropower schemes, oil exploration, and other industrial intrusions, not to mention the threats posed by global warming and by exposure to sharply increased levels of ultraviolet radiation. The wilderness idea, hopefully and enthusiastically popularized by John Muir's best-sellers at the close of the nineteenth century, has played itself out, here at the close of the twentieth, in the pessimism and despair of Bill McKibben's recent best-seller, *The End of Nature.* McKibben's thesis needs no elaboration by me because his title says it all.

Third, at the international level, the uniquely American wilderness idea is not a universalizable approach to conservation. But the environmental crisis, and particularly the erosion of biodiversity, is global in scope. Thus we need a conservation philosophy that *is* universalizable. In western Europe, conservation via wilderness preservation is meaningless. In India, Africa, and South America, American-style national parks have been created by forcibly evicting resident peoples, sometimes with tragic consequences. The Ik, for example, were hunter-gatherers living sustainably, from time immemorial, in the remote Kidepo Valley of northeast Uganda. In 1962 they were removed in order to create the Kidepo National Park, an area where the community of life would henceforth be untrammeled by man, where man would be a visitor who does not remain. When the Ik were forced to settle in crowded villages outside the park and to farm, their culture disintegrated and they degenerated into the travesty of humanity made infamous by Colin Turnbull.

Fourth, at the historical level, we are beginning to realize that wilderness is an ethnocentric concept. Europeans came to what they called the "new world" and since it did not look like the humanized landscape that they had left behind in the "old world," they thought it was a pristine wilderness, where, as David Brower put it, the hand of man had never set foot. But the Western Hemisphere was full of Indians when Columbus stumbled upon it. In 1492 the only continental-size wilderness on the planet was Antarctica. The aboriginal inhabitants of North and South America, further, were not passive denizens of the forests, prairies, and deserts; they actively managed their lands—principally with fire. Some paleoecologists believe that in the absence of Indian burning, the vast, biologically diverse open prairies of North and South America would not have existed, that the American heartland would instead have been grown over with brush. Some believe that the North American forests would not have been as rich and diverse in the absence of the Indian's pyrotechnology.

By the seventeenth century, when English colonists began to settle the eastern seaboard of North America, the native peoples had suffered the greatest demographic debacle of human history. Their populations were reduced by perhaps 90 percent due to the ravages of Old World diseases, which had swept through the hemisphere transmitted first from European to Indian and then from Indian to Indian. So the Pilgrims did find themselves in a relatively desolate and howling wilderness, as they lamented, but it was, ironically, an *artificial* wilderness—though that combination of words seems oxymoronic. Europeans inadvertently created the New World wilderness condition by means of an unintended but utterly devastating biological warfare on the aboriginal inhabitants.

Fifth, at the theoretical ecology level, ecosystems were once thought to remain stable unless they are disturbed, and if they are disturbed, to return eventually to their stable states, called climax communities. To be constantly changing and unstable is now believed to be their usual, rather than exceptional, condition. Thus, whether we humans interfere with them or not, ecosystems will undergo metamorphosis. But wilderness *preservation* has often meant freeze-framing the status quo ante, maintaining things as they were when the "white man" first came on the scene. Hence the wilderness ideal, so *interpreted,* represents a conservation goal that would be possible to attain, paradoxically, only through intensive management efforts to keep things the way they were in defiance of nature's inherent dynamism.

Sixth, at the philosophical level, the wilderness idea perpetuates the pre-Darwinian myth that "man" exists apart from nature. Our oldest and most influential cultural traditions have taught us that we human beings are exclusively created in the image of God, or that we are somehow uniquely endowed with divine rationality. Thus we, and all the products of our essentially supernatural minds, were thought to exist apart from and over-against nature. For wilderness purists, encountering any human artifact (not their own) in a wilderness setting spoils their experience of pristine nature. But Darwin broadcast the unwelcome news that we self-exalting human beings are mere accidents of natural selection, no less than any other large mammal. We are one of five living species of great ape. We are, to put it bluntly, just big monkeys—very precocious ones, to be sure, but monkeys nonetheless. And everything we do—from bowling and bungee-jumping to writing *Iliad*s and engineering space shuttles (and committing acts of ecotage, most definitely)—is monkey business. For many people, Darwin's news was bad news because it seemed to demean us and to undermine our noblest pretensions and aspirations. But I think it's good news. If we are a part of nature, then we have a rightful place and role in nature no less than any other creature—no less than elephants, or whales, or redwoods. And what we may do in and to nature—the transformations that we impose upon the environment—are in principle no better or no worse than what elephants, or whales, or redwoods, may do in and to nature.

I say "in principle" because I certainly do not wish to leave anyone with the impression that I think because we are just as natural as all other organisms, everything we do in and to nature—every change we impose upon the environment—is okay. Most anthropogenic change is certainly not okay. Indeed, most of what we do in and to nature is very destructive.

But other species, too, may have either beneficial or harmful effects on the rest of nature. If there were 6 billion elephants on the planet instead of 6 billion people (or, remembering that an adult elephant is more than a hundred times as heavy as an adult human, if there were as much elephant biomass as presently there is human biomass), then planet Earth would still be in the throes of an ecological crisis. Elephants, in other words, can also be very destructive citizens of their biotic communities. On the other hand, the biomass of bees and other insect pollinators of plants is probably greater than the human biomass (I don't know, I'm not a biologist) and certainly the bee population far exceeds the human population, but the ecological effect of all these bees is undoubtedly beneficial. So, if the ecological impact of the activities of bees and elephants can be either good or bad, then why can't the ecological impact of human activities be good as well as bad? Measured by the wilderness standard, all human impact is bad, not because human beings are inherently bad, but because human beings are not a part of nature—or so the wilderness idea assumes.

Personally, I hope that those of us affluent North Americans who wish to do so can go on enjoying the luxury of respectfully, worshipfully visiting wilderness areas. In my opinion, the greatest value of the Wilderness Act of 1964 is ethical. It formally acknowledges a human commitment to humility, forbearance, and restraint. But as the centerpiece of a nature *conservation* philosophy, we need to find an alternative to the wilderness idea. Fortunately, we need not look far. We find the appropriate alternative in the concept of biosphere reserves, a concept hatched in Europe, focused on the tropics, and given the imprimatur of the United Nations. Thus, it has genuine international currency. Further, biosphere reserves are selected not on the basis of scenic qualities and not because they are otherwise useless, but on the basis of ecological qualities. Such reserves, intended to preserve biological diversity and ecosystem health, should be designed to harbor not only the charismatic megafauna—bears, wolves, bison, and the like—but also the entire spectrum of indigenous species, invertebrates as well as vertebrates, plants as well as animals.

A policy of invasive human management—by means of, say, prescribed burning or carefully planned culling—is cognitively dissonant with the wilderness idea, but not with the biosphere (or biodiversity) reserve idea. Indeed, one of the signal differences between the old wilderness idea and the new concept of biosphere reserves is a provision for compatible human residence and economic activity in and around reserves. Had the Kidepo National Park been conceived as the Kidepo Biosphere Reserve (though of course to think that it actually might have been is anachronistic), then the Ik and their culture could have been part of what was preserved. Looking toward the future, the idea of a restored American Great Plains—the Buffalo Commons envisioned by Frank and Deborah Popper—was, upon first hearing, so violently opposed because it was originally uncritically cast in the wilderness mode. It is becoming politically more palatable, even attractive, as residents of the target regions see an opportunity to stay, not leave, and switch from farming and livestock ranching to various ways of sustainably exploiting bison, elk, deer, and pronghorn antelope. As I envision a Buffalo Commons, private herds of cattle and sheep would be removed all over the arid and semiarid West. Absent domestic stock, the native vegetation could reclothe the range. And with the fences down, the native ungulates could roam free and wild. Erstwhile ranchers and farmers could retain a home forty and form management co-ops to allot themselves culling rights, proportional perhaps to how much land each put into the commons. If the Blackfeet, Arapaho, Cheyenne, and Lakota could cull the unowned elk and buffalo herds without compromising biological diversity, why can't the contemporary residents of the same region?

The biosphere reserve idea may be the centerpiece of a coherent and universalizable conservation philosophy, but not the whole of such a philosophy. The wilderness idea is half of an either-or dichotomy: *either* devote an area to human inhabitation and destructive economic development, *or* preserve it in its pristine condition as wilderness. The classic wilderness advocates, such as Roderick Nash, in other words, envisioned no alternative to industrial civilization offset by wilderness preservation. As long as it stayed on its side of the fence, industrial civilization went unchallenged.

The core-buffer-corridor concept of the Wildlands Project is cast in the new biosphere reserve paradigm. But the authors of the 1992 "Wildlands Project Mission Statement" still, in my opinion, concede too much to industrial civilization as we know it when they write, "Intensive human activity associated with civilization— agriculture, industrial production, urban centers—could continue outside the buffers." Complementing the biodiversity reserve idea in a sound nature conservation philosophy are the ideas of appropriate technology and sustainable livelihood—*if* by "sustainable livelihood" is meant human economic activity that does not compromise ecological health and integrity. Solar alternatives to hydroelectric and fossil-fuel energy should be aggressively explored. Alternatives to industrial agriculture should be encouraged by means of policy changes. Urban sprawl should be controlled by better planning and stricter zoning. Timber reserves should be harvested ecologically as well as sustainably, as now ostensibly mandated by the new Forest Service policy on national forests. And so on. Thus some biological conservation might be integrated with economic activities in areas not designated as biodiversity reserves (cum buffers and corridors), just as some economic activities might be integrated with biological conservation in those that are.

I was impressed with how the Greater Yellowstone Ecosystem seemed to be a looming presence in the collective consciousness of Bozeman. Almost all the symposium speakers mentioned it. Some dwelled on it. A few spoke of nothing else. It being my spring break and all, I had set aside a few days afterward to go trekking. The park pulled me like a magnet. I rented a car and drove up the Paradise Valley to the north gate. Then I poked around the valley of the Yellowstone River and those of the Lamar and Gardiner, two of its tributaries, on foot.

Tired of a long, bitter Wisconsin winter and with my cross-country skis back home in my shack, I never got anywhere near the backcountry. Climbing up on McMinn Bench near Mount Everts, I could see the park headquarters village in the vicinity of Mammoth Hot Springs, the town of Gardiner off to the north, U.S. 89 running south to Norris Geyser Basin, and U.S. 212, which is kept open all winter as far east as Cooke City, Montana. But the difference between inside and outside the park boundaries was like the difference between night and day. Inside, the headquarters village, the roads, the campgrounds, all had hard edges. And there were no fences. Outside, the gate town had a long filament of gas stations, motels, fly shops, and whatnot strung out along the highway. New-looking houses were scattered here and there on the nearby bluffs. Though I was usually walking through a mixture of mud and elk manure, the park seemed clean. Beyond, the landscape seemed marred and cluttered.

Both outside and inside the park I saw elk, mule and white-tailed deer, and pronghorn. Inside the park I saw plenty of bison. At close range the evidence of elk overpopulation was ubiquitous: aspen were absent, an elk-eye-level browse line was on the Douglas-firs and whitebark pines, game trails traversed the slopes every fifty feet or so of elevation, the riverbanks were denuded and eroding, and every-where I stepped, I stepped in elk scat.

The Greater Yellowstone Ecosystem (comprising Yellowstone and Grand Teton National Parks, the Bridger-Teton, Targhee, Gallatin, Custer, Caribou, and Beaverhead National Forests, three national wild-life refuges, and BLM, state, and private lands) is the biggest relatively intact ecosystem in the Lower 48. The park is a listed UNESCO Biosphere Reserve and World Heritage Site. What the Yellowstone Biosphere Reserve lacks is a thoughtful buffer zone policy and well-articulated corridors connecting it with the Bitteroot, Bob Marshall, Glacier, and Cascade core habitats. I have no personal experience with potential corridors, but the Paradise Valley is an ideal candidate for a buffer zone on the north boundary of Yellowstone National Park. Under the new mandate for ecosystem management, the Forest Service should manage its "multiple use" forests as buffer zones to the adjoining parks and to its designated wilderness areas in the Greater Yellowstone Ecosystem. Up to now, the Forest Service has extensively roaded its lands and permitted clear-cut logging, especially in the Targhee and Gallatin National Forests, "treatments" not consistent with biosphere reserve buffer zone management. Stock grazing is permitted on nearly half the public lands in the ecosystem, including (incredibly) designated wilderness areas in the national forests and parts of Grand Teton National Park. But what hope can we entertain that the absolutely essential winter ungulate habitat represented by a multitude of private properties in the Paradise Valley will be managed as a buffer zone?

Let's look at what's going on in the valley now. With my first quart of cold beer in three days on the seat between my legs, my left hand on the wheel, and the right taking notes as I drove from Gardiner to Livingston, this is what I saw:

Immediately beyond the park boundaries a good deal of open land in the side hills between the Yellowstone River valley and the mountains has been bought for winter range by the Rocky Mountain Elk Foundation. But virtually within sight of the park gate and only a stone's throw from the river, some enterprising entrepreneur has dug a gravel pit. As I drove by, a bulldozer was pushing loose rock around in a cloud of dust.

The next notable manmark on the landscape is the former alpine estate, Royal Teton Ranch, of the late Malcolm Forbes, who must not have known that his view opened on the Gallatins, not the Tetons. As his last rite to Mammon, Forbes got top dollar for his prime Montana property from a California survivalist cult, the Church Universal and Triumphant. Right on the riverbank the hard core cultists live in a tacky shantytown (and the rest in places like Livingston and Bozeman). Back in the sidehills of the Gallatin Range they have erected bomb shelters whose fuel storage tanks were found leaking diesel oil. As I drove by at eventide, cult cattle were watering in the Yellowstone and trampling its banks. It so happens that the old Forbes place has geothermal "resources," and I saw steam rising near the little settlement. The "church" plans to develop these resources, putting the park's geysers at the risk of being extinguished.

Then, on the side of the road away from the river, I passed an "elk farm," a rundown house and some ramshackle outbuildings beside a small, grassless paddock enclosed by a high fence. I was told that game wardens had finally caught the wily proprietor luring hungry wild elk into his compound by night. Later he would sell them as pen-raised animals.

A little relief from this world of wounds came when I drove into Yankee Jim Canyon, most of which is part of the Gallatin National Forest, where the mountains on either side of the valley narrow and the river flows fast through a shallow gorge.

Down north of the Yankee Jim respite, the valley widens, framed on the east by the Absoroka and on the west by the Gallatin ranges. Once more the property is mostly private. Ranches. Cattle. I wasn't around long enough to know whether or not the ranchers in the Paradise Valley were conscientious land stewards, like Mr. Hibbard. But what I could see through the windshield at sixty miles per hour was the meaning of "trammeled"—to be caught or held in, or as if in, a net; to be enmeshed; to be prevented or impeded; to be confined, according to my dictionary. The valley was trammeled, enmeshed, and impeded by a network of fences.

Interspersed with the ranches, closer to a wide spot on the road called Emigrant and on into Livingston, are riparian smallholds with mansions sitting on them, belonging to gentry from elsewhere who found their little piece of paradise on the Yellowstone River. Two miles east of Emigrant on a big bend of the river is Chico, a hot springs resort. I didn't go there, since I had just had an *au naturel* soak in the park.

To accommodate itinerant pilgrims to the valley, someone was rearranging the river bluff with a bulldozer and building an RV "campground" farther down the road. The hookups were all installed. When I passed by, the driveways were just going in.

As I got closer to Livingston, the gentrification of the riparian zone became more intense. The mountains pinch in again and stop at the north end of Paradise Valley, near a place called Allen Spur. I rolled on into town—gradually. The highway is lined with modest houses along the river, lumberyards, gas stations, 7-Eleven stores, motels, fast-food joints, trashy empty lots—the usual mishmash of totally planless strip development, Anyplace, U.S.A.

And what could the valley become? A Buffalo Commons. Or, more precisely, an Ungulate Commons.

Most cults—the Branch Davidians were an especially spectacular example—eventually self-destruct. The Church Universal and Triumphant, one hopes, will be no exception to the rule. Then the federal government can do what it tried before to do, purchase the old Forbes place and devote it to wildlife.

The government thought it couldn't afford Forbes's asking price, and so probably would shrink from the thought of buying the whole Paradise Valley, much of which may not be for sale. So what can be done? Convince the ranchers to tear down their fences, the most ubiquitously trammeling presence on the land; get rid of their cattle; and invite in the elk, bison, antelope, and deer. Coyotes will keep the ground squirrels in check; black-footed ferrets will limit the prairie dog population; gray wolves and mountain lions will take out old, sick, and less fit large herbivores, leaving the cream of the free-ranging crop for the erstwhile cattle ranchers to skim. The gentry should love to look out their picture windows and see free wild animals, rather than their neighbors' fenced cattle. And the tourists might pay even more money to park a Winnebago in the midst of "free nature"—as Arne Naess dubs this fair mix of people and wildlife—instead of in just another roadside attraction.

But how to avoid the tragedy of the commons? Through co-operation. The Paradise Valley is well defined and self-contained. A ranchers' co-op could hire its own wildlife ecologists and, in consultation with the Fish and Wildlife, Forest, and Park Services, set their own sustainable harvest quotas.

After my talk at the wilderness symposium, Chase Hibbard was asked what he thought of my remarks about switching from cattle ranching to market-hunting native ungulates. He was opposed to it. Categorically. Why? I asked him, if market analyses suggest that such a scheme would be more economically attractive than cattle ranching. You know, business is business. Are cattle a religion in Montana, or what? Yes, he answered, they are. (This symposium was full of surprises.) And he went on to lay down the usual line of bullshit (pun intended) about how cattle are a part of what makes the West the West (in the Hollywood-mediated American mind), and how his family has been running cattle here a long time. A long time! I wanted to say, but didn't—a blip on the trajectory of the true history and future of the West, which belongs to the bison and to those whose livelihood once did and may soon again center on this shaggy symbol of North America's high, semiarid country and on the other native grazers and browsers.

Thinking over this exchange of opinions, I came to the conclusion that cattle were not the real cult object of the western ranchers' religion. Private property is. The Paradise Valley is not home to, in addition to the Church Universal and Triumphant, neo-Baal cultists. No, John Locke is the theologian of cattlepersons. As I envision a Paradise Valley Ungulate Commons—a key part of the Greater Yellowstone Biosphere Reserve Buffer Zone—private "real" property would remain in private hands. Privately owned "animal units" are what would go, along with fences, one purpose of which is to mark real estate boundaries and segregate one rancher's privately owned herd from another's.

Would this be so un-American? Not if we think more expansively, in historical terms. That's more or less the way the Indians—bona fide Americans if anyone is—did it. Each group had a territory to which they claimed and enforced the property rights. But the animals were their own bosses. And if, to get a hearing, we must confine ourselves to the short-term scale of Euro-American history, pelagic fisherpersons, traditionally, own their boats and tackle, but the fish go where they will, owned by no one. So the precedent and paradigm for an economically exploited native Ungulate Commons should perhaps be marine fisheries rather than terrestrial ranches. With this difference: A network of North American Ungulate Commons would be far less liable to overexploitation, because the stocks are composed of large, visible specimens that are fairly easy to count and they fall under national jurisdictions (those of the United States, Canada, and Mexico, now, for better or worse, coordinated by NAFTA).

The biosphere reserve conservation concept includes another, less often discussed zone, the transition zone. Here too, the key is appropriate technologies and sustainable economies. Starting at Livingston and going east, montane Montana gives way to high plains Montana. The Great Plains region is already moving in the direction of a Buffalo Commons. The fences are still up, but several big ranches—most famously, the one belonging to Ted Turner—are switching from cattle to buffalo. While buffalo are certainly less tractable and more difficult to contain, they need less care than cattle, and so are becoming an increasingly attractive alternative for imaginative and well-landed high plains entrepreneurs. And many Indian groups are expressing a keen interest in restoring buffalo herds to reservation land, with the added incentive of the bison's place in their histories, cultures, and religions.

WILDERNESS—NOW MORE THAN EVER
A RESPONSE TO CALLICOTT

REED F. NOSS *(1994)*

J. Baird Callicott's "A Critique of and an Alternative to the Wilderness Idea" is peculiar. It is nicely written and erudite, and it definitely provokes thought. But it also provokes, at least in me, a good deal of frustration. Many of us in the conservation movement have worked hard for years to promote ecological and evolutionary understanding as the logical foundation for land conservation (land in the sense Aldo Leopold used it, including air, soil, water, and biota), but coupled with the aesthetic and ethical appreciation of wild things and wild places for their own sakes. Following Leopold, we have tried to unite brain and heart, rationality and intuition, in the struggle to defend wild nature. Yet here comes Callicott, a leading environmental ethicist, a Leopold scholar, a professed lover of wildness, mounting an attack on the concept of wilderness. This article is only the latest in a series of essays in which Callicott assails the idea of wilderness as anachronistic, ecologically uninformed, ethnocentric, historically naive, and politically counterproductive. I believe Callicott is dead wrong and I will try to tell you why.

First, I must state emphatically that I agree with much of Callicott's essay. His progressive interpretations of biosphere reserves, buffer zones, transition zones, sustainable livelihood, and ecological management are all in line with what I and many others affiliated with the Wildlands Project have supported and proposed. But Callicott portrays all these integrative concepts as alternatives to wilderness protection, as things conservationists should spend their time on instead of defending wildlands. To support his contention that the wilderness idea no longer has merit, Callicott erects a straw man of wilderness (based essentially on the Wilderness Act of 1964) that is thirty years out of date. No one I know today thinks of wilderness in the way Callicott depicts it. Anyone with any brain knows that wilderness boundaries are permeable, that ecosystems are dynamic entities, that humans are fundamentally part of nature (though arguably a malignant part), and that ecological management is essential in most modern wilderness areas and other reserves if we want to maintain biodiversity and ecological integrity. To "let nature run its course" in small, isolated reserves burgeoning with alien species and uncontrolled herbivores is to watch passively while an accident victim bleeds to death.

Callicott claims that "several recent and not so recent realizations are subverting this simple philosophy of nature conservation through wilderness preservation." He goes on to provide a number of arguments in support of his thesis that the wilderness ideal is no longer useful. I will agree that "hands-off" wilderness areas in human-dominated landscapes often have minimal ecological value. But they do have some worth, for instance in serving as reference sites (though imperfect) for restoration and management experiments and as microrefugia for species sensitive to human disturbances. It is an overstatement to claim that wilderness preservation has failed. Indeed, one could more easily conclude from recent evidence over most of the continent that it is multiple-use management that has failed. Multiple-use areas, which constitute the vast majority of public lands, have been degraded far more than virtually any of our wilderness areas (Callicott himself provides several examples from the Greater Yellowstone Ecosystem). Roads run everywhere, the last old-growth forests are being converted to two-by-fours, cows munch and shit their way across public range-lands, and "ecosystem management" propaganda is being used to jus-tify continuation of the status quo under a new guise. This evidence only strengthens the argument that we need more—not less—area off-limits to intensive human exploitation. The more degraded the overall landscape becomes, the greater the value of real wilderness, even though it becomes ever harder to protect.

Callicott is absolutely correct that biological conservation was not a major consideration in the designation of existing wilderness areas. The biased allocation of land to wilderness—where areas of little economic value, except for recreation and tourism, are protected instead of more productive and biodiverse areas—is well known. That warped, unecological approach to wilderness protection has been thoroughly exposed in the technical and popular literature of conservation. Modern conservation programs, from mainstream government projects such as the National Biological Survey's Gap Analysis to avant-garde efforts such as the Wildlands Project, are trying to correct this imbalance and better represent the full spectrum of biodiversity in protected areas. Callicott's criticism of the wilderness movement on these grounds is disingenuous; we have learned and we have matured. We will no longer tolerate sacrifices of productive wildlands in exchange for a few scraps of rock and ice. Callicott's claim that wilderness preservation is purely "defensive" only reflects the assaults wild areas face everywhere. Of course we are defensive. If we did not defend the last remaining wild areas, they would soon be gone. We lose most battles as it is; if we gave up, nothing would remain for long. Anyway, the wilderness movement today is not purely defensive. Indeed, the Wildlands Project seeks to move away from defensive, last-ditch efforts, away from saying what should not be done toward saying what should be done to restore whole ecosystems in all regions.

Callicott devotes quite a bit of space in his essay to the problem of excluding humans from wilderness when humans are really part of nature. I know of no philosophical problem more recalcitrant than the whole question of "what is natural." Hell if I know. But Callicott doesn't make much headway toward resolving this issue either. I agree that it was a mistake to extend the standard American model of national parks to developing countries and exclude indigenous hunter-gatherer cultures from these areas. The idea that wilderness can include all primates except for the genus *Homo* is ridiculous. It is not ridiculous, however, to exclude people living profligate, subsidized, unsustainable, industrial lifestyles (including Callicott and me) from permanent habitation in wilderness areas. Even to exclude "native" people from some reserves is not ridiculous when these people have acquired guns, snowmobiles, all-terrain vehicles, bulldozers, and modern medicine. It is not exclusion from these reserves that separates us from nature; it is our culture and our lifestyles, which had already separated us long before we began designating wilderness areas. Yes, the Darwinian revolution united us with nature intellectually; but we have been trying our damnedest to separate ourselves from nature emotionally and physically since Neolithic times (at least).

The problem of our estrangement from nature may lie in the increasing dominance of cultural over biological evolution in the past few millennia of our history. This cultural-biological schism also requires that we take measures to protect wild areas and other species from human exploitation, if they are to survive. The adaptations of most species are determined by biological evolution acting through natural selection. Except for bacteria species and some invertebrate species that have very short "generation" times, biological evolution is much slower than cultural evolution, taking hundreds or thousands of years to express itself. Through cultural evolution humans can respond much faster than most other species to environmental change. Because most environmental change today is human generated, we have created a situation in which our short-term survival is much more assured than that of less adaptable species. Some of these species are extremely sensitive to human activities. It seems to me that an environmental ethic, as Leopold, Callicott, and others have expressed it, gives us an obligation to protect species that depend on wilderness because they are sensitive to human persecution and harassment. I hasten to add that few species "depend" on wilderness because they prefer wilderness over human-occupied lands; rather, they require wilderness because humans exterminate them elsewhere. Roadlessness defines wilderness. Where there are roads or other means of human access, large carnivores and other species vulnerable to human persecution often cannot survive.

Callicott correctly criticizes the idea of wilderness as a totally "unmanaged" landscape. I differ from some modern wilderness advocates in emphasizing that most wilderness areas today must be actively managed if they are to maintain the "natural" conditions for which they were set aside (see my book with Allen Cooperrider, *Saving Nature's Legacy: Protecting and Restoring Biodiversity,* Island Press, 1994). Certainly Native Americans managed the ecosystems in which they lived, principally through the use of fire. I think the evidence is plain that at some level of management *Homo sapiens* can be a true "keystone species" in the most positive sense, in that we can enrich the diversity of habitats and species in the landscape. We can play a role similar to that of the beaver, prairie dog, bison, woodpecker, or gopher tortoise, by providing habitats upon which many other species depend. Above some threshold of manipulation, though, biodiversity enhancement becomes biodiversity destruction. Diversification becomes homogenization. Man as part of nature becomes man at war with nature. We become too damn clever for our own good. I do not believe that human management or technology is inherently bad; but once we have crossed the threshold, we become a tumor instead of a vital part of the ecosystem. Again, this transformation provides all the more reason to set wild areas aside and protect them from human invasion. Those wild areas may very well require management, but the most positive management will usually be protection from overuse by people, restoration of structures and processes damaged by past human activities, and disturbance management (for instance, prescribed burning) to substitute for natural processes that have been disrupted.

Callicott's straw man of wilderness reaches its zenith in his statement that "wilderness *preservation* [his emphasis] suggests freeze-framing the status quo ante, maintaining things as they were when the 'white man' first came on the scene." While it is logically consistent, such an interpretation of the wilderness ideal is idiotic. No ecologist interprets wilderness in the static, pristine, climax sense that Callicott caricatures it. Nonetheless, to throw out knowledge of the historical, pre-European condition of North American landscapes would be equally stupid. Those presettlement ecosystems developed through thousands and even millions of years of evolution of their component species without significant human intervention [excepting the possible role of human hunters in eliminating many of North America's large mammals 10,000 to 15,000 years ago]. Sure, the environment in which these communities developed was dynamic, but the rate and magnitude of change was nothing like that experienced today. As ecologists Stewart Pickett, Tom Parker, and Peggy Fiedler (in *Conservation Biology*, edited by P. L. Fiedler and S. K. Jain, Chapman and Hall 1991) pointed out with regard to the "new paradigm in ecology," the knowledge that nature is a shifting mosaic in essentially continuous flux should not be misconstrued to suggest that human-generated changes are nothing to worry about. Instead, "human-generated changes must be constrained because nature has functional, historical, and evolutionary limits. Nature has a range of ways to be, but there is a limit to those ways, and therefore, human changes must be within those limits."

Yes, many North American ecosystems were managed by Indian burning for perhaps as long as 10,000 years; but in most cases, the Indians did not create new ecosystems. They simply maintained and expanded grasslands and savannas that developed naturally during climatic periods with high fire frequency. Furthermore, the importance of Indian burning is often exaggerated. As many ecologists have pointed out, the natural thunderstorm frequency in some regions, such as the Southeastern Coastal Plain, is more than enough to explain the dominance of pyrogenic vegetation there. In any case, the native Americans in most cases (megafaunal extinctions of the late Pleistocene aside) clearly operated more within the functional, historical, and evolutionary limits of their ecosystems than did the Europeans, who transformed most of the North American continent in less than 200 years. The modern wilderness idea, as embodied in the Wildlands Project, does not say humans are apart from nature. It simply says, in line with Leopold's land ethic, that we need to impose restraints on our actions. We need to keep ourselves within the limits set by the evolutionary histories of the landscapes we inhabit. Until we can bring our numbers down and walk humbly everywhere, let us at least do so within our remaining wild areas.

Callicott discusses the biosphere reserve model as if it were an alternative to wilderness. I agree that the biosphere reserve model is useful—we base our wildlands network proposals on an extension of that model. Biosphere reserves are not, however, an alternative to wilderness. In fact, wilderness is the central part of the biosphere reserve model: the core area. Without a wilderness core, a biosphere reserve could not fulfill its function of maintaining the full suite of native species and natural processes. A wilderness core area may still require ecological management, especially if it is too small to take care of itself (less than several million acres). A healthy long-term goal is to recreate core areas (ideally at least one in every ecoregion) big enough to be essentially self-managing, areas that do not require our constant vigilance and nurturing. Those true wilderness areas will have much to teach us about how we might dwell harmoniously with nature in the buffer zones.

Callicott's alleged dichotomy of "either devote an area to human inhabitation and destructive economic development, or preserve it in its pristine condition as wilderness" is false. The reserve network model applied by the Wildlands Project recognizes a gradient of wild to developed land, but encourages a continual movement toward the wild end of the gradient over time as the scale and intensity of human activities decline. And human activities must decline if Earth is to have any future. Callicott's idea of "sustainable livelihood" is entirely consistent with this model. But how are we to figure out how to manage resources sustainably (while sustaining all native species and ecological processes) without wild areas as benchmarks and blueprints? How are we to show restraint in our management of resources in the landscape matrix when we don't have enough respect to set aside big, wild areas for their own sake?

We need no alternative to wilderness. Rather, we need to incorporate the wilderness ideal into a broader vision of recovered but dynamic landscapes dominated by wildland but complemented by true civilization. As Ed Abbey stated, a society worthy of the name of civilization is one that recognizes the values of keeping much of its land as wilderness. We need the wilderness ideal in these days of frivolous "ecosystem management" more than ever before. We need it to provide a "base-datum of normality," as Leopold put it, to give us reference sites for comparison with more intensively managed lands. We need it to counter the arrogant belief that we can manage and control everything. We need it to inspire us, to put our lives at risk, to humble us. And, more importantly, the bears need it too.

IS NATURE REAL?

GARY SNYDER *(1996)*

I'm getting grumpy about the slippery arguments being put forth by high-paid intellectuals trying to knock nature and knock the people who value nature and still come out smelling smart and progressive.

The idea of nature as a "social construction"—a shared cultural projection seen and shaped in the light of social values and priorities— if carried out to the full bright light of philosophy, would look like a subset of the world view best developed in Mahayana Buddhism or Advaita Vedanta, which declares (as just one part of its strategy) the universe to be *maya,* or illusion. In doing so the Asian philosophers are not saying that the universe is ontologically without some kind of reality. They are arguing that, across the board, our seeing of the world is biological (based on the particular qualities of our species' body-mind), psychological (reflecting subjective projections), and cultural construction. And they go on to suggest how to examine one's own seeing, so as to see the one who sees and thus make seeing more true.

The current use of the "social construction" terminology, how-ever, cannot go deeper, because it is based on the logic of European science and the "enlightenment." This thought-pod, in pursuing some new kind of meta-narrative, has failed to cop to its own story—which is the same old occidental view of nature as a realm of resources that has been handed over to humanity for its own use. As a spiritually (politically) fallen realm, this socially constructed nature finally has no reality other than the quantification provided by economists and re-source managers. This is indeed the ultimate commodification of na-ture, done by supposedly advanced theorists, who prove to be simply the high end of the "wise use" movement. Deconstruction, done with a compassionate heart and the intention of gaining wisdom, becomes the Mahayana Buddhist logical and philosophical exercise that plumbs to the bottom of deconstructing and comes back with compassion for all beings. Deconstruction without compassion is self-aggrandizement.

So we understand the point about wilderness being in one sense a cultural construct, for what isn't? What's more to the point, and what I fail to find in the writings of the anti-nature crowd, is the awareness that wilderness is the locus of big rich ecosystems, and is thus (among other things) a living place for beings who can survive in no other sort of habitat. Recreation, spirituality, aesthetics—good for people—also make wilderness valuable, but these are secondary to the importance of biodiversity. The protection of natural variety is essential to plane-tary health for all.

Some of these critical scholars set up, then attack, the notion of "pristine wilderness" and this again is beating a dead horse. It is well known that humans and proto-humans have lived virtually every-where for hundreds of millenia. "Pristine" is only a relative term, but humanly used as the landscape may have been, up until ninety years ago the planet still had huge territories of wild terrain that are now woefully shrunken. Much of the wild land was also the territory of in-digenous cultures that fit well into what were inhabited wildernesses.

The attacks on nature and wilderness from the ivory towers come at just the right time to bolster global developers, the resurgent timber companies (here in California the Charles Hurwitz Suits at Pacific Lumber) and those who would trash the Endangered Species Act. It looks like an unholy alliance of Capitalist Materialist and Marxist Idealists in an attack on the rural world that Marx reputedly found idiotic and boring.

Heraclitus, the Stoics, the Buddhists, scientists, and your average alert older person all know that everything in this world is ephemeral and unpredictable. Even the earlier ecologists who worked with

Clementsian succession theory knew that! Yet now a generation of re-source biologists, inspired by the thin milk of Daniel Botkin's theoriz-ing, are promoting what they think is a new paradigm that relegates the concept of climax to the dustheap of ideas. Surely none of the ear-lier scientific ecologists ever doubted that disturbances come and go. It looks like this particular bit of bullying also comes just in time to sup-port the corporate clear-cutters and land-developers. (Despite blow-downs, bugs, fires, drought, and landslides, vast plant communities lasted in essence for multimillions of years prior to human times.)

It's a real pity that many in the humanities and social sciences are finding it so difficult to handle the rise of "nature" as an intellectu-ally serious territory. For all the talk of "the other" in everybody's theory these days, when confronted with a genuine Other, the non-human realm, the response of the come-lately anti-nature intellectuals is to circle the wagons and declare that nature is really part of culture. Which maybe is just a strategy to keep the budget within their specialties.

A lot of this rhetoric, if translated into human politics, would be like saying "African-American people are the social construction of whites." And then they might as well declare that South Central Los Angeles is a problematic realm that has been exaggerated by some white liberals, a realm whose apparent moral issues are also illusory, and that the real exercise in regard to African Americans is a better under-standing of how white writers and readers made them up. But liberal critical theorists don't talk this way when it comes to fellow human beings because they know what kind of heat they'd get. In the case of nature, because they are still under the illusion that it isn't seriously *there,* they indulge themselves in this moral and political shallowness.

Conservationists and environmentalists have brought some of this on themselves. We still have not communicated the importance of biodiversity. Many if not most citizens are genuinely confused over why such importance appears to be placed on hitherto unheard-of owls or fish. Scientists have to be heard from, but the writers and philosophers among us (myself included) should speak our deep feelings for the value of the nonhuman with greater clarity. We need to stay fresh, write clean prose, reject obscurity, and not intentionally exaggerate. And we need to comprehend the pain and distress of working people everywhere.

A *Wilderness* is always a specific place, because it is there for the local critters that live in it. In some cases a few humans will be living in it too. Such places are scarce and must be rigorously defended. *Wild* is the process that surrounds us all, self-organizing nature: creating plant-zones, humans and their societies, all ultimately resilient beyond our wildest imagination. Human societies create a variety of dreams, notions, and images about the nature of nature. But it is not impossible to get a pretty accurate picture of nature with a little first-hand application—no big deal, I'd take these doubting professors out for a walk, show them a bit of the passing ecosystem show, and maybe get them to help clean up a creek.

ECOFORESTRY OR PROTECTED STATUS?
SOME WORDS IN DEFENSE OF PARKS

KEN WU *(1996)*

In the 1990s, the tremendous growth in the environmental movement
has been accompanied by numerous changes within the movement,
many for the better but some for the worse. Among the detrimental
changes has been an increasing tendency among activists to downplay
the need for parks and protected areas. Many such individuals and
groups are either fighting wilderness destruction in a vacuum, that is,
with no clear alternative to the destruction, or are calling for "ecoforestry" and other forms of supposedly benign, environmentally
friendly resource extraction. I hope to show here that a call for anything other than protected status in priority wild areas is to the detriment of native biodiversity. I'll examine the primary arguments against
park establishment that some environmentalists use and the strategic
consequences of not advocating for parks.

A REBUTTAL TO SOME PRIMARY ARGUMENTS
AGAINST PARKS

Much of the lack of advocacy for protected areas can be attributed to
ignorance. Many activists simply do not have an overview of the status
of endangered ecosystems in North America and are unaware that it is
precisely in parks and protected areas that ecosystems are healthiest
and most secure from environmental destruction. Hence, they do not
understand the importance of directly campaigning for protected status,
as opposed to mere moratoria on destruction that usually get lifted later.

It is the philosophical criticisms of parks and protected areas that must be most vigorously addressed, however, for the development of such antiwilderness environmental arguments is on the rise, as exemplified by William Cronon's essay, "The Trouble with Wilderness," in the recent anthology *Uncommon Ground: Toward Reinventing Nature.* Dave Foreman, David Johns, George Wuerthner, Mike Matz, and Reed Noss have already responded to many critiques of the wilderness concept and wilderness areas in the Wildlands Project anthology, *Place of the Wild,* as well as in *Wild Earth,* and there is no need for me to repeat their refutations. Still, I would like to add a few insights of my own, because I think it is crucial that such misguided criticisms of parks (the most common Canadian wilderness designation) are refuted once and for all before they gain a further foothold in the movement. The environmentalist arguments against protected areas, and my rebuttals, are as follows:

1. The concepts of parks and wilderness separate humans from nature when, in fact, humans are a part of nature. Thus, parks reinforce the man/nature dualism of Western civilization.

Of all the arguments against protected areas, this one takes the cake for being ill-considered and just plain illogical. That human society *should be* in harmony with nature does not mean it *is* in harmony—far from it, thus the whole environmental crisis. There's a difference between what *should be* and what *is.* Industrial society with its automobiles, factories, DDT, and shopping malls is certainly not one with nature, and by using the word *wilderness* we are not somehow creating a dualism; a dualism already exists. There is a world of difference between a parking lot and a prairie, a clear-cut and an old-growth forest. Human civilization has already separated from nature, from the wilderness; the task is to put humans back into harmony with nature by developing an environmentally harmonious society *and* by protecting nature in wilderness parks *while industrial society still exists.* Wilderness advocates didn't create the human/nature dualism; agriculture, technology, and industrial society did by destroying nature, thereby creating an obvious distinction between wilderness and human society. We must recognize this wilderness/civilization dichotomy if we are to overcome it. Creating parks, protecting the nature that people are supposed to be a part of, is the most important step in transcending that dualism.

2. "Ecoforestry" and environmentally harmonious lifestyles and practices are needed, not more parks. It is not humans per se that are at fault, but rather the ways we live that are destructive.

Fair enough. Hunting-gathering lifestyles have more or less allowed the ecosystems in which they occur to remain intact. Arguably, such lifestyles are environmentally harmonious. However, ecoforestry, permaculture, and organic agriculture with the use of today's advanced technologies and with the present human overpopulation are far cries from hunter-gatherer lifestyles.

In ecoforestry, large numbers of trees, up to the annual growth of the forest, are removed and used for lumber. This is in contrast to the small number of trees, if any, removed by hunter-gatherers to make the odd boat or building. True, where a swidden (slash and burn) agricultural system is also practiced along with hunting and gathering, as in many tropical aboriginal cultures, many more trees are taken. This may represent the beginning of a primarily agricultural lifestyle in such peoples, which would certainly be ecologically destructive, as with all agriculture. Agriculture is the destruction of native organisms in an area and their replacement by one or a few species useful for humans.

In *primarily* hunting-gathering societies, however, swidden takes only tiny fractions of the forest cover, which are quickly reclaimed when the small patch clearings are abandoned in a couple of years. In contrast, through selection logging and commercial thinning, which are much more practical possibilities than ecoforestry in an industrial society, trees far in excess of the annual growth may be removed, to the point where forest interior conditions are lost. Tree removal aside, problems of road building, habitat fragmentation, soil compaction, erosion, stream damage, and the introduction of exotic species arise even with selective forestry practices. Nor should indigenous practices of burning tracts of forest to provide better grazing for ungulate prey be used to justify alternative forestry practices. Increasing numbers of studies are revealing the differences between logged and burned areas (Noss 1993), such as changes in soil chemistry, successional species composition, and the presence of gradients of defoliation in burned areas but not logged areas. Clearly, wild nature and areas used for forestry are not the same. Ecoforestry may be needed in areas not available for protection, but such practices are not appropriate everywhere and are not a replication of natural processes.

Some opponents of protected areas cite the example of indigenous peoples living in harmony with nature to deny the necessity of protected areas in which human habitation is prohibited. Fine, let's have protected areas that include the protection of native hunting-gathering tribes. Most wilderness advocates would support the continuance of indigenous hunter-gatherers living in protected wilderness areas, as long as the native peoples possess traditional technologies and population levels (as with several tribes in tropical Africa, Asia, and South America). Few protected area advocates, however, would support native peoples with industrial technologies and larger populations harvesting resources in protected areas, especially not for commercial purposes. This is where ecocentric environmentalists often differ from more anthropocentric environmentalists, who support native peoples with chain saws, bulldozers, rifles, steel traps, and snowmobiles extracting resources in proposed protected areas. Support of native hunting-gathering lifestyles does not negate the need for protected areas. Rather, it is a justification for protected areas that include hunter-gatherers.

Proponents of native sovereignty may object to the notion of native people living in parks controlled by colonial governments, whether here in North America or elsewhere in the world. Native sovereignty may be a legitimate right; but in the meantime, before the ruling governments are either pressured into accepting native sovereignty or are overthrown, it does neither the environment nor native people any good to have corporations destroy wilderness. Parks are the best means within the present society to prevent this.

3. Changing society to become environmentally harmonious is the crucial task, not creating more parks that exist parallel to consumer society without challenging its fundamental basis. Industrial society will eventually destroy protected areas anyway through pollution (ozone layer depletion, greenhouse effect, acid rain, etc.) and by opening park borders in times of resource scarcity.

This is a critique used by both reformists and radicals. Its two main problems are that it confuses the means with the ends and that it is strategically unsound. First, from an ecocentric perspective, the continued existence of Earth's complete natural biodiversity is the most fundamental goal. To achieve this goal, we must advocate *both* the protection of this biodiversity in wilderness parks—a particular means that is also identical to the ends—and the establishment of an environmentally harmonious society so that pollution and population growth don't destroy protected areas and the rest of nature. Thus, when one pushes for new environmental laws to regulate logging practices or to curb pollution or, more fundamentally, when one works to dismantle industrial society, it is to ensure the long-term security of protected areas and all species, including humans. Yet the critics of protected areas, believing the primary task is the survival of the human species, do not see any reason to protect wilderness; a world with the basic necessities for survival—clean air, water, soil, and renewable agriculture—is all that is needed to secure human existence. The existence of the world's vast array of biodiversity in functioning ecosystems (some species may be reserved in genetic banks) is for the most part not a necessity for human survival; the garden vision, as critiqued by Roderick Nash (1982), is seen as sufficient.

To some critics, wilderness protection is simply a means to "save the planet," meaning to secure human existence, while the reform or replacement of industrial society is the most crucial task for ensuring human survival. Such people have confused the means of creating a green society to secure wilderness with the ends.

In addition to being anthropocentric, this critique is strategically unsound. If, as many confused park critics claim, protection of more wilderness would be great but society must be changed first, then it will simply be too late for most wild areas and species by the time the revolution succeeds. Already, most of the parks and designated wilderness areas in the United States and in southern Canada are surrounded by agriculture, clear-cuts, and urban development. If it weren't for the protective designations, these natural areas would be long since destroyed.

4. Our parks have failed miserably in halting the loss of biodiversity. Most parks, too small to begin with, are located in high-elevation areas of rock and ice or lands otherwise unsuited for human use, while the most productive and diverse low-elevation ecosystems have been largely left out. In addition, parks have been subject to industrial tourism, which has destroyed much of their biotic integrity.

As George Wuerthner (1994) points out, "The fact that our present preserve system does not work as well as it should does not mean that it could not work." That our parks are too small to maintain healthy populations of all their species doesn't mean we should not advocate parks; it means we fight to get bigger parks, as in the proposed Northern Rockies Ecosystem Protection Act. That parks are rarely established in old-growth forests or prairie grasslands doesn't mean we stop advocating the creation of parks; it means we work to get old-growth forests and prairie grasslands protected. For example, here in British Columbia, the tremendous push by the public to protect old-growth rain forests has resulted in recent years in significant tracts of prime, low-elevation old growth being protected: the Carmanah,

Megin, Stein, Khutzeymateen, Boise, Kitlope, Mehatl, Skagit, Clendenning, and Niagara Valleys, as well as South Moresby. These are not lands marginal for human use; they are worth billions of dollars in timber value. That some parks contain ski resorts, livestock grazing, and logging doesn't mean parks are useless; it means we fight against ski resorts, livestock, and logging in parks.

Moreover, to say that parks have failed is to accept a very narrow and uninformed view of ecosystem protection. Alpine and sub-alpine ecosystems, which have their own unique species that are just as important in their own right as old-growth endemics, have been reasonably well protected. All other ecosystems partly protected by parks—including the small and moderate-sized tracts of productive, economically valuable lands—also represent partial victories. Park creation is a process in which all areas protected thus far are victories while still more and larger parks must be created to complete an ecologically viable system of protected areas.

Ultimately, if one believes that nature has intrinsic value and that humans cannot improve it, then there really is no truly sound option other than to leave wilderness as is, and to secure it from future human alteration; this is the definition of a protected area, or what is often called a "park." Some people have a problem with the word *park*, because it holds a connotation that wilderness is for human recreation; fine, then let's call them "ecological reserves" or "wilderness reserves." But to not advocate the protection of an endangered ecosystem because of a name, and thus allow it to be clear-cut or strip-mined, is a crime.

5. Nature needs human management to stay healthy. For example, exotic species must often be controlled, prescribed burns must be set in isolated habitats, predators must sometimes be controlled to allow endangered species to recover their populations, and new individuals must be introduced into small, isolated populations to prevent inbreeding. Thus, because nature must be managed, there is fundamentally nothing wrong with managing a landscape through selection forestry, controlled grazing, or limited agriculture.

This argument is made by some conservation biologists and land managers who realize that active management of some wild areas is necessary to maintain their natural character. Humans have so disrupted natural populations and processes that human intervention is often needed to correct past mistakes. The difference between correcting and managing *human-induced mistakes* on nature and managing *nature itself,* however, is huge. One can still advocate parks even if the areas of concern need such corrective management; their protected status should nonetheless forbid the managing of nature itself. Unfortunately, some people lump both managing human mistakes and managing nature under the general concept of "management" and support "alternative" forms of commodity extraction in place of full protection, thinking that such activities are fundamentally no different from prescribed burns or the elimination of exotics.

IMPLICATIONS OF FAILING TO ADVOCATE PARKS

With the main philosophical arguments against protected areas out of the way, the strategic implications of not calling for full protection can be examined. Environmentalists' failure to call for protected status commonly has one of two "best-case" consequences:

1. A moratorium on destruction, by court injunction (in the United States) or by simple government decree (in Canada). Moratoria can always be lifted, so the same fight will be repeated all over again, except that political circumstances may not be as favorable the next time around; new antienvironmental politicians may be in power, the "wise use" backlash may have grown, or the environmental movement may be on the downswing. Moratoria are not solutions.

2. A half-baked solution in which the pristine status of the area is

compromised. This may include smaller clear-cuts, limited road building, or, very unlikely, implementing the alternative forestry suggested by the environmental group (which, as already discussed, is not a replication of nature). These half-baked solutions are often harder to overturn than full-scale onslaughts, since they may render complacent much of the more moderate environmental movement. Meanwhile, the wilderness is progressively eaten away at a reduced pace.

CONCLUSION

Clearly, direct calls for the establishment of protected areas are necessary if wilderness areas are to be saved once and for all. Of course, there is no guarantee that protected areas will not be opened up for development in the future, but there is no guarantee on anything in society; protected status is the most secure way to ensure the survival of native biodiversity.

Sometimes in building a coalition with nonenvironmental groups that share opposition to a proposed development, a direct call for protected status may destroy the alliance. Some locals may be against the development of gas wells in their area but still want to continue grazing their cattle, or may oppose logging plans but still want to trap commercially. In such areas, conservationists must use their judgment in deciding whether the coalition is worth temporarily forfeiting a protected area. In any case, the ultimate goal of the campaign should be complete protection once the immediate threats are defeated. In addition, one must question whether a coalition with other groups is desirable in the context of the overall campaign, especially if such groups oppose all protective designations and will end up becoming the opposition after the common threat is defeated. As a general principle in wilderness campaigns, the sooner one calls for complete protection, the better.

SOURCES

Cronon, W. 1995. The trouble with wilderness. In *Uncommon Ground: Toward Reinventing Nature,* ed. William Cronon. New York: Norton.

Foreman, D. 1994. Where man is a visitor. In *Place of the Wild,* ed. David Clarke Burks. Washington, D.C.: Island Press.

Foreman, D. 1995. Wilderness areas are vital. *Wild Earth* 4(4): 64–68.

Johns, D. 1994. Wilderness and human habitation. In *Place of the Wild,* ed. David Clarke Burks. Washington, D.C.: Island Press.

Matz, M. 1995. Lock it up. *Wild Earth* 4(4): 6–8.

Nash, R. 1982. *Wilderness and the American Mind.* New Haven, Conn.: Yale University Press.

Noss, R. F. 1993. *The Wildlands Project: Yellowstone to the Yukon.* Canadian Parks and Wilderness Society. Video.

Noss, R. F. 1995. Wilderness—Now more than ever. *Wild Earth* 4(4): 60–63.

Wuerthner, G. 1994. A new vision for the West. In *Place of the Wild,* ed. David Clarke Burks. Washington, D.C.: Island Press.

Returning to Our Animal Senses

David Abram *(1997)*

I'm beginning these thoughts during the winter solstice, the dark of
the year, during a night so long that even the trees and the rocks are
falling asleep. Moon has glanced at us through the thick blanket of
clouds once or twice, but mostly left us to dream and drift through the
shadowed night. Those of us who hunger for the light are beginning
to taste the wild darkness, and to swallow it—taking the night, quietly,
into our bodies.

According to a tale told in various ways by diverse indigenous
peoples, the fiery sun is held, at this moment, inside the body of the
earth. Each evening, at sunset, the sun slips down into the ground;
during the night it journeys through the density underfoot, and in the
morning we watch it, far to the east, rise up out of the ground and
climb into the sky. But during the long nights of winter, and especially
during the solstice, the sun lingers longer in the ground, feeding the
dark earth with its fire, impregnating the depths with the diverse life
that will soon, after several moons of gestation, blossom forth upon the
earth's surface.

It is a tale born of a way of thinking very different from the ways
most of us think today. A story that has, we might say, very little to do
with "the facts" of the matter. And yet the tale of the sun's journey
within the earth has a curious resonance for many of us who hear it,
despite our awareness that the events it describes are not literally true.
For the story brings us close to our senses, and to our direct, bodily
awareness of the world around us.

Our spontaneous, sensory experience of the sun is indeed of a fiery presence that rises and sets. Despite all that we have learned about the stability of the sun relative to the earth, no matter how thoroughly we have convinced our intellects that it is the *earth* that is really moving while the sun basically holds its place, our unaided animal senses still experience the sun as rising up from the distant earth every morning, and sinking beneath the ground every evening. Whether we are scientists or slackers, we all speak of the "rising" and the "setting" of the sun, for this remains our primary experience of the matter. Which is why I am pausing, at this moment, to feel the sun's fire nourishing the deep earth far below my feet.

Going to grade school in the sixties and seventies, I was taught not to trust my senses—*the senses,* I was told again and again, *are deceptive.* This was a common theme in science classes at a time when all the sciences seemed to aspire to the pure precision of physics—we learned that truth is never in the appearances but elsewhere, whether in a mysterious, submicroscopic realm that we could reach only by means of complex instruments, or in an apparently disembodied domain of numbers and abstract equations. The world to which our senses gave us direct access came to seem a kind of illusory, derivative dimension, less essential than that truer realm hidden behind the appearances.

In my first year at college I had a rather inane physics professor who would periodically try to shock the class by exclaiming, wild-eyed, that the chair on which he was sitting was not really solid at all, but was constituted almost entirely of empty space! "Why, then, don't you fall on your ass?" I would think. And I began to wonder whether we didn't have it all backwards. I began to wonder if by our continual put-down of the senses, and of the sensuous world—by our endless *dissing* of the world of direct experience—we were not disparaging the truest world of all, the only world we could really count on, the primary realm that secretly supports all those other "realities," sub-atomic or otherwise.

The sensory world, to be sure, is ambiguous and open-ended, filled with uncertainty. There are good reasons to be cautious in this enigmatic realm, and so to look always more closely, to listen more attentively, trying to sense things more deeply. Nothing here is ever completely certain or fixed: the cloud-shadows darkening the large boulder across the field turn out, when I step closer, to be crinkly black lichens radiating across the rock's surface; the discarded tire half buried in the beach suddenly transforms into a dozing seal that barks at our approach and galumphs into the water. The world we experience with our unaided senses is fluid and animate, shifting and transforming in response to our own shifts of position and of mood. A memory from a hike on the south coast of Java: It is a sweltering hot day, yet a strong wind is clearly stirring the branches and leaves of some trees across the field. As I step toward those trees in order to taste the moving air, the wind rustling the leaves abruptly metamorphoses into a bunch of monkeys foraging for food among the branches!

Such encounters, and the lack of certainty they induce, may indeed lead us to reject sensory experience entirely, and to quest for "truth" in some other, less ambiguous, dimension. Alternatively, these experiences might lead us to assume that truth itself is a kind of trickster—shape-shifting and Coyote-like—and that the senses are our finest guides to its approach.

It seems to me that those of us who work to preserve wild nature must work as well for a return to our senses, and for a renewed respect for sensorial modes of knowing. For the senses are our most immediate access to the more-than-human natural world. The eyes, the ears, the nostrils catching faint whiffs of sea salt on the breeze, the fingertips grazing the smooth bark of a madrone, this porous skin rippling with chills at the felt presence of another animal—our bodily senses bring us into relation with the breathing earth at every moment. If humankind has forgotten its thorough dependence upon the earthly community of beings, it can only be because we've forgotten (or dismissed as irrelevant) the sensory dimension of our lives. The senses are what is most wild in us—capacities we share, in some manner, not only with other primates but also with most other entities in the living landscape, from earthworms to eagles. Flowers responding to sunlight, tree roots extending rootlets in search of water, even the chemotaxis of a simple bacterium—here, too, are sensation and sensitivity, distant variants of our own sentience. Apart from breathing and eating, the senses are our most intimate link with the living land, the primary way that the earth has of influencing our moods and of guiding our actions.

Think of a honeybee drawn by vision and a kind of olfaction into the heart of a wildflower—sensory perception thus effecting the intimate coupling between this organism and its local world. Our own senses, too, have coevolved with the sensuous earth that enfolds us. Our eyes have taken shape in subtle interaction with oceans and air, formed and informed by the shifting patterns of the visible world. Our ears are now tuned, by their very structure, to the howling of wolves and the honking of geese. Sensory experience, we might say, is the way that our body binds its life to the other lives that surround it, the way the earth couples itself to our thoughts and our dreams. *Perception is the glue that binds our separate nervous systems into the larger, encompassing ecosystem.* As the bee's compound eye draws it close to the wildflower, as a salmon dreams its way through gradients of scent toward its home stream, so our own senses have long tuned our awareness to particular aspects and shifts in the land, inducing particular moods, insights, and even actions that we mistakenly attribute solely to ourselves. If we ignore or devalue sensory experience, we lose our primary source of alignment with the larger ecology, imperiling both ourselves and the earth in the process.

I'm not saying that we should renounce abstract reason and simply abandon ourselves to our senses, or that we should halt our scientific questioning and the patient, careful analysis of evidence. Not at all: I'm saying that as thinkers and as scientists we should strive to let our insights be informed by our direct, sensory experience of the world around us; and further, that we should strive to express our experimental conclusions in a language accessible to direct experience, and so to gradually bring our science into accord with the animal intelligence of our breathing bodies. (I think of Howie Wolke's superb essay, a few years back in *Wild Earth*, on how science that lacks a visceral connection to what it studies is lousy science. He's right! For such science denies the scientists' own embeddedness in the very world that they seek to study. Such science is not really Darwinian enough—it pretends that we humans, by virtue of our capacity for cool reason, can somehow spring ourselves free from our coevolved, carnal embedment in a more-than-human web of influences.) Sensory experience, when it is honored, renews the bond between our bodies and the breathing earth. Only a culture that disdains and dismisses the senses could neglect the living land as thoroughly as our culture neglects the land.

Many factors have precipitated our current estrangement from the sensuous surroundings, and many more factors prolong and perpetuate this estrangement. One of the most potent of these powers is also one of the least recognized: our everyday language, our ways of speaking. What we *say* has such a profound influence upon what we *see,* and *hear,* and *taste* of the world! To be sure, there are ways of speaking that keep us close to our senses, styles of speaking that encourage and enhance the sensory reciprocity between our bodies and the body of the earth. But there are also ways of wielding words that simply deaden our senses, rendering us oblivious to the sensuous surroundings, and hence impervious to the voice of the land. Perhaps the most pervasive of these is the habit of endlessly *objectifying* the more-than-human world around us, writing and speaking of every earthly entity (moss, mantis, or mountain) as though it were a determinate, quantifiable object lacking all sensations and desires—as though in order to describe another being with any precision we first had to strip it of its living otherness, or had to envision it as a set of passive mechanisms with no spontaneity, no subjectivity, *no active agency of its own*. As though a toad or a cottonwood was a fixed and finished entity waiting to be figured out by us, rather than an enigmatic presence with whom we have been drawn into a living relationship.

Actually, when we are really awake to the life of our senses— when we are really watching with our animal eyes and listening with our animal ears—we discover that *nothing* in the world around us is directly experienced as a passive or inanimate object. Each thing, each entity meets our gaze with its own secrets, and if we lend it our attention we are drawn into a dynamic interaction wherein we are taught and sometimes transformed by this other being. In the realm of direct, sensorial experience, everything is animate, everything *moves* (although, of course, some things—like stones and mountains—move much slower than other things). If while walking along the river I find myself suddenly moved, deeply, by the sheer wall of granite towering above the opposite bank, how, then, can I claim that the granite rock is inanimate, that that rock does not move? It moves *me* every time that I encounter it! Shall I claim that this movement is entirely subjective, a purely mental experience that has nothing to do with that actual rock? Or shall I admit that it is a physical, bodily experience induced by the powerful presence of this other being, that indeed my body is palpably moved by this other body—and hence that I and the rock are not related as a mental "subject" to a material "object" but rather as one kind of dynamism to another kind of dynamism, as two different ways of being animate, two very different ways of being earth?

If we speak of matter as essentially inanimate, or inert, we establish the need for a graded hierarchy of beings: stones have no agency or experience whatsoever; bacteria have a minimal degree of life; plants have a bit more life, with a rudimentary degree of sensitivity; "lower" animals are more sentient, yet still stuck in their instincts; "higher" animals are more aware; while humans alone are really awake and intelligent. In this manner we continually isolate human awareness above, and apart from, the sensuous world. If, however, we assume that matter is animate (or "self-organizing") from the get-go, then hierarchies vanish, and we are left with a diversely differentiated field of animate beings, each of which has its own gifts relative to the others. And we find ourselves not above but in the very midst of this living web, our own sentience part and parcel of the sensuous landscape.

If we continue to speak of other animals as less mysterious than ourselves, if we speak of the forests as insentient systems, and of rivers and winds as basically passive elements, then we deny our direct, visceral experience of those forces. And so we close down our senses, and come to live more and more in our heads. We seal our intelligence in on itself, and begin to look out at the world only as spectators—never as participants.

If, on the other hand, we wish to recall what it is like to feel fully a part of this wild earth—if, that is, we wish to reclaim our place as plain members of the biotic community—then we shall have to start speaking somewhat differently. It will be a difficult change, given the intransigence of old habits, and will probably take decades of careful attention and experimentation before we begin to get it right. But it will also be curiously simple, and strangely familiar, something our children can help us remember. If we really wish to awaken our senses, and so to renew the solidarity between ourselves and the rest of the earth, then we must acknowledge that the myriad things around us have their own active agency, their own active influence upon our lives and our thoughts—and also, of course, upon one another. We must begin to speak of the sensuous surroundings in the way that our breathing bodies really experience them—as active, as animate, as alive.

CONTACT AND THE SOLID EARTH

CHRISTOPHER MANES *(1997)*

The theme of estrangement from nature has a venerable history in the West, from Genesis to Rousseau to *Jurassic Park*. We could probably continue for a couple more millennia drawing inspiration for great literature and bleak philosophy from our sense of distance from the natural world, were we not rapidly running out of nature to lament losing. The attitudes and actions of modern people toward the environment matter in a way that St. Augustine, looking out from his monastery window at a virtually pristine Mediterranean Sea, never could have imagined in his most troubled musings about the fallen state of the world. This generation's ability to restore a meaningful relationship with the wild may well determine whether anything wild, human or otherwise, survives the next century.

But just when we need to cultivate our sensibilities toward the nonhuman world, we have become estranged even from our estrangement. In his book *The Abstract Wild,* Jack Turner makes the biting observation that the distress people feel over the abuse of nature in most cases springs not from firsthand experience, but from viewing wildlife programs on television. Our sense of loss is often the emotion of sad entertainment, indistinguishable from the experience of melodramatic films, and just as powerless to change the way we live.

Some postmodern and conservative thinkers would even deny us the solace of this ineffectual anguish. They argue that nature is simply a creation of culture and our estrangement nothing more than a nostalgic misbelief.

Serious thinkers know better. Like a Wagnerian leitmotif,

alienation from nature follows us around in every aspect of our lives, virtually defining what it means to be a modern person. David Abram's pioneering book *The Spell of the Sensuous* has helped rescue the problem from the trivializers by rigorously exploring how deeply human understanding, even the most abstract thinking, depends on our participation in the nonhuman world. According to Abram, it is not so much that we entertain wrongheaded ideas about nature (though surely our society does), but rather that the dazzling, all-encompassing power of literacy and texts has beguiled us into thinking that meaning belongs to humans and not to the world.

And it continues to beguile us. Like the optical illusion that makes a straight line look bent, explaining the trick doesn't make it go away. We are so embedded in a culture of texts displacing nature that even the most enlightened ideas honoring the wild do little to end our sense of estrangement, since they cycle through the literate understanding that always holds nature at bay. We cannot simply talk ourselves out of this problem with better philosophy. What Abram, Turner, and a few other innovative thinkers have done is raise the issue in a new way that goes beyond the search for better ideas to a more interesting question: What can we do to transcend our literate, abstract experience of nature?

Of course, the immediate answer is, *no one knows.* But when in doubt, tell a story . . .

I was hunting deer along the North Middle Fork of the Willamette River in Oregon's Cascades. As usual I didn't get any deer, but I did get lost. Very lost. I was alone and it started to rain so hard even my Marmot rain gear and Herman Survivors couldn't keep me dry. After flailing around in the muck for a couple of hours looking for my camp, I concluded I was going to die of hypothermia unless I made it back over the river to my car—no mean feat, since the bridge washed out years ago and the only way in or out of the area was to shimmy over a fifty-foot trunk of the pine tree that had conveniently fallen from one bank to the next.

So I turned my back on my expensive equipment (ultralight down Gore-Tex sleeping bag, ultralight tent, ultralight stove, etc.) and bushwhacked along the river, getting lashed and soaked. I was really attached to that fancy stuff. Ironically, I stumbled across the remains of an elk calf carcass: the luckless denouement of my hunting talents. There were mountain lion tracks nearby. With the foreboding that I might be next on the menu, I continued my endless journey, taking a couple of elk teeth for luck (I still keep them in a box).

By the time I got to the serendipitous log, it was almost dark. The trunk had a crust of ice and the river roared with runoff. I wanted to tie a line, but I couldn't because my fingers were numb and my teeth chattered like castanets. I remember slamming my hands against a boulder to try to arouse the nerve endings, without success, and no-ticed they looked and sounded like pork chops on a cutting board. Half frozen, I shimmied across the dead tree, holding on for dear life, while I balanced a pack and an aught-six on my back (like a fool I couldn't bring myself to leave my gun and oranges). The old wood sagged and creaked in the middle under my weight.

But I made it across. I found my car and drove to the moribund logging town of Oakridge, proudly trudging into my favorite restau-rant wearing only my long johns and a sweater, my last dry clothing. I beamed inwardly as I drank a pot of coffee: once again I had survived my own stupidity.

I can't remember what I ate for dinner last Tuesday, but I recall every minute of my costly excursion to the North Middle Fork. I also remember the solo trek I made across the interior tundra of Iceland, and the time I pulled a leg muscle alone in the Panamints above Death Valley. As to the hundreds of trips I've made with friends into wilder-ness or national parks, they all seem to run together.

The difference is, in the latter excursions, nature really didn't matter. I was a tourist and the landscape a spectacle. If push came to shove, and we got injured or lost our supplies, civilization was just a phone call and a medevac helicopter away. We could always hit the panic button and end the ride.

Not so in the North Middle Fork. At that moment, the forest, river, and wildlife had my rapt attention, because they meant literally everything to me. How I comported myself in relation to my surroundings held my future in the balance. Every twig, every track, every twist in the landscape signaled meanings to me, while the abstractions of literate culture that could move armies across the world dwindled into nothing.

I'm not suggesting that taking life-threatening trips into unforgiving country is the only way to revive a direct relationship with nature. But I am convinced that participation in the world beyond civilization, real involvement that has something at stake (building a home, raising animals, climbing a mountain), is the precondition for overcoming our estrangement.

This conclusion is nothing new. It is simply a reprise, perhaps a more desperate one, of what Thoreau understood a century and a half ago. In "Ktaadn," an essay in *The Maine Woods*, Thoreau wrote: "Talk of mysteries! Think of our life in nature,—rocks, trees, wind on our cheeks! the *solid* earth! the *actual* world! the *common sense!* Contact! Contact!"

What we lack, Thoreau knew even back then, was not correct thinking *about* nature, but contact, a life *in* nature.

"But Thoreau didn't live in nature," I can hear the critical philosopher in back shout. "He was a literate man, just like us, who saw the natural world through the lens of his culture."

Well, yes. Thoreau stayed only a couple of years at Walden, just a mile or so from downtown Concord. And his trips to the woods were just that: trips. Like us, he always had in the back of his head the whir of American civilization, as a counterpoint, perhaps even a premise, to his contact with the solid earth.

This dual perspective is called irony. Sometimes irony in bad situations is the best we can do. But for however brief a moment, irony becomes moot when you reach the icy, groaning middle of a rotten log poised over a raging river. That's Thoreau's contact. It changes things. To what, we can't know, sitting as we do in the smug certainty of our literal civilization. Which is why Thoreau rightly called it a mystery.

THE WILDERNESS OF HISTORY

DONALD WORSTER *(1997)*

I live in northern Kansas, a part of America without any wilderness—
no large tracts of land existing within hundreds of miles that are free of
producing a commodity. This country used to be wild prairie running
north all the way to the Saskatchewan; now, we have less than 1 percent of the original tallgrass prairie left, and much of the shortgrass is
gone too.

Two years ago, it is true, Kansas finally got a prairie protected
area. The struggle was long and tough against the Farm Bureau, the
cattlemen's association, and former senator Robert Dole (who balked
at spending $10 million for an addition to the National Park System
but not at $1 billion for National Guard aircraft to beat back our ene-
mies). Even now, with the Tallgrass Prairie National Preserve a legisla-
tive reality, a Texas businessman has his cattle out there, on a lease, and
the antipark forces are insisting that the cattle stay there; they demand
it be a monument to the beef industry rather than returning it to bison
and pronghorn. Anyway, they say, that land was never wilderness.

Such assertions are getting support, unintended though it may be,
from some of my colleagues in environmental history, many of whom
I fear have not spent enough time among the good folks who claim to
"work for a living"—members of the Farm Bureau, for example—
and do not sufficiently appreciate how hard it is to establish an ethic
of environmental restraint and responsibility among fierce private
property and marketplace advocates. Otherwise, my colleagues would
be a little more careful about the sensational headlines they encourage,
like "Wilderness Is a Bankrupt Idea."

That is not the headline that William Cronon really wanted to see when he wrote his controversial essay "The Trouble with Wilderness, or Getting Back to the Wrong Nature," published in the book *Uncommon Ground: Toward Reinventing Nature* (1995). What he meant to say, I think, was that sometimes wilderness defenders have hurt their cause by sophomoric rhetoric that alienates thoughtful people and lacks any social compassion. He is right on that score. The wilderness movement needs more self-scrutiny, needs a larger commitment to social justice—and, above all, needs the patience to read its critics more carefully. On the other hand, Cronon and some of the other authors in *Uncommon Ground* should take a dose of their own medicine. They have at times inflamed the discourse, missed the more profound ethical core of the movement, and made a few weak arguments of their own—arguments that need critical scrutiny and exposure. Therefore, with hope for a more mutually respectful and probing debate than we have had so far, I examine some of those arguments. Here is my list of major errors about wilderness being committed by some environmental historians.

Error #1: North America (we are told) was never a "wilderness"—not any part of it.

Some revisionist historians now argue that ignorant Europeans, animated by "virgin land" fantasies and racial prejudices, had it all wrong. The continent was not a wilderness; it was a landscape thoroughly domesticated and managed by the native peoples. Indians, not low rainfall and high evaporation rates, created a vast sweep of grassland all the way from the Mississippi River to the Rocky Mountains, and they did so by constant burning. They herded the bison like domesticates in a big pasture. They cultivated the wild plants and made a garden of the place. All over the continent, they completely civilized the wasteland long before the white man got here.

I respect Native American stewardship and would not take credit away from any of their considerable achievements, but such characterizations by historians are huge extrapolations from limited examples. Two million people spread over what is now Canada and the United States, a people armed with primitive stone tools, simply could not have truly "domesticated" the whole continent.[1] By comparison, 300 million Americans and Canadians today, armed with far more powerful technology, have not wholly domesticated the continent yet; in the United States, by a strict standard of evaluation, roughly 100 million acres of virtually pristine wilderness exist under protection while more are without protection, and in Canada areas with no roads, towns, mines, or mills still dominate most of the north.

We are further told by some historians that the Indians were pushed out of their domesticated homeland in order to *create* a wilderness for the white man. There certainly was a massive dispossession, often bloody and ruthless. But if our national parks, wilderness areas, and wildlife refuges were once claimed by Native Americans, shifting in tribal identity over time, so once were our cities, farms, universities, indeed the very house lots on which we dwell. What are we now to do about that fact? Should we give all national park and wilderness areas back to the Native Americans? Or open them for subsistence hunting (by people likely to be armed with modern rifles and snowmobiles) or for agriculture? If we do that, then we are logically bound to permit the same repossession of our campuses, suburbs, and cornfields. I have not heard anyone, however, seriously propose that Los Angeles or Stanford University be returned to their "rightful owners." Why not? Why are parks and wilderness areas viewed as suspect forms of expropriation while the vast portion of the country under modern American economic use is not really questioned? Obviously, Indian land claims are not the real issue here; debunking preservationists is.

A more sensible policy would be to find out whether any of the 100 million acres of currently protected wilderness are in violation of valid treaty rights and, if they are, to settle in court or get the lands returned to their proper owners, as we should be doing with all contested lands. But I haven't seen any historian actually undertake that research project into land claims within the wilderness system. Nor do I see any definite, clear proposal coming from scholars about where and how to alter the size, shape, or rules governing our wilderness areas. Meanwhile, let it be noted that any American citizen, Indian or non-Indian, has free and equal access to the nation's wilderness, which is more than can be said about access to universities or suburbia.

Error #2: The wilderness is nothing real but is only a cultural construct dreamed up by rich white romantics.

I trace some of that oversimplified thinking to Roderick Nash's book *Wilderness and the American Mind,* which (for all its many virtues) set up a flawed narrative that environmental historians have cribbed from ever since. The now-standard story starts with an ancient, intense Judeo-Christian hostility toward the wild, an antiwilderness culture of spectacular proportions and longevity. That hostility supposedly reached a crescendo in Puritan New England, where every farmer stepped out of his saltbox scowling at the forest. Then the story moves on to a dramatic reversal of attitudes as affluent, white, educated, secular, urban Americans became sensitive romantic lovers of nature. Part of the scarcely hidden moral in that story is that ordinary people, without education or income, have been in serious cultural lag and cannot be depended on for any significant environmental change. But a more complicated reading of the past would suggest that the love of wilderness was not simply the "discovery" or "invention" of a few rich men with Harvard or Yale degrees coming at the end of a long dark age.

If you assume that standard account, then it becomes very easy to turn the entire story into a polemic against elitist snobs who seek the sanctuary of wilderness at the expense of peasants, workers, Indians, or the poor of the world. Of course there were and are people like that. If the story didn't have a kernel of truth in it, the revisionists would not get any kind of hearing at all. But it is a small kernel, not the whole complicated truth of what wilderness has meant to people through the ages or of what draws them to protect wilderness today.

Contrary to the established story, the love of nature (i.e., wilderness) was not merely a "cultural construct" of the romantic period in Europe. It has much older cultural roots, and it may even have roots in the very structure of human feelings and consciousness going far back into the evolutionary past, transcending any cultural patterns. Historians of late have been far too quick to dismiss as "essentialist" any deep residuum of humanity and to reduce all thought and feeling to shifting tides of "culture." Nineteenth-century romanticism, with its glorification of the sublime, was indeed an important cultural expression, but it also may be understood as an effort to recover and express those deeper feelings that in all sorts of cultures have linked the beauty of the natural world to a sense of wholeness and spirituality. The enthusiasm for wilderness in America was undeniably a cultural fashion, but it also drew on that other-than-cultural hunger for the natural world that persists across time and space. Finally, it drew in the United States on a frontier-nourished spirit of liberty, which itself reflected both cultural and biological needs. Most importantly, that enthusiasm was felt by poor folks as well as rich.

Historians have tended to miss the broad social appeal of the wilderness movement, particularly in the twentieth century. They like to feature that brash, big-game-hunting, monied New Yorker, Teddy Roosevelt, especially if they want to do a little lampooning, and ignore all the men and women from more humble origins, before and after him, who played an important role in saving the wilderness. John Muir and Ed Abbey, to be sure, get plenty of attention, though historians have seldom appreciated the fact of their rural, nonelite roots. Nor do they give much emphasis to the millions of wilderness seekers who do not like to kill big animals or thump their chests or order from Eddie Bauer catalogs. And then, after reading the poorer class of people out of the wilderness "construct," the historians turn around and proclaim: "See, wilderness has been an upper-class fetish all along." Finally, with no little condescension and inconsistency, they set out to correct the "naive," popular, grassroots "misunderstanding" of these matters.

Error #3: The preservation of wilderness has been a distraction from addressing other, more important environmental problems.

Precisely what are those problems? The protection of less exalted beauty close to home, we are told, not only in the remote, western public lands. The health and well-being of urban people, particularly impoverished minority people, in the neighborhoods where they live. The wise, efficient use of natural resources that furnish our means of living. I grant that all these are important problems for environmental-ists to face. They are in many ways linked, and they should not be sev-ered and rigidly compartmentalized one from one another. Actually, I don't know any wilderness advocates who are so single-minded, who deny the existence or importance or interconnectedness of those other environmental problems. There may be some, but I have never met them. But I have met, and will defend, the person who, out of deep moral conviction, believes that the preservation of the world's last wilderness is a higher obligation than cleaning up the Hudson River or preventing soil erosion. Someone who gives his or her life to wilderness issues instead of those other problems is not necessarily misguided or immoral or needing to be "reeducated."

But the main historical issue here is whether the wilderness movement has in fact significantly diminished American interest in other environmental problems. The claim that it has is repeatedly made; outside the carefully hoarded wilderness areas, it is charged, the country is a mess and their wilderness "obsession" encourages many environmentalists to do nothing about it. It is sometimes argued that preserving wilderness gave Americans a green light for exploiting other less pristine environments with no compunction. But where is the evidence that this has been so on any important scale? The major reason we abuse land, as Aldo Leopold told us a while back, is "because we regard it as a commodity belonging to us" rather than "a community to which we belong." Protecting wilderness by itself may not change that situation, but neither is it responsible for it.

Since the Wilderness Act was passed in 1964, the United States has seen an extraordinary increase in the number of people who call themselves environmentalists, and the issues they are working on range from preserving remnant wetlands threatened by shopping malls to stopping toxic dumping on Indian reservations to getting emission controls on smokestacks. The movement has become more and more diverse, inclusive, and pervasive. Far from being a distraction, the example of wilderness activism may even have encouraged that diversification of environmental concern occurring across the whole country!

I live in a place where the immediate, compelling, and most practical need is to create an agriculture that is less destructive to soil, water, and biota, along with preventing real estate developers from turning our towns into cultural and biological deserts. I serve on the board of directors of the Land Institute, which is trying to meet that important environmental need. Yet I can still cherish the thought of large, unmanipulated wilderness on this continent where the processes of evolution can go on more or less as they have for millennia. Does my commitment to saving wilderness in Alaska "alienate" me from the place where I live? Some historians say it must, but people are more complicated than that. Like millions of other Americans, I have a whole spectrum of concerns, near and far. I can support the Library of Congress without losing interest in my local public library.

We do have a legacy of using land badly all over this country. It has left us with degraded forests, grasslands, and cities, and that legacy requires profound reform along a broad front. Developing an ethic of care and restraint wherever we live and wherever we take our resources—on that 95 percent of the nation's land area not protected as wilderness—is a clear, important need. How do we address it and move toward intelligent, just, and wise use of the land beyond wilderness areas? Our recent history does not suggest that we need to get rid of the wilderness "fetish" in order to do so, or that we need to trash the leading, popular arguments for preserving wilderness, which on the whole have worked pretty well against implacable opposition.

The wilderness has been a symbol of freedom for many people, and it is a primordial as well as cultural sense of freedom that they have sought. Freedom, it must be granted, can become another word for irresponsibility. Yet almost always the preservation of wilderness freedom in the United States has been interwoven with a counterbalancing principle of moral restraint. In fact, this linkage of freedom and restraint may be the most important feature of the wilderness movement. Those 100 million acres exist not only as a place where evolution can continue on its own terms, where we humans can take refuge from our technological creations, but also as a place where we can learn the virtue of restraint: this far we drive, plow, mine, cut, and no farther.

Old-time religions enforced moral restraint on their followers by the practice of tithing, a practice that has almost completely disappeared under the impact of the market revolution. But the practice of tithing is too good an idea to lose. Without saying so, we have created in the form of wilderness a new, more secular form of the ancient religious tithe. We have set aside a small portion of the country as the part we return to the earth that supports us, the earth that was here before any of us. We are not yet up to a full tithe, but we are still working on it.

A place of restraint as well as a place of freedom for all living things, the wilderness has promoted, I believe, a broader ethic of environmental responsibility all across this nation. Far from being an indefensible obsession, wilderness preservation has been one of our most noble achievements as a people. With no broad claims to American exceptionalism, I will say that here is a model of virtuous action for other societies to study and emulate. This is not to say that historians have been wrong to criticize weaknesses in the wilderness movement. They have only been wrong when they have denigrated the movement as a whole, carelessly encouraged its enemies, and made bad historical arguments. The real danger we face as a nation, we should remember, is not loving wilderness too much but loving our pocketbooks more.

NOTE

1. I am using the cautious but authoritative estimate of Douglas H. Ubelaker of the Smithsonian Institution, in his 1988 article "North American Indian Population Size, A.D. 1500 to 1985," *American Journal of Physical Anthropology* 77: 291. He calculates an average density of eleven people per 100 square kilometers, ranging from a low of two or three in the arctic and subarctic regions to a high of seventy-five in California. Much larger and more controversial are the estimates of H. F. Dobyns in *Their Number Become Thinned* (Knoxville: University of Tennessee Press, 1983).

THE MYTHS WE LIVE BY

GEORGE WUERTHNER *(1998)*

A few years ago, I spent an entire day in Yellowstone National Park
with one of the most outspoken critics of the park's wildlife policies.
He believed park officials were guilty of malfeasance for permitting elk
and other wildlife to self-regulate their populations. Such a policy, he
felt, was destroying the park's vegetation and jeopardized the park's
landscapes. Although I had been to Yellowstone many times, my own
observations didn't jibe with his perspective. So, thinking that perhaps
I was missing something, I asked him to spend a day with me in the
park and make his best case, an invitation he eagerly accepted.

As we wandered the northern range looking at plants and talking about management policies, I began to learn his "story" of the role
of people and nature in the West. It became evident to me that the
park's natural regulation policy, the root of the elk "problem" he perceived, actually represented a deeper, more fundamental challenge to
his belief system. What he really didn't like about Yellowstone is that
nature appeared to be out of control—specifically, beyond human
control.

He didn't like it that elk died from starvation or were killed by
bears and wolves, and thus were "wasted"—unavailable to be taken
by hunters and consumed by people. And to let "timber" (rather than
trees) burn up in fires seemed to him to be the equivalent of a holocaust against forests. As he explained to me while we were driving
back to Bozeman, "God put those trees on the hillside for people to
use, and to just let them rot or burn up is going against His teachings."

His views on nature, particularly their obvious religious

foundation, may represent the extreme end of a particular perspective, but are not, at their heart, all that uncommon. Indeed, to one degree or another his perspective represents the dominant worldview of most natural resource managers, loggers, ranchers, miners, and other commercial users of the land. Their livelihoods depend upon control and manipulation of the land and its wildlife to meet human ends. All require "domestication" of the landscape.

This is distinctly different from the goals of wildlands preservationists, who seek to protect or restore self-generating and self-regulating landscapes and wildlife populations. Wild landscapes are those where human control and manipulation is minimal; as such, they threaten the values of those who seek to domesticate our forests and grasslands. These divergent views on how the world is ordered, and how humans fit into that world, are at the core of most environmental conflicts.

The controversy over wolf restoration exemplifies the divergent parables. Anyone who sees this debate as solely about biology or economics misses a very important point: ranchers and others who advocate human control of the landscape fear the wolf not only because it may occasionally consume one of their cows or sheep, but also because it represents a challenge to the dominant cultural myth of the western frontier—a bucolic agricultural landscape where livestock are tended by "hardworking" cowboys.

While conservationists may base their advocacy of wolf recovery primarily upon ecological arguments, wolf restoration is also an attempt to "rewrite" the story of the West. It requires humans to give up willingly and freely a certain degree of control and manipulation of the land. Thus, wolf restoration is accurately viewed by wolf opponents as a direct attack upon the dominant parable that organizes their lives. The passions that lie behind the battle over wolf restoration are so fierce because they involve fundamental assumptions about the human–nature compact.

Ironically, although this conflict (like most other natural resources

conflicts) is primarily about *values,* wolf advocates and opponents both
rely extensively upon scientific studies to bolster the legitimacy of
their positions. Unfortunately, this debate cannot be resolved by science. Decisions about wolf restoration, whether to graze cattle in the
arid West, whether to kill bison outside of parks, whether to log forests
to "save" them, or "protect" landscapes as "wilderness," and other current controversies are, at their roots, debates over the stories we want
to tell ourselves. We may give science a holy place at the altar, but in
reality, what guides our decisions and fuels our passions are the myths
we live by. Science may be able to tell us that cows trampling a riparian
zone results in fewer fish in our streams, or that logging old-growth
forests causes spotted owls to go extinct, but whether that is perceived
as a problem or not depends upon one's values—and these values are
shaped by the stories we use to our guide our lives.

Certainly, science is a powerful tool to help us see connections
and relationships; but it is the vision and the way it is interpreted—not
the science—that will capture people's hearts, and ultimately their
minds. Because many environmental issues involve deeply held ideas
about our perception of nature and the human relationship to the
natural world, the idea that science and rational debate can sway the
outcome seems a bit optimistic, perhaps even naive.

Rather, it may be the poets, musicians, writers, and artists who
will communicate a new vision of the American West as a place where
people live among bison herds, streams full of trout flow without being
dewatered, and wolves are more than token animals in a few national
parks. It is the *storytellers* who ultimately may change the Western
parable and, thus, our relationship to the land and nature.

Coming Home to the Wild

Florence R. Shepard *(1999)*

Paul Shepard's book *Coming Home to the Pleistocene,* written during the last months of his life, is like a mirror held before us "thinking animals" that reflects our primal human being. This image, if it is comprehended and lived fully, Paul counseled, can make us at home on Planet Earth, rather than ecological misfits. We recognize this image, for at the heart of our identity is a fundamentally wild being, one who finds in the whole of wild nature all that is true and beautiful in this world.

In his address at the Fifth World Wilderness Congress in 1993, Paul put forth more assertively than ever before an idea he had been tracking for years. We are, he proclaimed, wild to the core. Furthermore, our self-consciousness and worldview are based not on the teachings of civilization, but rather on the biological legacy as well as the cultural influences passed on from our ancestors, the Pleistocene hunter-gatherers.

He elaborated further: Our genome, the genetic inheritance that identifies us as humans, has remained relatively unchanged for the past 10,000 years. When we walked out of the Pleistocene we were essentially the same beings we are today. In fact, because of the slow mutation rate of genes in humans, our genome is essentially as it was 100,000 years ago when ancestral humans roamed the earth. And that genome, in turn, was the culmination of the evolutionary change in still more ancient primate ancestors whose brain size and body weight increased threefold in the relatively short span of 2 million years. We are, for the most part, he insisted, the same creatures who came down out of the trees on the forest edges, placed our feet firmly on the ground, looked around in an innately suspicious primate fashion, and began the game of chasing and being chased.

Much smaller than the large carnivores, we developed the acumen to watch predators and prey around us, for we were both, and we learned from our adept fellow creatures. Animals became our teachers, shaped our perception and cognition, and gave us the basis for music, dance, ceremony, and language.

From the beginning we were omnivorous and gathered what was plentiful to eat, understood the phenology of the seasons, hunted accessible small animals, and scavenged large dead bodies. Paul insisted that our most prized cognitive skills—the ability to think and plan ahead, to match our intellect with others in collaboration, to synthesize many bits of information in appraising situations, to read signs, to create symbols that convey information, to design beautiful artistic expressions, to find joy in music and celebration and communion, to overcome obstacles through the use of cunning, and to relate existence to the cosmos and acknowledge the spirit world—were not the legacy of civilization but were bequeathed us by our hunter-gatherer forebears.

But our cunning has turned against us in these last 10,000 years as we have overstepped our human bounds and ignored the "limits of the natural order" (Turner 1998). We have changed the face of the earth more rapidly and more destructively than any meteoric catastrophe; our mindless exploitation of Earth's limited resources has placed this planet in an ecological crisis since the beginning of the twentieth century. These changes came about as the result of two concomitant movements:

• the domestication of plants and animals and the sedentary life that agriculture promulgated;

• pastoralism, the keeping of herds that created the conditions for ownership, surplus, and scarcity that stratified humans into classes. And with the horse and its harnessed power came the capacity for invading and conquering others.

Along with these changes in lifestyle arose a different spirituality. Mounted powerfully on prancing steeds, we turned our eyes and hearts away from the spiritual and ecological sustenance of the earth and looked skyward for a god or gods to save us from earthly existence. We began to see life not as a seamless intertwining of past and present, but as a linear set of chronological events beginning in the past, coming to the present, and leading on to the future. This life was not enough to satisfy us; we wanted paradise and immortality. We abandoned the wisdom of our own instincts, denied death as a part of the ever-renewing cycle of life, and, in the end, rejected the numinous earth as the source of life in favor of a material world where we were supreme, rational beings.

This turning away from the wisdom of the earth worried Paul Shepard in his later years. During the first two decades of his adulthood, however, he lived an optimistic, tempestuous life of environmental activism. In the early 1970s, he "became disillusioned with the environmental movement . . . and no longer believed that understanding the meaning of ecology would make any difference in turning the public's consumptive mind to a more sustainable economy" (Shepard 1998). At that time he began looking deeper into the origins of our problems and in his writing presented what some think was a prophetic and visionary message. This thoughtful enterprise led him to explain Western perceptions of ecology, animals as the language of nature, and the ontological (developmental) framework of the human life cycle. Through his research he became firmly bonded to the ancient hunter-gatherers and dreamed of a time when there was no distinction between the wild and the tame. This thinking led him to discern the differences between the concepts of wildness and wilderness.

Wildness, he said, is the state of our genome, our evolved genetic endowment that has been honed by evolution over millions of years. Like other uncontrolled creatures on Earth, he maintained, we are a wild species because our genome has not been altered with certain ends in mind as have the genomes of domesticated plants and animals that humans have manipulated for our own purposes. Paul agreed with philosopher Holmes Rolston, who said that wildness is not just something "behind" and separated from ourselves, but is the "generating matrix" for what we are (Rolston 1983). Although we have taught each other social and cultural conventions in order to live together, and although we are creatures that can adapt to deficient environments, we are more at peace, less stressed, and more sane in environments that resemble the ones in which we evolved. The primal landscape, Paul reminded us, is still etched on our brains and is recognizable and familiar to us. Without it, he insisted, we are ecological misfits and often physical and mental wrecks.

Wilderness, on the other hand, is both a cognitive construction and a place we have dedicated to wildness that provides the optimal conditions for elaboration of the wild genome. We think of it as a place set aside, a realm of purification outside civilization with beneficial, therapeutic qualities, a release from the overdeveloped environment and the disease of domestication. But we take wilderness too literally, too legalistically, he advised, and in the process we lose the meaning for which it was intended, the place where wildness can flourish.

Early in his career Paul Shepard gave up writing and thinking about wilderness landscapes as a key to our sense of nature. He felt we had been corrupted not only by domestication but also by the conventions of nature aesthetics, where we had been steered by Freud's psychology depicting us as creatures destined to suppress sexual or combative urges. Nature, Paul asserted, has been oversold for four centuries as an aesthetic as opposed to a religious experience—even the spiritual uplift of wilderness is burdened with our egocentric human purposes. When wilderness became a subject matter in art, the criteria of excellence became technique. In such a context the real landscape is objectified and distanced through photography or landscape painting or, for that matter, through nature writing. As a consequence of this abstraction of nature as art, masses of people who are not interested in art analysis regard the extinction of animals, destruction of old-growth forests, pollution of the sea, and the whole range of environmentalist angst as "elitist." Wildness, he cautioned, cannot be captured on film or on canvas; wildness is what we kill and eat because we, too, are wild and are also eaten. We are a part of a sacred trophic community.

Paul warned us that the corporate world has drawn our attention away from wildness by negotiating parcels of wilderness too small to allow random play of genes. This establishes a dichotomy of places and banishes wild forms to enclaves where they are encountered by audiences, while the business of domesticating and denuding the planet proceeds unabated.

In a closing statement in *Coming Home to the Pleistocene*, Paul declared his own "primal closure." "We go back," he said, "with each day . . . with the rising and setting of the sun, each turning of the globe . . . to forms of earlier generations. . . . We cannot avoid the inherent and essential demands of an ancient, repetitive pattern." He implored us to return to the integrity of our genes, to trust them and follow their lead, and to acknowledge our ontogeny, the biological pattern of growth and development during our life cycle that we inherited from our primal ancestors.

Our lifelong development brings physical changes that occur rapidly during the first years of life, and with these changes come differing psychosocial responses. To these changes within each of us, however, there must be appropriate responses in the culture to mitigate our neoteny. Neoteny is that strange immaturity retained by humans that makes us dependent on others and on the culture for help and support throughout our life cycle as we confront critical life passages.

Young children require the firm nurturing of loving caregivers, but as they grow and become more self-sufficient they increasingly need opportunities for exploration in nature. Their cognitive development begins with the taxonomy of animals, who are like us and yet so different, who provide not only the basis for language categories but also the psychological basis for otherness, the understanding of difference apart from the self. These initial explorations in childhood promote identity formation as well as develop our capacity for symbolic and metaphoric thought.

Progressively more independent explorations in familiar terrain widen and deepen children's experience. These explorations begin with the topography of their mothers' and their own bodies and move outward until their identity takes in other creatures as well as their surroundings. The recognition of universe and cosmos blossoms in adolescents, and, at this time, their astonishing zeal should be accompanied by story and music and celebration from the adult community to match their expanding cognition and spirituality.

In the ideal world of our ancestors, children, youth, and adults live lives richly textured with play, sound, and movement and shared in common with people of various ages. Segregation by age groups is not a wise practice, Paul advised. Without close contact and mentoring—preferably by adults who are not parents—youths, longing for affiliation, congregate in groups (gangs) and try in their own immature ways to "grow themselves up." But without guidance and bonding to nature and its wild creatures, they grow into immature adults, ignorant of their place in an ecologically sustainable community.

In a neoprimal community centered in place, adults find full and active lives with emphasis on small group collaboration, some independent family subsistence and sharing, self-restraint in accumulation of material wealth, diverse activities, and less emphasis upon the individual household and more on the sharing community. Prestige comes from integrity rather than from inheritance or fame. Participation and broad representation in the political realm is expected of all. Leadership is dispersed, emergent, and dynamic, and gender relations are egalitarian. Elders are important keepers of stories and are revered and cared for.

Paul used the "fire circle" as both metaphor and literal example of community in which a small, cohesive group is bonded in discourse, communion, celebration, mutual support, and enlightenment—an interesting idea around which we can fashion families, communities, and work groups. Important events like birth and death are seen as the binding matrix of spiritual existence. In such a plan no one is neglected. No one is unimportant. We each take responsibility for others and they for us, as we give care, support, recognition, and respect.

The primal community has many applications in our modern world. It means living more firmly in place but allows for periodic peregrinations or pilgrimages. With rapid communication, we have opportunities to keep our fire circle cohesive and the members strongly supportive of each other even when they are separated by continents. Narrative is a central motif. An integrated spirituality pervades all aspects of life and brings a respect for otherness. In a healthy and active community, members acknowledge their need for ceremony that makes explicit their interdependence. Welfare of other creatures and of the earth comes first, not last, in the order of business in all arenas of decision making. Paul Shepard saw this community closely tied to sacred trophism through the practices of hunting and gathering, where omnivory is the dietary plan, with sacramental rather than sacrificial trophism. Rather than on restrictions, more emphasis is placed on the freedom of people to make choices to accommodate their developing psyches. This is the life cycle we inherited. This is the life cycle we should acknowledge, Paul Shepard implored.

In terms of the larger view, Paul saw a world made up of three composite systems: genetic systems, ecosystems, and cultures. Each system is a mosaic of independent and distinct parts that are portable yet embedded and that can be exchanged and recombined in an "integrated and lively conglomerate." These three systems lie in horizontal proximity, each affecting the others and responding to the others. Although the genes dictate the range of feasibility, they carry millions of years of possibilities for the interwebbing of creatures in ecosystems. Cultures arise in response to the elaborations of genes and ecosystems and can result in rich, diverse human- and creature-friendly societies and environments.

We should not ignore what is possible in our own lives, within our family groups, and among our neighborhood communities. Here in this essential matrix, appropriate cultural responses can stabilize our home place and spill out into the world at large. But our purpose in formulating plans must be to be true to wild nature within and outside of ourselves. Our wildness, as Paul saw it, is not some dream of a future paradise, but aspects of community within which our primal ancestors lived. We have only to go back to this wisdom and bring it into our lives in every way possible.

We are all brothers and sisters in our genetic endowments, essentially alike, essentially wild. Cultures may differ in their ecological integrity and practices, but individuals within those cultures are made from the same stuff, feel in the same way, and think and communicate in surprisingly similar modes. In his life work, Paul Shepard chose to think about our wild nature within a greater ecological community. He worked through the errors we have made, pointed them out to us, and hoped that we will pick up his work and carry it forward. Throughout his life, his writing was a model of consilience, the unity of knowledge that E. O. Wilson has told us in his recent book is needed if we are going to preserve life on Earth (Wilson 1998).

I spend some time each year in a cabin in the Hoback Basin in the Greater Yellowstone Bioregion of the Northern Rockies of North America. Designated wilderness areas as well as healthy public lands and national parks abound in this region. The headwaters of three great western rivers are here. If anyone were to say to me that wilderness areas are a thing of the past, that they cannot be sustained, that they are not important or needed, or that it is too late for wilderness,

I would argue steadfastly. Granted, my idea of wilderness is unique to the place where I live; there are other definitions of wilderness throughout the world, appropriate to other cultures and other bioregions. But, as Paul Shepard told us, at base they must have one common purpose. They must be places that sustain wildness, where the free play of genes is allowed to take its course.

We can view and define wilderness from differing cultural perspectives, but when we talk about the wild, we are, I believe, of one heart and mind. There is nothing relativistic about wildness, nothing to be negotiated. Genes are either wild or they have been tamed. Wildness does not depend on the context. It is something fundamental to all our understandings; it is not culturally based or socially constructed. We can all recognize wildness when we see and hear it, for it resonates within our own essential wild nature. Wildness is the reason we are here. It is the reason we are fighting for endangered species, for wilderness designations, and for our human being.

LITERATURE CITED

Rolston, H., III. 1983. Values gone wild. *Inquiry* 26(2): 181–207.

Shepard, P. 1998. *Coming Home to the Pleistocene*. Washington, D.C.: Island Press/Shearwater Books.

Turner, J. 1998. Jacket cover of *Coming Home to the Pleistocene*. Washington, D.C.: Island Press/Shearwater Books.

Wilson, E. O. 1998. *Consilience*. New York: Knopf.

WILD PLACES AND CREATURES

ISLE ROYALE FRAGMENTS

every beautiful morning of the world
I choose the fog,
I choose the wolf,
I choose to learn to walk again
on moss with the moose through
water in air,
water under foot,
breathing the breath of the world
on every beautiful morning.

———————

Nothing but moosetrails in the mist,
today's fog and wind,
trees against sky.
I want to disappear into cloud,
wander my way to sunlight,
follow the moose down
secret trails in the woods
to reach the places where the wolves
rest above the ridges, within us,
where the heart wanders, wild.

—GARY LAWLESS

FELLOW TRAVELERS

MOLLIE YONEKO MATTESON *(1994)*

When the Pleiades and the wind in the grass are no longer a part of the human spirit, a part of very flesh and bone, man becomes, as it were, a kind of cosmic outlaw, having neither the completeness and the integrity of the animals nor the birthright of a true humanity.

—HENRY BESTON, *THE OUTERMOST HOUSE*

After a three-day ski trip in the Absaroka-Beartooth Wilderness, I was driving home through Yellowstone Park. It was still midwinter, but the sun lingered, as if relenting of its terseness the previous month. In the Lamar Valley, a distant herd of elk swept up a treeless hillside. One followed the other in a sinuous path, like the bows of a river. Closer, a small group of cows and calves watched my car with buttery eyes. Cows and calves: I wished there were more graceful words for mother elk and their young, with their supple-stalwart bodies like modern dancers. Only some atrophied mind, viewing these animals as stock for harvest, could have placed the terms for penned and prodded bovines on these elegant ungulates.

Bison slumbered on the snowy ground, resembling haphazardly placed leather couches. A coyote, fat and fluffy as a panda, stared at me as I cruised by. "Hi, sweetie!" I shouted out the window on impulse. The instant internal retort: "Oh, God, you're becoming a sappy old lady before you're thirty." The dreaded anthropomorphism: it wouldn't be long before I was dressing Lhasa apsos in overcoats and rhinestone collars, and why didn't the Park Service supply those poor coyotes with little vinyl ponchos?

My husband teases me when I blurt "Bun-bun!" at passing hares and cottontails. I speak familiarly to the lazuli bunting that frequents our feeder and the kingfisher perching above the bridge we cross on our daily run. I must sound alternately like a child and a victim of senility. But I care less about that than I once did. I did not call to the coyote because it needed something from me. Rather, I was glad to see it, and joyous that (though I do, at times, participate in "research" myself) this one wore no collar save its own luxurious ruff. If shouting greetings to coyotes signaled the early onset of my dotage, I thought, then I would hope for a long life of such mental instability.

I continued north, scouting the cliffs along the Gardiner River for bighorn sheep. No sheep, but a few napping "bull" elk. I was puzzled by their ability to sleep while balancing four-foot-high candelabras atop their heads. On windswept, chocolate-colored hills above the Yellowstone River, antelope grazed. I was out of the park now, and without being conscious of it, I had begun a mental checklist. Next: mule deer. Then: bald eagle. A rough-legged hawk on a fence post. And another. When I spotted the goldeneyes swimming along the icy margin of the river, like punctuation marks on an ancient scroll, I felt a distant easing in my chest, an involuntary sigh. I realized then I'd not simply been observing the passing scene. I had been searching for those little round ducks, expectant and anxious, like a passenger disembarking from a train and searching the crowd for a familiar face.

Ever since I'd left the trail, the piles of bills at home, letters unanswered, the maw of my office door loomed larger with every mile. I'd sought those creatures like one trapped in a nightmare, flailing subconsciously for the sweet reality of another's warm back, the reassurance of a shoulder, a leg, an embracing arm. These animals, not mine in any sense, were nonetheless compatriots, fellow travelers. What could my freedom to move about, my ability to speak, to study, to contemplate, to effect change, mean in a world without chickadees, pine martens, spiders, and salamanders? I might as well live in a box: that darkest, most silent space, inside my own skull.

A friend of mine recently called an employee of Animal Damage Control [the federal predator killing agency, now renamed, incongruously, Wildlife Services] to ask if he would speak at a conference she was organizing. Their conversation stretched to an hour, as he railed against the biases, illogic, and misinformation of activists opposed to "predator control." "He said he hated emotions getting involved with management decisions," my friend reported.

"Isn't that a contradictory sentence?" I asked. "He 'hated' emotions?" I felt sorry for the man. Feeling frustrated, angry, resentful, yet thinking solutions lay in the direction of elimination, denial, and repression of emotions, just as his agency eliminates, denies, and represses other species. What would happen if for one day that man were required to walk out in the woods and sing hello to the ravens, wave to a deer, whisper to a coyote? He would probably rather die than have to behave that way. Why? Would he fear that a breath of compassion, of friendliness, might brush his skin and weaken his stern "objectivity"?

It is a truism that only humans divided within themselves can commit acts of barbarism. We deny feelings of compassion and identification in order to justify brutality and isolation. We claim noble goals (knowledge, management, order, progress) to mask our desire, our desperation, for control. David W. Orr writes in the December 1992 issue of *Conservation Biology* about teaching "the love of life." His essay (insightful, bold, and honest, as his writings always are) makes the point that we do not come to science, or to conservation, as two-legged computers. Yet almost no scientists or bureaucrats, not even many environmentalists, dare to speak loudly, if at all, such words as *kindness, caring, joy, wonder, love*. If these words are used, they are used as weapons to beat back the "emotional" types.

I once spent an entire afternoon rescuing tadpoles from shrinking, shallow pools in a gravel quarry. My best friend and I—we were about eight or nine—fetched Tupperware from her mother's cabinets and ferried the hapless baby frogs from the doomed pools to the biggest, deepest ones. Perhaps we would have done the species a favor by letting the descendants of imprudent mother frogs desiccate and die. Perhaps we overcrowded the bigger pools, and thus caused more tadpole deaths than we prevented. Perhaps. Yet surely it is not an over-abundance of human kindness—unwitting though it can be—that is threatening the world.

People judge others by the company they keep. I judge people by those they consider to be their company. How far-flung or confined is their net of inclusion? To whom do they speak greetings? For whom do they mourn? Are finches and frogs and elm trees part of their circle? Would they pause to grieve for a shattered deer by the side of a highway? We are warned against personalizing, anthropomorphizing, caring. I will warn others, for my part, against not personalizing, not caring enough. Conservation, as David Orr tells us, will not happen without the impetus of love. For me, though, it really comes down to this. I do not like traveling alone. When I greet coyotes, elk, a river, I am reminding myself—and rejoicing—that once again, I have found plenty of good company.

Loss of Place

Howie Wolke *(1995)*

For many of us, some places are just a bit more special than all others. One of my special, *sacred* places is within a rough-hewn land of long ridges, rounded hills, cliffs, lakes, peaks, and plunging river canyons. It's a raw asymmetrical land, lacking the scenic appeal of colorful Colorado's alpine peaks. It's a land clothed in a quiltwork of lodgepole pine, Engelmann spruce, subalpine fir, and Douglas-fir, with heroic patches of alpine larch and whitebark pine hugging the highest, rockiest slopes and basins. Old-growth ponderosa pine, grand fir, and other montane species grace the nearby canyons of the Main Salmon and upper Selway Rivers. Scattered meadows and a few low-elevation grasslands are the other major biotic communities.

This is the Big Wild, the heart of the Greater Salmon-Selway Ecosystem, mostly in central Idaho far from the nearest potato field. Though it's not my only sacred country, it's my first and foremost. Within that country is an extra special place. It is an isolated lake basin a thousand feet below tree line deep within this contorted land. Near as I can tell, this is the center of the universe.

The clear emerald-hued lake is surrounded by alpine larch, whitebark pine, subalpine fir, a few spruce, and big chunks of metamorphosed granites plunging into the icy water. Larch and boulder-strewn slopes of beargrass rise above the inlet to a 9,000-foot peak. The outlet plunges over cliffs into the great green blanket of mystery that defines the Salmon-Selway. Just north of the basin's lip is an open slope with a clear view into an ancient world of conifers, part of the biggest remaining expanse of virgin forest left in temperate North

America. That's where I sit, gazing at the real world as I jot down these words on my laptop notepad.

This morning I climbed the peak above the lake. From its summit, no towns, ranches, roads, reservoirs, or power lines can be seen. Forested mountain wilderness sprawls in every direction. To the southeast are the Bighorn Crags, rising 7,000 feet above the Salmon River's Middle Fork. Far to the east, on the Continental Divide, is the jagged top of the Beaverhead Range, which segregates Idaho and Montana. To the northeast the Bitterroots are monoliths of naked granite belying the lush hybrid forests of Pacific Northwest and Rocky Mountain biota that cover their lower slopes, canyons, and basins. Well over a hundred miles north is the southern terminus of the Mission Range. Northwest is an endless sprawl of forested ridges of the Selway. To the west, across virtually unbroken forest, is the isolated Gospel Hump, and farther southwest is the still wild Payette Crest. To the south, more mountains: rolling and occasionally near-alpine, stretching into the eternal blue today of an unusually hot, late July noon. Despite the archipelago of alpine peak clusters scattered around the compass and rising above the forested ridge and canyon matrix, the real theme here is habitat, not alpine scenery. On a more basic level, my sacred lake basin speaks of a wildness found nowhere else in the United States south of Alaska.

There's been no rain for two weeks, and it's been hot. To the south, big cumuli build and bulge against the cobalt-blue sky. They float slowly north. To the west, mares' tails slowly encroach, foretelling a possible Pacific front. Will the building storm cells set the woods ablaze in a fury of thunder and lightning before a Pacific storm can soak the desiccated duff? As I write under the darkening sky, the verdict is out. I root for neither water nor fire, content with either. Who am I to say which is better? Both just are. We humans can judge by our own peculiar standards, but these standards are irrelevant to nature's forces. This forest is shaped by periodic fire, but nurtured by water in a landscape created by molten magma, flowing water, and glacial ice.

The geologic story of the Idaho Batholith is overshadowed now, though, by the story of today's humans who surround it. For it is they who determine its fate.

From the summit of my peak in the Frank Church River of No Return Wilderness (RNR), until now there was no visual evidence of human idiocy, except for a few tiny fire lookout buildings atop scattered summits visible only to the trained eye. But a Nez Perce National Forest supervisor named Tom Kovalicky (now retired and masquerading as a conservationist Forest Service reformer) ended that peace. By signing a legal document called "Decision Notice, Cove and Mallard Timber Sales," Kovalicky condemned the heart of the Big Wild to a massive invasion of bulldozers and chain saws, roads and clear-cuts. The Cove and Mallard roadless areas are in an unprotected enclave formerly called Jersey Jack, forty miles west of my sacred lake basin. Cove-Mallard abuts the RNR and Gospel Hump Wilderness Areas, and it is just over the canyon rim of the Main Salmon River. Cove and Mallard may be the worst timber sales in the sordid history of the U.S. Forest Service.

I visit the summit of my sacred peak once or twice each year, sometimes with a small group. I tell no one that this is the center of the universe. But atop the mountain this morning, the center of the universe shattered into the pieces of a broken heart. This happened because in 1978, Cove and Mallard were denied designated wilderness status when conservationists cut a political deal: protection for the high ridges of the Gospel Hump and standard multiple abuse for the forested enclave just to the east. This compromise, orchestrated by a now retired Sierra Club and Wilderness Society careerist named Douglas Scott, set the stage for the infamous Cove and Mallard timber sales.

Atop the mountain this morning I was gazing across melting patches of snow into the green-blue ridges to the west when I spotted the distant squares in the unprotected enclave. I counted eight new clear-cuts.

This cannot be, I thought. Hoping I was wrong, I turned around, confused. My feelings became a tangle of overwhelming loss, sorrow, and raging anger. The anger quickly overtook all else. Images of green-uniformed bureaucrats lined up for execution flashed before me. Rational thought be damned. I wanted to *get* the responsible bastards. Of course, retaliation isn't the answer. But neither is pretending that conservation is an intellectual crapshoot. This is the real world; coursing through my veins is real blood. If anger, and even violent thoughts, aren't appropriate at times like this, then we humans are truly worthless, and we may as well curl up and die. For despite the distance to the clear-cuts, the center of the universe is cheapened, made a bit more like every other human-gouged place on Earth, more mediocre, less special.

It is rare, in this society, to find people who grieve for loss of *place*. We grieve for the loss of loved ones, but not for loss of place, or for the loss of the essence of place. Why don't we? True, my lake basin remains intact, buffered from the bulldozer and chain saw by a few million acres of designated wilderness, still silent, alive, and wild. This basin still commands the wonderful view of the surrounding Salmon-Selway wilds, where few humans have trod. As I write I hear a northern pygmy owl. On the quartz-striated ridge above, bighorn sheep and maybe even wolverine hide in the larches. Do the lynx and the golden eagle sense the travesty?

Cove and Mallard are forty miles distant, yes, and the loss of a chance to gaze at unspoiled wilderness for 360 degrees from a favorite mountain pales in comparison with the biological impacts of the butchering of the forest: habitat fragmentation; erosion; fewer salmon, wolves, fisher, marten, lynx, varied thrushes, Townsend's warblers, golden eagles; less old growth . . .

But for now, I simply grieve for this loss of place, mourn the loss of some of the essence of my center of the universe. It's a loss that heroes tried to prevent, and it is a loss that is duplicated throughout the West, across America, and around the globe. As the U.S. Forest Service and other agencies and multinational corporations mow down the public domain, how many others also mourn the loss of the irreplaceable, the wasting of something that cannot be retrieved?

Wilderness must survive for its own sake. Insofar as anything, including humans, has a "right" to thrive, so does wilderness and all of its dependent life. Intrinsic worth. Inherent value. I grasp hold of these phrases like a falling cat might grasp the limb of a dying tree. Such biocentrism is the only view that makes sense to me. Nonetheless, I cannot help but wonder: What becomes of a people who continue to destroy the irreplaceable, the sacred? In the temperate United States there simply is no other place where so much unbroken wilderness can be seen at once. Yet it was desecrated with relatively little fanfare, just business as usual for the Forest Service. Strange.

Lightning bolts belt the distant ridge tops. Processes carry on. Blue sky tops the basin's edge. Fire will likely win and that's OK; there is little rain in today's sky. I feel despair, and now, hours and pages later, tempered anger. I feel lost and I grieve by writing this essay. I don't know what else to do. Perhaps when we, as a people, learn to mourn the loss of place, we will halt the losses and render meaningless the phrase "nothing is sacred."

THE POLLINATOR AND THE PREDATOR

GARY PAUL NABHAN *(1996)*

As I camp alone in a narrow canyon, waiting for a nocturnal pollina-tor to visit an endangered wildflower, I recite the names of threatened pollinators from around the world. I recite this litany not simply as a way to stay awake; it is also for the pure pleasure of the images they evoke:

Mahogany gliders, honey possums, dibblers, Marianas flying-foxes, little flying cows, moss-forest blossom bats, crowned lemurs, golden-mantled saddle-backed tamarins, little woodstars, purple-backed sunbeams, turquoise-throated pufflegs, marvelous spatuletails, yellow-footed honeyguides, four-colored flowerpeckers, apricot-breasted sunbirds, Bishop's oos, regent honeyeaters, and Duvaucel's geckos.

As I mull over the music of their names, I shudder with the recognition that those sounds may be all I ever get to know of these critters. Many of these pollinators are known by just a few diligent zo-ologists who have had the fleeting luck to be in the right place at the right time; such times are becoming less and less frequent. A number of these threatened pollinators—some eighty-two mammal species, a hundred and three birds, and one reptile—have dwindled down to fewer than a thousand individuals.

Little is known about the endangered wildflower I am baby-sitting this evening, and little is known of these pollinators' life histories: their rates of reproduction under favorable conditions, their longevity, their responsiveness to rainy years, or to years of drought like this one. They are almost gone, yet all we can say about their way of life is that they have been attracted to flowers for millennia. We presume that they were effective pollinators of certain loosely coevolved blossoms, but some of them may merely be casual floral visitors. Or perhaps all we know is that one individual in one species in their genus was once documented ducking its head into the blooms of a certain flower. What range of flowers it visited before invasive weeds arrived in its home, I don't know, but its beak or nose and its behavior suggest it may be a legitimate pollinator. ("Legitimate" here distinguishes it from an animal that feeds on a plant's nectar or pollen without aiding in cross-pollination of the plant.)

Three nights ago, while suffering insomnia and a fever due either to flu or to biophilia, I stayed up through the twilight hours counting how many of the vertebrate wildlife species in the 1994 World Conservation Union (IUCN) *Red List of Threatened Animals* were likely to be pollinators. The 186 vertebrate species that I tallied are but needles in the haystack compared to the total number of pollinators on this planet—some 100,000 invertebrate species are definitely involved in pollinating the 240,000 species of flowering plants that depend upon animal vectors for pollen transfer. We are decades away from knowing with any confidence what percentage of these 100,000 invertebrate pollinators are imperiled. Instead, I had to focus on the 186 imperiled pollinating vertebrates, which are in genera that include 1,035 to 1,220 species that may serve as pollen vectors. My late-night calculation was that 15 to 18 percent of those potential pollinators are already of conservation concern; that is, they are listed by the World Conservation Union as rare, threatened, endangered, or possibly extinct. At least 100 genera of the 165 vertebrate genera of floral visitors now include threatened species.

Tonight, I am not laboring over the numbers in superficial global surveys of threatened species; instead, I am camping in their midst within a national wildlife refuge perched on the line between the United States and Mexico. I have been watching whippoorwills

diving after hawkmoths, bats darting across the canyon, and micro-
moths landing on the flowers of the rare Kearney's blue star. As I reach
to clamp a mason jar over an insect crawling on the blue star's inflores-
cence, I hear a scream echoing off the canyon walls above me. Somewhere on the higher ridges behind my back, a female mountain lion is
caterwauling—*yowling her heart out*—while I clumsily screw the lid back
on a glass jar filled with nectar-feeding insects. "Forty-five seconds of
screaming, presumably puma," I write in my field journal at 8:54 P.M.,
in case I end up in the kill jar of *Felis concolor* later on this night.

An insight flashes into my adrenaline-inundated mind: while
the relative rarity of carnivores such as cougars is well recognized by
scientists and laypersons alike, the worsening scarcity of pollinators
has remained beyond the reach of our society's antennae. I can affirm,
"This is the first cougar I've heard caterwauling in my quarter century
of living in the Southwest." My wife can assert, "I've lived in puma
country my entire life, and only once, in Big Bend, did I ever see
one." But who on this Earth (other than the chiroptophiles over at Bat
Conservation International in Austin) has a visceral sense of pollinator
scarcity? And yet, when Martin Burd sorted out hundreds of case studies of low seed set in flowering plants, he attributed 62 percent of these
reproductive shortfalls to pollinator scarcity. An offhand comment by
Burd may be even more telling: the very showiness of flowers might
be an indication that good pollinators are hard to come by.

Big, fierce carnivores may be naturally rare. If so, the last century's declines in seldom-seen nectar-feeding vertebrates may be even
scarier than those that meat eaters have suffered. A roost site in the
Philippines once housed hundreds of thousands of flying-foxes; today
you can witness a few hundred on the best of nights. The Panay giant
fruit bat is altogether gone from the Philippines. The Okinawa flying-
fox is extinct; so are the ones from Palau and Reunion. The Solomon
Islands have lost their endemic tube-nosed fruit bat, while Puerto Rico
has lost its flower bat.

Cuba has lost its red macaw. No one is sure whether turquoise-throated pufflegs occur in Colombia or Ecuador anymore. When was the last time any birder you know spotted a robust white-eye? Or an Oahu oo? A kloea? A Koha grosbeak? A black mamo? Ula-ai-hawane? To add insult to injury, only two reptiles have ever been studied as being legitimate pollinators and one of them—Duvaucel's gecko, on a small island off New Zealand—is already red-listed.

While rare carnivores and scarce nectar feeders may differ in their *salience* (or their *intrinsic* perceptibility to humans, as the bio-philiacs say), they are similar in another way. Both groups of vertebrates demonstrate the *connectivity* between species essential to the healthy functioning and cohesive structuring of biotic communities. If pollinator guilds are defaunated, animal-pollinated plants that formerly dominated a mature community are likely to decline, while weedy wind-pollinated plants are likely to find open niches. If carnivore guilds are defaunated, grazing or browsing populations may explode, eliminating herbaceous understories or crippling the recruitment of woody canopy plants. In either case, a shift in vegetation structure results from declines in animal populations that most of us seldom see. In both cases, the natural functioning of a biotic community is disrupted by the demise of ecological relationships between diffusely coevolved associates.

The pollination relationship is between plants and their animal mutualists, and the predation relationship is between carnivorous animals and their prey; but *connectivity* is the unifying principle. Just as most carnivores rely upon a relatively modest list of prey, most pollinators depend upon a rather narrow range of flowering plants that feature certain fragrances, forms, presentations, and nutritional rewards. Coyotes and honeybees may be extreme generalists, but the majority of carnivores and nectar feeders have limits to what they can opportunistically feed upon; their food choices are not random. In fact, pollinators may generally be more restricted in food choices—and thus potentially more vulnerable—than carnivores, since bears, cats, dogs, weasels, and others of their order tend toward opportunism.

As the dawn light begins to seep into the canyon shadows, I realize that I have not been selected as a puma prey item at this time. Costa's and broad-billed hummingbirds arrive to visit the pale blossoms of the Kearney's blue star. So do bee flies and skippers. Not every visitor is an effective pollinator; not every live hunk of meat to visit this canyon gets to sacrifice itself as cougar food. Some interactions between species are more probable than others.

I backpacked into this canyon, miles above the nearest inhabited cabin, because I had the urge to camp alone. As I awake in my sleeping bag at dawn, I remember how I am strung together with many other lives—from plant to pollinator to predator—in a hammock of interconnected threads.

Traveling the Logging Road, Coast Range

KATHLEEN DEAN MOORE *(1997)*

I'm driving between banks of forest duff, through a leafy tunnel lined with sword ferns and foxgloves. Morning fog spreads through the trees and along the narrow road, like milk poured in water. I turn on the windshield wipers and swerve to avoid a salamander. Huckleberry bushes and rhododendrons grow thick under cedars reaching over the road. I'm not sure how tall these trees are; their top branches have disappeared in the fog. I don't know how old the forest is either, but along this road, I have seen scars on the uphill sides of cedars, where Siuslaw people peeled strips of bark more than three hundred years ago. In the undergrowth, in the fog, these are trees without beginning, trees without end: an eternity of forest.

The road has only one lane for most of its length, but every mile or so there's a wider space where a driver can pull over to let a log truck past. There are pink plastic ribbons dangling from branches here and there, and sometimes a mileage number on a plastic post. Thickly paved with asphalt and built to last, the road follows its fogline around the shoulders of mountains and along ridge tops in Oregon's Coast Range. It's surprisingly well built for a one-way road that, as far as I can tell from my topographic map, ends on the top of a hill in the middle of nowhere.

MILEPOST 19

I crest a hill, startle, and hit the brakes. Bare hillside falls away on my left, bare hillside rises sharply to my right, nothing but mud, acres and

261

acres of steep hillside stripped and sodden. A few blackened spars fall across the hill at odd angles, a few more stand upright—each a stake burned to its base. Far up the hillside, a bulldozer is working slowly. I can hear it shifting and wheezing and powering in low gear, gouging into the earth to tear at a root ball, then shoving the broken end of a tree into a pile of slash. A single strand of smoke rises from a smoldering slash pile and spreads out brown against the bottom of the clouds.

I pull off the road onto a landing littered with tree bark. The tracks of heavy equipment have cut the ground into muddy stripes. Through the clear fans of my windshield, everything has been reduced to shades of gray except, far away, the dull orange smudge of the bulldozer. I have seen a landscape like this before, but it takes me a minute to search my memory. It isn't Central America; nothing I have seen in the slash-and-burn agriculture of third-world countries comes close to this kind of devastation, on this scale. Eventually, I pull back to mind a photograph of a scene from Europe—a cloud-shrouded moonscape of burned and broken snags, where even the ground is churned into craters and thrown into pressure waves of mud and slash. In the foreground, a burned-out tank, and below the photograph, the label: "The Forest of Ardennes, 1945."

Fog turns into rain and within minutes gullies are channeling gray water into larger gullies and digging ditches that spill a slurry of mud onto the road. The mud runs under my car, drops off the roadbed, and slides down a ravine toward the river where salmon are pooling up, waiting to move onto spawning beds.

Before I saw the effects of clear-cutting the great Northwest forests, I imagined a romantic picture: Lumberjacks come in and cut down trees, everyone has clean, sharp-smelling lumber for homes and schools, families have jobs and, where there had been a forest, there is a flower-filled meadow, which is nice for the deer and thus for the hunters; and after a time, the forest grows back and the lumberjacks can cut it again. Then I came to Oregon and saw clear-cutting with my own eyes.

Do people know about the bulldozers? Do they know about the fires and the poison sprayed from small planes to kill whatever brush may have survived? Do people know about the steepness of the bare hills and the crumbling edges of eroded ravines, the silt in the spawning beds? Do they know about the absolute, ground-zero devastation? Logging companies don't just cut the trees and haul them away. In clear-cuts I have seen, not only the trees, but the huckleberries, ferns, moss, the fuss of the chickadees, the silver whistle of the varied thrush, even the rich forest duff that holds on to winter rains, the nourishing soil itself, are all gone—hauled off, sawed up, starved out, plowed under, buried, compacted, or burned. All that's left after clear-cutting are steep hillsides of churned-up mud, a few half-burned piles of slash, and a high-quality asphalt road.

MILEPOST 34

On a line drawn as sharply on the landscape as a boundary line on a map, the clear-cut ends and so does the rain. Ahead are steep scrubland hills, steaming in hard light. I pull off the road, pack up my lunch, and push through the brush down a steep grade toward a stream that shows on my map. But after struggling for almost an hour through blackberry canes and nettles, I find myself less than halfway down the hill, stranded on a stump in the middle of a briar patch. I look around cautiously, shading my eyes with my hand. Hot light and harsh shadows make it hard to see. Nothing on this hillside is taller than I am. There are waist-high salmonberry bushes, their stems fuzzy with thorns, Oregon grape as sharp as English holly, and thick tangles of blackberries reaching over everything, like cobwebs.

I jump from the stump onto the root ball of a sword fern and grab for a fir sapling. The fern's roots break free and the whole clump slides ten feet down the slope. I ride it down, landing on my back, my feet out in front of me, one arm wrapped in a blackberry vine that has scraped from my wrist to my shoulder. The hillside buzzes in the sun. I give up on the hike to the stream, and start the climb back to my car.

When I finally push through a last thicket and emerge, hot and wobbly at the top of the slope, I sit down in the only shade on the hillside, shade cast by a wooden sign. The sign reads, TREES: A RENEWABLE RESOURCE. PLANTED IN 1985.

Sure enough, I can see a few young Douglas-fir trees here and there, light green and frothy, about my height. I can also see every alien, invasive, thorned or poisonous plant that ever grew in hot sun on disturbed soil in this part of the country: Himalayan blackberries, Scotch broom, poison oak, tansy ragwort, Russian thistles, nettles. I wonder if people understand that forests don't just grow back. Plants grow all right; plants always grow in Oregon. But what you get is not what you had before—not by a distance, not in a hundred years.

A pickup truck grinds by, slowing as it passes. I wonder what the driver thinks of me, sitting alone in the dirt, glowering at the scrub.

MILEPOST 39

I pull over next to a grove where I can see nothing but Douglas-firs ranging off in all directions. They grow tall, straight and thin, closely spaced, evenly ranked, each almost the diameter of a fence post. For ten feet off the ground, the branches are bare spikes. Then the trees leaf out into a canopy that exhales piney air and a slow drift of dry needles. The forest has the feel of a park—the light dusty and even, the afternoon simple and silent. I walk deeper into the trees, brushing a few needles out of my hair.

I am well out of sight of the road, not thinking much, when the silence finally catches my attention. I stop walking to listen. Where are the chickadees, the bees, the flies? I look behind me. What happened to the hemlocks, the big-leaf maples, the low salal? I take a step backward. Douglas-firs five inches across, everywhere I look. Ten feet apart.

Three hundred trees per acre. This isn't a forest. This is a farm. I am trespassing on a fence-post farm. Poisoned and plowed and planted and fertilized as deliberately as a wheat field, this lumber will be harvested as routinely as wheat is cut and threshed. I feel like a grasshopper— nervous, scratching one leg against another, tiptoeing across dusty ground below tall yellow stalks.

It wasn't very long ago that trucks carried one-log loads through my town. Standing in line at the five-and-dime, customers would pass the word. "One-log load goin' by." We would crane our necks and peer past the fabric bolts and Valentine's candy, through the dusty window and, sure enough, a truck would rumble past carrying a section of log so massive, it was all the truck could haul on a single load. I try to remember now what I thought then, and it seems to me that I felt admiration for the log, but had no understanding that in the place where the tree had grown, another like it would not grow in my lifetime, nor my children's, nor my grandchildren's . . . not in fifteen generations.

The five-and-dime is a used bookstore now, and the trucks that come by carry thirty, forty logs a load—thin logs, destined for pulp or fence posts. Logs hang out the back and flap up and down whenever the truck hits a bump in the road.

MILEPOST 46

The road climbs in a spiral around a bare mountain and finally ends at the top of the hill in a broad expanse of gravel. I get out of my car to look around. I'm guessing that a high-line used to work about where I am standing. Although the hill has grown up in brambles, the earth still bears the marks of skid trails where cables pulled logs up the hill to the yard. This high up, I can see all the way to the afternoon sun and the white line that marks the ocean. From the top of the range to the edge of the sea, the landscape is a patchwork of clear-cuts, replants, landings, bare earth, and a few reserves of old-growth cedar and hemlock along the coast.

When I walk to the far edge of the hill, I learn that I am not alone up here. A man sits in the cab of an old pickup truck, staring out over the fading hills, never looking my way. The hair on the back of his neck is gray and curling, the skin moist and brown from the sun. He wears a plaid shirt covered with a quilted vest and his hands, still gripping the steering wheel, are enormous.

What does he hear, listening so intently? Faint on an old wind, the creak of cables maybe, the shriek of the whistle-pig, shouted commands, men calling out, chain saws shaking with power. Trucks gearing up, logs thudding onto huge log-decks, and the cracking, cracking, as a tree falls through the forest, breaking off limbs, rending the long fibers of its trunk, then silence—a long, terrible silence—and a great thud as the tree drives its limbs into the earth, rises once, settles. Faint on an old wind, the smells of lubricating oil, diesel exhaust, coffee, dust, and the sweetness of new-cut cedar, as beautiful as Christmas.

A few patches of forest are left on old homesteads and in locked-up forest reserves on federal land. A few more plots to cut, a couple of lawsuits pending that may release some logs, some salvage logging after burns in the Siskiyous and Cascades. Three years maybe. Maybe four. Then the logging companies will pull up stakes and look for somewhere else to cut. His children will leave then, too; there's no work for timber workers where there's no timber. One son off to the fish-packing plants in Alaska maybe. Another to California. Once the daughter with the new baby leaves—for Portland? Spokane?—what will he hold in those great rough hands?

Both he and I can see clear to the sea. The view from the end of the road is a landscape of irretrievable loss.

EXTINCTION
PASSENGER PIGEON CHEWING LOUSE
(COLUMBICOLA EXTINCTA)

PETER FRIEDERICI *(1997)*

It is the most famous extinction in North American history. From a continental population that may have exceeded 3 billion in 1800, the passenger pigeon *(Ectopistes migratorius)* declined to a handful of captive birds within a century. The last reputable sighting of a wild bird occurred in Ohio in 1900; the last captive specimen, dubbed Martha, died at the Cincinnati Zoo in 1914.

The well-known pigeon took with it an entirely unknown organism, the passenger pigeon chewing louse *(Columbicola extincta),* a creature whose scientific name reveals the melancholy fact that our knowledge of its existence has been defined by its extinction. The louse remained unknown to science until the 1930s, when Richard Malcomson, an entomologist at the University of Illinois, found several long-dead specimens clinging to a passenger pigeon study skin in the university's collection (Malcomson 1937). The study skin was collected in 1895 in Urbana, Illinois, and must have belonged to one of the last passenger pigeons shot in the wild. (In those days, collecting the last specimens of a dying species was typically a higher priority than attempting to save them.)

ECOLOGY

Passenger pigeon chewing lice belonged to the Order Mallophaga, which contains over 2,000 species of lice that parasitize birds and mammals. Many, like *Columbicola extincta,* appear to be restricted to a single host species.

Almost nothing is known of the life cycle of *Columbicola extincta.* But a few entomologists have studied other Mallophaga, including the closely related *Columbicola columbae,* which parasitizes the common rock dove or urban pigeon *(Columba livia)* (Martin 1934). Such lice spend their entire life cycle within their host's substrate of feathers. Their biting mouth parts are not able to penetrate skin, and they feed almost entirely on feathers, to which they cling tenaciously.

Columbicola columbae nymphs hatch from eggs glued to feather shafts. They undergo incomplete metamorphosis and reach maturity about twenty days after hatching. Adults, which are between two and three millimeters long, have survived as long as fifty-one days in the laboratory. The insulation of feathers protects them from swings in temperature, to which they are quite sensitive. In response to changes in temperature, food availability, or mating needs, they run swiftly from one part of their host's body to another. In some species—especially, perhaps, in cold climates—Mallophaga appear to overwinter on their hosts in the egg stage (Foster 1969).

Parasitism rates of wild birds have varied widely in published studies. Foster (1969) found that just over 20 percent of museum specimens of orange-crowned warblers *(Vermivora celata)* showed evidence of Mallophaga parasitism. Ash (1960) reported that 95 percent of shorebirds banded during a study in Sweden were infested. Most infestations are light. Only in rare cases do Mallophaga detrimentally affect their hosts (Ash 1960). Lice do some damage to feathers, but old feathers are replaced anyway during regular molts. Typically birds control populations of external parasites through regular maintenance, including preening, dust bathing, and perhaps rubbing ants over their plumage (Ehrlich et al. 1988).

Passenger pigeon chewing lice must have been abundant. Like their hosts, they exploited an ecological niche that allowed their numbers to swell. Some researchers have speculated that passenger pigeons, before their population decline began, may have comprised as much as 40 percent of the total bird life of North America north of Mexico (Schorger 1955). Fantastically sociable, they thrived only in huge flocks that numbered in the millions and even billions. The early American ornithologist Alexander Wilson painstakingly estimated the size of one flock that passed overhead for four hours in Kentucky at 2,230,272,000 individuals. Pigeons fed, roosted, and nested in massive congregations. More than a hundred nests were often found in a single tree.

These conditions must have been favorable for the passenger pigeon chewing louse's transmission from one bird to another. When their host dies, Mallophaga individuals leave the cooling body and search for another living host. Some chewing lice also travel from one bird to another on Hippoboscid flies (also known as "louse flies"), which themselves are parasitic on birds. During large-scale passenger pigeon hunts at roost or nest sites, hundreds of thousands of birds were killed. The migration of *Columbicola extincta* individuals from freshly killed birds to still-living ones must have been a remarkable phenomenon that, alas, went entirely unobserved.

EXTINCTION

The passenger pigeon went extinct with breathtaking rapidity. In 1878 the bird's last great nesting colony occupied an estimated 100,000 acres near Petoskey, Michigan. A decade later only small flocks roamed the shrinking patches of eastern deciduous forest that provided them with food and roosts. Though biologists still debate the exact mechanism of the passenger pigeon's extinction, it is clear that the decline came through some combination of gross overhunting, habitat destruction, and disruption of the species's social structure. Individual pigeons may have been stimulated to breed only in massive flocks. Once flock sizes dropped below a certain threshold, the species was doomed—even though it might still have appeared abundant to observers.

The passenger pigeon chewing louse, of course, experienced the same quick decline. With diminished opportunities for spreading from one individual to another, it may have vanished even before the last of its hosts did.

LESSONS

Modern-day critics of endangered-species protection might label concern for such an unheralded species as literal nit-picking. But in fact the extinction of the passenger pigeon and its louse has important echoes. It is remarkable that not a single nineteenth-century observer recorded the presence of passenger pigeon chewing lice, considering that hundreds of millions of passenger pigeons were shot, trapped, knocked from trees with long poles, or captured when nest trees were set afire. For all the awestruck commentaries on the abundance of the host species, that oversight certainly bespeaks a lack of interest in the quotidian details of the life of individuals of the species.

It took almost as long for the import of the passenger pigeon's extinction to sink in as it did for the species to decline from abundance to vanishing. Throughout the early part of the twentieth century some Americans claimed that the pigeons had not been wiped out by humans: they had flown en masse to South America, or to Canada's boreal forest; they had all drowned while trying to cross the Gulf of Mexico; they would show up again somewhere. As late as the 1950s some observers believed they would reappear—somber evidence of a type of public denial that is surely instructive for those working to forestall today's extinction crisis (Shoemaker 1958).

Finally, the sad case of *Columbicola extincta* should remind us that the natural world is perennially more complex than we know. Not until more than twenty years after its host's extinction did the louse's existence—and extinction—become known. The louse's story is a reminder that we don't know what other creatures, or what intricate interrelationships, are lost when a known plant or animal disappears.

LITERATURE CITED

Ash, J. S. 1960. A study of the Mallophaga of birds with particular reference to their ecology. *Ibis* 102: 93–110.

Ehrlich, P. R., D. S. Dobkin, and D. Wheye. 1988. *The Birder's Handbook*. New York: Simon & Schuster.

Foster, M. S. 1969. Synchronized life cycles in the orange-crowned warbler and its Mallophagan parasites. *Ecology* 50: 315–23.

Malcomson, R. O. 1937. Two new Mallophaga. *Annals of the Entomological Society of America* 30: 53–56.

Martin, M. 1934. Life history and habits of the pigeon louse (*Columbicola columbae* [Linnaeus]). *Canadian Entomologist* 66: 6–16.

Schorger, A. W. 1955. *The Passenger Pigeon: Its Natural History and Extinction*. Madison: University of Wisconsin Press.

Shoemaker, H. W. 1958. *The Last of the Passenger Pigeons*. Ross County Historical Society, Chillicothe, Ohio.

Field Report
Yellowstone Bison Slaughter

Doug Peacock *(1997)*

I have been unable to live without wild things from my earliest memories as a boy growing up in northern Michigan. During my twenties, this requirement for turtles, swamps, and geese took a surly turn and I discovered that without big dangerous animals ranging freely over huge hunks of wild habitat, my prior life paled and I despaired. More recently, the addiction twisted again and I found it difficult to get out of bed without the anticipation of the daily fix of physical and psychic proximity to some big native animal. It was no longer good enough just to know they were out there. Others, probably more mature and better adapted, seem to do just fine with whatever nature they find around their backyards. I don't think anyone is wrong in determining their own minimum wild needs, and I tend to think of mine as merely a personal problem, born of violence in and to the planet, an accident of history to one who remains a second-rate human if I'm deprived of regular contact with the wild ones. I see this pattern less as a singular trait of quirky characters than as a personality defect, which occasionally approaches true perversion (because there are dark sides) in its need for wild and sometimes dangerous critters.

How the cumulative effects of this individual compulsion affect wild ecosystems is a subject for another time best written by somebody else. To chart your occasional spiritual success by conserving wildness is not the only measure of gratification in the late twentieth century; yet for me, many of these small victories have come when I remembered the fragrance of walking through a place, the stare of a particular wild animal, my own fear in its presence. The supposition here might be that it is necessary to know something in order to save it.

I offer this personal observation because this winter I ran into something I couldn't save, a conservation problem I could not solve, indeed none of us could. It concerned bison in Yellowstone National Park. Despite the efforts of hundreds of individuals—good people— many preservation groups and conservation organizations, we failed to save a single wild bison during the brutal winter of 1996–97.

The nation's only wild free-ranging bison herd was savaged by agencies and bureaucrats cheered on by regional politicians, and we couldn't find a way to stop them. Of the park's estimated 3,500 bison, over 1,100 were shipped to slaughter by the National Park Service or blown away by shooters of the Montana Departments of Livestock and Fish, Game, and Parks. An estimated 1,400 more were winter-killed by early April. The dying continues today, and it is possible we will be left with so few bison that the viability of the population is in question. The starving bison's only crime was looking north across the park's border down the valley where I lived.

From my home some forty-five miles north of the park, down the Yellowstone River in the valley they call Paradise, I watched as one of the worst slaughters of North American wildlife in recent history unfolded.

Yellowstone's bison had been important in my own life. I had camped with them in the backcountry of Yellowstone Park for three or four months each year for over fifteen years during the two decades after Vietnam when I lived with grizzly bears. Sometimes I didn't see grizzlies for weeks but the bison were there every day, offering me the wild gift of their companionship, kicking, romping, rolling in the dirt and shaking off clouds of dust, bellowing and grunting as the summer proceeded.

These creatures were remnants of the greatest herds of game animals ever to roam the face of the earth—greater than the wildebeests of the Serengeti or the caribou of the Yukon—the American bison of the High Plains. Numbering perhaps 70 million at the beginning of the nineteenth century, the American bison was slaughtered into near extinction by 1900.

This was no hunt, but butchery. In less than a hundred years, we European Americans reduced the quintessential animal of the continent by 99.999 percent. Both the magnitude of this milling, vibrant animal spectacle and the rapidity with which the herds were slaughtered are unprecedented in human history; I'm saying no other people, maybe no other species on Earth, ever had the impact on the planet's biomass that we had on the bison in the late nineteenth century.

Seventy million were reduced to a few dozen wild bison that survived by finding refuge in Yellowstone National Park. In 1902, twenty-three bison eluded Yellowstone Park managers' efforts to capture them. Another seven hundred or so lived in captivity at the turn of the century. Those were all that was left of them.

Since that cold spring in 1902, the buffalo has made a small recovery and, indeed, the origins of the American conservation movement are connected with its return. The Lacy Act of 1894, a precursor to the Endangered Species Act, made it illegal to kill bison. In 1905 President Theodore Roosevelt helped found the American Bison Society. Protective measures were implemented, and in 1909 the National Bison Range was established in Montana. Today, more than 150,000 bison live in private herds, on Indian reservations, and in a few parks. But only in Yellowstone have these animals always been free to roam, especially once the park committed in 1966 to a policy of natural regulation, allowing nature to take her course. Descendants of the only free-ranging bison in the country increased their numbers to about 3,500 by 1996.

This historic connection was what first attracted me to Yellowstone's wild bison and held my attention for three decades. They were the great-great-grandchildren of the last and only wild ones. This kinship lent me abiding pleasure, a gift. I owed these animals and I had a personal stake in their survival. During the killer winter of 1996–97, I visited these animals every week, bearing witness to this un-precedented twentieth–century wildlife disaster.

It went something like this: Winter slammed down on Yellowstone Park early, ending wildlife grazing. In late December, snowpack measured twice the normal depth. Worse for the bison and elk who winter here, a rare freezing rain had blasted the high plateau with an impenetrable ice layer just before New Year. Grazing was im-possible. The animals had to get out, migrate down off the plateau to lower habitats, or starve. This habitat was mostly on public land outside the park, national forest land. The elk were welcome here, but not the bison. The bison would be killed for trying to cross the park boundary. Stay or leave, the bison were dead.

The danger compounding the death inflicted by winter was a new government policy known as the Interim Bison Plan. Agreed to by the U.S. Departments of Agriculture and Interior and the state of Montana, Yellowstone National Park officials reluctantly implemented the new agreement in December 1996. Bison were no longer free to roam. Under the interim plan, all bison that appeared to be headed across the northern park boundary were to be rounded up, captured, and shipped to slaughterhouses. On the west border of Yellowstone, the wild bison that couldn't be corralled (90 percent of them) were simply shot by sharpshooters of Montana's Department of Livestock.

The ostensible reason for this slaughter is a disease called brucel-losis, a contagious bacterium present in both domestic animals and wildlife. A European disease, it was probably brought over by domestic animals, though humans can also contract it. Cattle infected with bru-cellosis often miscarry their first calf. Montana livestock interests are concerned about losing the state's brucellosis-free status—a threat made by the federal Animal and Plant Health Inspection Service (APHIS), a threat the Montana Department of Livestock (DOL) took very seriously. Never mind that there has never been a documented case of bison infecting cattle with brucellosis in the wild.

The killing began in earnest in late December. Nearly every day, three or four dozen bison were shipped to slaughter from inside the park's northern boundary. Those left in the park's interior were reduced to browsing on pine needles and bark—starvation food. On the west border, the Montana DOL shot another 200 during this brief period. Yellowstone's superintendent and the governor of Montana argued publicly about "whose bison problem" it was. By the third week of January, the number of bison killed by humans exceeded the previous late-twentieth-century record of 569 (for the winter of 1988–89). The superintendent had earlier stated with great accuracy: "If we managed AIDS the way brucellosis is being managed here, you'd be shot when you left your house."

On February 1, APHIS announced it would back off and allow some bison on public land without stripping Montana of its disease-free status. But the state wouldn't hear it and the killing continued. Lying just north of Yellowstone Park, and arguably the bison's worst neighbor, the Church Universal and Triumphant once again whined about gut piles of bison left on their private property adjacent to Yellowstone Park, even though these buffalo had been shot by the DOL in response to the New Age cult's request. When the number of bison dead approached 800 in late January, the National Park Service announced a moratorium on killing. Just two weeks later, Yellowstone National Park's superintendent said the program of shooting and shipping to slaughter would resume with a few modifications. The park spokesperson reported that Yellowstone had no choice but to return to its policy of killing bison. "We're between a rock and a hard place," she said. By the end of February, 1,000 of Yellowstone's estimated 3,500 bison had been shot by government sharpshooters or shipped to the slaughterhouse. An aerial survey conducted on February 21 counted 1,720 bison left, meaning 800 had starved to death with winter barely half over.

During March, the Department of Livestock continued to blow away nearly all bison crossing the western park border. Montana's chief veterinarian had made the DOL position clear: "The one thing I'm going to tell you is exposure (of wild bison) to livestock is not a negotiating point." Of course, there were no cattle in the area and wouldn't be until June 15. The killing persisted even after APHIS, in a letter signed by heads of the Park and Forest Services, wrote Montana's governor saying tolerance for bison would not endanger the state's brucellosis-free status. Department of Livestock shooters killed eighty-three more bison after that communication, all but one on public land, including forty-one bulls, which present the least threat of transmitting the disease. About the only way the bulls could contaminate a beef cow, the state veterinarian had stated, was if a bison bull tried to breed the cow and injured her in the process. Since no cattle were in the area, precluding this most unlikely of unnatural acts, the forty-one bulls died just to show, once again, that the Montana DOL could kill them anyway if they damned well pleased, with or without APHIS's blessing. The most recent aerial survey counted less than 1,100 bison.

Spring equinox arrived and the public began to tire of this muddy controversy with no apparent human heroes. As late as March 17, 1997, the press was still reporting that the issue was simply poor diseased bison who sadly had to be killed. "Yellowstone's Bison Biting the Dust as Brucellosis Spreads," read a front-page article in the *Salt Lake Tribune*. Elsewhere, the slaughter of Yellowstone's bison was being widely reported as a states' rights issue, portraying mismanaged federal animals invading the blameless state of Montana. By late March, a chinook blew in, the weather warmed, and, although bison continued to winter-kill within the interior of Yellowstone Park, the regional press forgot about the bison massacre and dropped its coverage. By the end of March, we had lost more than 2,500 of the estimated 3,500 Yellowstone bison. Winter up there wasn't over. Down here, in paradise, an abrupt and heavy silence lay over the land: the protests and outrage evaporated and the popular media abandoned the issue altogether.

It is now April. Winter lingers on the high plateau. The high peaks of Yellowstone Park's Absaroka Range, which run behind my house, are encased again in fresh hoarfrost, a terrifying white beauty with the wind chill at twelve degrees below zero. The dying continues. Combined with the natural mortality of the harsh winter, this government policy has led to the most deadly year the American bison have faced since being slaughtered into near extinction in the late nineteenth century.

A couple of observations may be appropriate here; the issues engulfing the slaughter were lost in the murk and smokescreen of brucellosis. The rights of native wildlife on public and other lands were scarcely discussed. The media culmination of the bison issue was a town meeting on March 23 in Gardiner, Montana, which was attended by three U.S. senators and Montana's governor for the sole benefit and edification of the U.S. secretary of agriculture. Wildlife personnel were not present. Yellowstone's superintendent was permitted a two-minute reply. The driving management forces throughout this butchery of wild animals were the Department of Agriculture's APHIS and Montana's Department of Livestock—agricultural agents managing wildlife as domestic chattel, a holy war in the endless taming of the Earth whose victory would be the replacement of wild America with a zoo.

Conservation groups were ineffective, though not necessarily inactive. The Fund for Animals wrote papers and threatened to file lawsuits; in late January the fund took out an ad in *USA Today* calling for a tourist boycott of Montana. The Sierra Club Legal Defense Fund did file against the National Park Service but lost the case on appeal. Groups that do good jobs on land use seemed less directed: the Greater Yellowstone Coalition republished in their newsletter a color insert that called for allowing bison to roam on national forest land; and the

Jackson Hole Alliance received a $3,000 grant from Patagonia to do a bison public service announcement, but they couldn't get it together in time for this winter. Cold Mountains, Cold Rivers provided invaluable and ghastly video of the slaughter that was widely viewed, especially by Native Americans. The local Bison Action Group, a tiny bunch of impoverished activists from Bozeman and Missoula, got the most press by their collective protests and for trying to douse Montana's governor with rancid bison guts at the Gardiner meeting.

On Valentine's Day 1997, seven conservation groups finally presented their long-term plan for handling bison migrating out of Yellowstone National Park. The plan, presented in a letter to the governor of Montana and President Bill Clinton, calls for the park to stop grooming the snowmobile trails that have facilitated the exodus of bison. Outside the park, the letter suggests, the U.S. Forest Service should allow bison to graze public lands and APHIS should guarantee its coveted brucellosis-free status if the bison are in a quarantine facility or on state lands. Other suggestions include a state bison hunt and the acquisition of easements or leases from private landowners allowing bison to use and migrate through their lands. The letter was signed by representatives from the Greater Yellowstone Coalition, Defenders of Wildlife, Natural Resources Defense Council, Sierra Club Legal Defense Fund, Intertribal Bison Cooperative, and Jackson Hole Alliance. Presumably because of the recommendation for a hunt, the Fund for Animals did not sign on.

These sound recommendations came too late to make any difference. The Yellowstone bison population had already "crashed."

For myself, I stayed put much of the winter just north of Yellowstone, making mostly ineffective phone calls to people I thought might help: many Native Americans, especially the Intertribal Bison people; I went so far as to call American Indian Movement activist Russell Means, who was busy being a movie star but who said he'd make some calls. I accomplished nothing beyond my weekly travels into Yellowstone Park to visit my shaggy brothers and bear witness to their plight.

What are the implications of the Yellowstone bison crisis for us conservationists? Each group or organization might look at its own goals and agenda and see how it did. How many animals were saved by Earth First!, the Fund for Animals, or Defenders of Wildlife; how much ecosystem management or natural regulation was advanced by the efforts of the Jackson Hole Alliance or the Greater Yellowstone Coalition; how much support was garnered for corridor linkage by groups like the Alliance for the Wild Rockies or the Wildlands Project. That sort of thing. By every standard I can think of, we took—by what it's known as up here in bison country—an asskicking.

We lost on every level. Eleven hundred native wild bison were blown away for crossing an artificial boundary, in defense of an unproven threat to privately owned domestic livestock who weren't even present on public land grazing allotments. The easy talk about restoring grizzlies to California and Nebraska, of linking wolves from Maine to Mexico, sounds in this context like empty ecobabble. It was a major defeat handed to us by midlevel bureaucrats and local politicians leering for media attention.

Among the voices missing in loudly protesting the slaughter—the ones I noticed—were hunting groups, sportsmen, guides, those whose outrage would have been thunderous if elk, instead of bison, were being killed. Also noticeably silent here were the collective spokespersons of the Wildlands Project, though Dave Foreman was immensely supportive in his public lectures. A quote in the national press or a letter of protest would have been useful. Nothing much came in beyond the protests of the activists, Native Americans, and the Intertribal Bison Cooperative, Joe Gutkoski of the American Buffalo Foundation, and finally a letter to the editor of the Livingston paper, from George Wuerthner, a bit late, but, as usual for George, right on the money.

And accountability? Read the papers and magazines. Listen to what the bureaucrats and politicians say. Where was the Clinton-Gore White House on all this? They sound clueless on issues of American wildlife and wilderness. Why couldn't they rein in the rogue agency APHIS, and why was the Agriculture Department handling wildlife issues anyway? Who advises the president? The secretary of interior's silence was deafening. The director of Greater Yellowstone Coalition reported that Secretary Babbitt had got his butt kicked once on grazing reform and, being from a ranching family, didn't want another livestock defeat. The regional spokesman for the National Park Service talked about the need for Yellowstone to be a "good neighbor"; part of being a good neighbor, he said, was being sensitive to the APHIS threat to strip Montana of its brucellosis-free status (therefore, having won on the wolf reintroduction and the New World Mine, it was time to lose on the third issue, bison).

At the Yellowstone Park level, the chief scientist correctly characterized the controversy as "a struggle between the park and agribusiness and we're losing badly. They did not like us winning the wolf issue and they are determined not to lose this one."

Park managers were counting heavily on public opinion to bail them out of a bad deal. They hated what they were doing but did it anyway. I think park officials figured no more than a hundred or so bison might wander north out of the park and actually end up at the slaughterhouse. The media coverage of the corralling, trucking, and butchering and subsequent public outcry would force intervention from above and thus slam the lid on the operation. A more enlightened bison management plan could then be formulated by next winter. Yellowstone National Park officials miscalculated badly, and nobody could have predicted the killer winter.

The agency responsible for most of the bison killing was the Montana Department of Livestock. Once control of wild bison was turned over to agricultural agencies, their fate was sealed. Most intractable has been the core of the operation run by DOL, with little or no supervision, answering to none, headed up by director Larry Peterson and the state veterinarian, Clarence Sirochi. Local activists have called Sirochi "the Eichmann of Yellowstone."

Even more corrupt than the DOL, who were after all only doing their job with striking efficiency, were Montana's governor and congressmen, who got on the bandwagon only after sensing the feds were bleeding and they could safely make political hay out of blaming the Park Service. Though not all equally of course, they did collectively aid and abet a false presentation of the brucellosis issue and a phony substitution of legitimate ranching interests by bureaucratic power brokers within the livestock department. All these agencies and officials, incidentally, claimed to be "caught in the middle," a most cowardly contradiction of ethical configurations.

Late this winter, livestock associations from the states of Oregon and, especially, Colorado took cheap shots at bison through dishonest representation of a brucellosis threat. All of these people, as well as the politicians and agencies, got off scot free. What could be done, then, to put some heat on these cold executioners and professional spit dribblers? Perhaps a mainstream conservation group could take on the task of sorting out wildlife interests from the legitimate interests of livestock growers (neither state livestock associations nor departments of agriculture necessarily speak for regional ranchers here). The right of bison to lead a wild bovid life on America's wildlands must be a given. Ideally, the model would be the dolphin-safe label on the tuna can. People who eat beef should have a choice beyond "organic" raised meat. This will not be easy because current packaging and labeling does not permit identification of where or how such food arrives nor if it's bison friendly. Many cattle raisers from the Yellowstone to the Malpais would endorse such accountability. Livestock raisers who deal responsibly with the issues of native habitats and wildlife should be rewarded, not lumped with welfare ranchers.

Finally, I don't think this is a time to merely talk conservation and ecology. I feel close enough to the legacy of Ed Abbey to believe this is not what he had in mind when he said, "Sentiment without action is the ruin of the soul." A wilderness strategy for the twenty-first century cannot be successful without fighting like hell all through the twentieth. What is called for is closer to the metaphorical equivalent of a lynching. I don't believe in lynching, but I believe in retribution appropriate to the deed. It may not be practical or positive, but there are times to lay down your imaging software and pick up a baseball bat. Or perhaps pick up the moral arms of your own choices—including, but not limited to, prayers, letters, and tomahawks—in defense of native wild rights.

The ease with which the second slaughter of 1,100 wild American bison went down took all of us by surprise. How could this happen again? I believe the American bison has never entered our consciousness as a sentient creature, but somehow lies in our history as a black hole of denial, an obstacle to Manifest Destiny that we expediently slaughtered as part of the final solution to the Indian Problem, not unlike how colonial cultures treated subordinate races. How else could we kill them so easily? The Yellowstone slaughter went far beyond any notion of "wildlife management" in both scale and brutality. All through this winter, officials made a point of delineating between individual bison and the "population." Yellowstone's superintendent said that even the secretary of interior got it: "It's the population, stupid." The park's senior bison biologist called the winterkill a "critical ecological need" because the Yellowstone bison population had become "inflated." Even conservation biologists, if I read them right, subscribe to such detachment, which so facilitates extermination of undesired nonhumans or "sub"humans. Ask Pol Pot. The ribs and pelvis of the starving bison shot four times at the Sheridan, Wyoming, slaughterhouse looked like emancipation day at Auschwitz. Do My Lai and Yellowstone share this convenience? I've been both places and I think so. The lightning efficiency with which we butchered our 70 million bison boggles the mind and lingers yet, I believe, near the heart of our flawed relationship with the American wilderness and its wild inhabitants.

We never really knew these animals.

The Gift of Silence

Anne LaBastille *(1997)*

Silence is the invisible, intangible, exquisitely fragile natural resource that no one thinks about. No one makes an effort to save it, and no one donates to preserve it. There is no Citizens Group to Save Silence, no Washington lobby to fight for silence, no Coalition to Reduce Loud Manmade Sounds in the Environment.

Silence is an integral part of every climbing, camping, or canoeing trip. It is the heart and soul of the wilderness experience. It is the perfect prescription for a good night's sleep, and the oldest Rx for stress. It may be a partial cure for workers subjected to high noise levels in factories, who are prone to increased heart disease and nervous disorders.

Once silence stretched over New York's Adirondack Mountains from shore to shore, peak to peak, like a velvet mantle. It was broken by wind soughing through great white pines, by August thunderstorms and February blizzards. It was disrupted by trout splashing, deer snorting, owls hooting, and wolves howling. These sounds melded and molded with silence for 10,000 years and more.

With the invention of gunpowder, steam and electric engines, and gasoline motors, the erosion of silence began. This erosion has accelerated dramatically in the past twenty years.

On a typical Adirondack Park summer day, an inhabitant may hear the following: Around 7:00 A.M., sounds of vehicular traffic increase as workers and tourists take to the roads. Then outboard and inboard motorboats start cruising the lakes. From 9:00 to 10:00, mail trucks and mail boats cover their routes. Seaplanes fly over, carrying fishermen or sightseers. Or an F-16 makes a sonic boom while A-10s roar above the treetops on military training flights. Camp owners engaged in repairs work with electric skill saws and drills. At intervals, commercial jetliners pass overhead. As the day warms, water-skiers and jet-skiers start streaking up and down the lakes. (In winter, it's snowmobilers.) In the afternoon, chain saws rev up as people cut firewood. By twilight, most human noises diminish. A few late cars and boats go by. Finally, night's noises can preside—except for those infernal bug zappers!

Who among us today can say that they have spent a day totally free of sounds generated by motors, engines, and guns? Only the deaf, those in solitary confinement, and dedicated wilderness campers. The disappearance of silence in the Adirondacks, in America, and in every other First World country has been gradual, invasive, and continual. It will get worse as our materialistic society produces more and more mechanized gadgets.

The Adirondack Park can still offer substantial time blocks of silence. With it come those blessed feelings of solitude, contemplation, and creativity. Silence in the natural world has inspired humans as diverse as the biblical prophets, famous poets and musicians, and great conservationists such as John Muir, Teddy Roosevelt, Sigurd Olson, and Aldo Leopold.

We need silence. We need it to be reminded of the vastness of the stars and space that surround our tiny planet. Of the awesome beauty of wilderness. Of the implacability of nature's laws. In short, silence helps put us in our place. It makes humans humble and reverent.

I consider it a gift to spend a summer's night with only the sound of a loon's tremolo on a silent lake. And to walk through the flaming leaves in late September. And to lie for a moment at midnight on an icebound lake, wondering at the aurora borealis, and hear nothing but the trees cracking in the cold.

I fear the gift of silence will become precious and rare as we enter the twenty-first century.

Job and Wilderness

Bill McKibben *(1997)*

The first attempt of which I'm aware to answer the question "Why are wild places valuable?" comes in the Hebrew Bible, in the book of Job. Job, of course, suffers wretchedly and unfairly; he loses his family and his lands, and is reduced to lying in a dung heap at the edge of town, covered with oozing sores. Knowing that he has behaved justly, and puzzled at his travails, Job demands an audience with God—demands that God justify Himself. Job's is the first modern voice in the Bible, really in all of literature. And the answer that God, speaking from a whirlwind, gives him is a curious one.

God says nothing about justice, about evenhandedness, about sin, about any of the current metaphysical categories that usually occupy our attention. Instead, He conducts a tour of the physical Earth— its tides and storms and forests and waters, its magnificent animals. He speaks sarcastically some of the time, taunting Job with the man's insignificance: Where were you when I laid down the boundaries of the oceans? When I placed the very stars in the heavens? But He also speaks with great tenderness:

> Do you tell the antelope to calve
> or ease her when she is in labor?
> Do you count the months of her fullness
> and know when her time has come?
> She kneels; she tightens her womb;
> she pants, she presses, gives birth.
> Her little ones grow up;
> they leave and never return.

287

When Job asks why he must suffer, God talks about antelopes, vultures, lions, ostriches. God points out that it is He who cuts a path for the thunderstorm to "water the desolate wasteland, the land where no man lives, to make the wilderness blossom." The clear and overpowering implication of his speech—God's longest sustained speech in the whole Bible—is that Job and people in general are but a part of creation, not its central feature. Even our notions of justice fit into something very much larger and less tame.

I recite this story simply to say that one value wilderness has *for us* (clearly subsidiary to the many values it has for other creatures) is that it allows us to remember how big we are. We live, at the end of the twentieth century, in a world designed to constantly make us seem large and important. The television natters at us constantly about the importance of our desires; we can scarcely drive down a road in this country without a sign to flatter and cajole us. The marks of our power are everywhere about us, especially in the ways that we annihilate space and time through our technology.

Yet the marks of our infatuation are everywhere about us too, in a culture of instant gratification that descends easily into selfishness and violence. Wilderness is one of the few places (along with soup kitchens and hospitals and other places that transcendent human love can be practiced) that remind us there are other definitions of what it means to be a man or a woman. Wilderness allows us to entertain the possibility that instead of being constantly at the center of the world, we might be more comfortable as one part among many. In this way, it helps preserve a diversity of human identities just as it helps preserve a diversity of other creatures.

Most of my work deals with the largest environmental problems, forces like global climate change. The data convince me we will be unable to deal with these challenges until we manage to shift, subtly but powerfully, our estimation of how big, how central, how important we should be; until we find other ways of living that suit us better, and that suit the planet better as well. Wilderness, the kind of wilderness that surrounds Vermont's Wallingford Pond, is a crucial schoolhouse for this transformation. A clear-cut next to it would be the equivalent of a boombox blaring static in one corner of that schoolhouse. It would keep us from hearing the voice from the whirlwind, the voice from our heart, the voice that says we are a small part of something very wonderful and very right.

Bill McKibben wrote this essay on behalf of Wallingford Pond, one of the largest undeveloped water bodies in Vermont. Green Mountain National Forest managers were planning a large timber sale next to the pond. Pressure from conservationists, led by the organization Forest Watch (www.forestwatch.org), forced the Forest Service to reconsider and the proposed logging did not occur.

THE LEAST NAVIGABLE CRAFT
WHALES AT THE MILLENNIUM

PHOEBE WRAY *(1997)*

The oceans cover about 71 percent of Earth's surface. They contain
an estimated 301,471,060,000,000,000,000 gallons of water. What is
striking about this figure is not the enormousness of it but the fact that
it can be measured. The seas are finite. They are not the "limitless resource" our fables would have us believe, but a measurable entity with
numbers of the kind we have come to bandy about in this age of computers and rockets into the universe.

　　Standing on the shores, we measure the oceans against our own
bodies and are rightly humbled. They seem big enough to never die,
big enough to feed us all, big enough to hold both our endless wastes
and our hope. Despite what many scientists, naturalists, and soothsayers
tell us about the dying seas, we embrace our memories of the time
of hardy, independent people clinging like barnacles to their watery
towns: braving storms, mourning their unreturned dead, writing sad
songs to the Mother Sea. We say the sea has secrets. We know the sea
has laws.

　　One sacred, which is to say consistently acknowledged, law of
the sea is that the least navigable craft has the right of way. Surely, at
the end of the twentieth century, whales are the least navigable craft.
We can herd them into shallows, throw nets across their passage, outrun them in the open ocean, stop them dead with our weaponry, spy
on them from satellites. We do all these things. But the design of a fin
whale drives a marine engineer to despair. Our vessels are not as
sleek, as resilient, as radical in design, as elegant as the simplest, most

primitive cetacean. But we can outmaneuver them and, in a flash, turn them belly up in the bright water.

The greatest of mammals, the blue whale *(Balaenoptera musculus),* is a marvel of sinew and strength and beauty. It can reach lengths over 100 feet, much longer than a bowling alley. The blue whale requires the two-inch marine animal with a romantic name, *Euphasia superba.* Without that spit of life the blue whale couldn't exist. That's what it eats. This exigency makes the blue whale a least navigable craft.

Euphasia superba is one of the largest of the minute sea creatures known collectively as "krill." It resembles a shrimp. Krill is a prime candidate to be harvested in enormous volumes for people food; although it is 75 percent water, it is 13 percent protein. Whales eat it by the ton. The Japanese and Russians are already processing krill into something edible for humans. This animal is the thick soup of the oceans, the staple of any number of marine species. It is not spread uniformly (nothing is), but is particularly abundant in the Antarctic, where whaler's guns have reduced krill-eating blue, humpback, and fin whales to insignificant numbers.

The vast and growing human population needs to be fed, thus we go more and more to sea. We compete increasingly with aquatic life for food and space. Our conquest of the land relatively complete, we approach the seas with questionable credentials and with the knowledge that random, unregulated exploitation and alteration of the hydrosphere is dangerous and unthinkable. At least some people, sensitive to the size and finiteness of this planet, think so.

Most of our fisheries technology is based on the principle of maximizing profit. Such an idea leads resolutely to degradation of the resource. It has encouraged, for instance, the "walls of death" nets, drifting miles long, drowning everything that swims against them, commercially "valuable" or not. There is much "or not," including dolphins, other marine mammals and turtles, and millions of fish, that is discarded. It also encouraged overexploitation of the great whales until a halt was called to the slaughter by the moratorium on commercial whaling, passed with some protest by the International Whaling Commission (IWC) in 1982, taking effect in 1986.

Since the passage of the moratorium, a concerted attack against it has been launched by the remaining whaling nations, Japan and Norway, abetted by Iceland and by small nations such as the Solomon Islands and Dominica, recruited by Japan. This attack is pursued not just at annual IWC meetings, but throughout the year, enhanced by several well-funded nongovernmental organizations that claim to be adherents of the neo-Cartesian philosophy dubbed, inexplicably but ironically, "wise use." Under the banner of reasserting commercial whaling interests as rights, the wise-use groups claim that whale populations are increasing as a result of protection, and ought to be killed by anyone who wants to use them. Whaling is presented as a traditional human endeavor; its appropriateness is not questioned. And much of the wise-use agenda is based on economics, fisheries economics.

Here at the end of the millennium, if we have learned anything it is that all life is a complex, interconnected web, and that diversity sustains the structure. In our expanding fisheries exploitation, we would do well to remember that variety in nature is not the spice, it is the meat and potatoes. The educational effort to promote such an idea is incomplete and inadequate, and people still speak of "desirable" and "undesirable" species. Predicating the existence of all that is not human on whether or not one group of people happens to like it, finds it edible, pretty, or capable of becoming something useful when dead, is an arrogance the planet should not have to endure. Such philosophy is not wisely useful.

Even in the face of a hopeful trend—the growing support for establishment of marine ecological reserves—this utilitarian bent is evident. As scientists and conservation activists work to establish such reserves, it is apparent that thus far the support of governments and fishing industry representatives is driven by a concern to restore depleted commercial fisheries to exploitable levels, not to restore eco-system functioning itself.

At the IWC meeting in Dublin, Ireland, in 1995, a helpful summary paper called "The International Whaling Commission Now" was distributed. It was written by the IWC secretary, Dr. Ray Gambell. The first paragraph of his conclusions deserves quoting:

> Commercial whaling has a long history of over-exploitation of each species and stock of whales as they were discovered or the technology advanced to permit capture. No regulations have been successful in preventing this in the face of the economic demands from the industry.

Moreover, for years the regulations were based on questionable data. During the most intense years of commercial whaling, the former Soviet Union habitually lied about the numbers of whales it took. This falsification was revealed by a courageous and respected Russian scientist in 1993, when the political climate allowed the release of secret data showing that Russian fleets operating in the Antarctic routinely took nearly double the number of whales they reported, including protected and endangered species. They did this even while Japanese "inspectors" aboard the ships presumably monitored the killing. More than 90,000 whales were killed but not reported. The illegally killed whales were, it is said, sold at sea by the Russians to the Japanese for cash.

Whales are the least navigable in other ways. Climate change may be affecting them. Southern right whales have been seen with sunburn (likely attributable to ozone depletion). Whales that come close to shore encounter toxins and heavy metals at dangerous levels; the Mediterranean is notable for such pollution. Vessel traffic in migratory paths used both by whales and humans has increased exponentially, resulting in collisions and death to the whales. This is especially harmful to the slow-moving, greatly endangered Atlantic right whale, present off the North American coast and now represented by a few hundred animals. Lobster pots and fishing nets tangle and drown whales around the world.

The California gray whale, a conservation success story in which protection has resulted in what appears to be complete recovery of the species, is off the endangered list but still threatened at both ends of its long annual migration between the Bering and Chukchi Seas and Baja California. The gray whale journeys to the salty shallow lagoons of Baja to breed and to bear its young. Huge and expanding salt-mining operations that threaten the breeding lagoons are sanctioned by the Mexican government and are funded partially by Mitsubishi, the ubiquitous Japanese megacompany. In the north, American gas and oil exploration continues. The migratory path is busy and noisy with vessels of all kinds.

The indigenous people of Russian Siberia use the gray whales, under special quota from the IWC, primarily as food for their mink farms but do not kill the whales themselves; government catcher boats take the whales for them. In 1996 Russia reported its kill to the IWC and revealed the whales were taken with an antitank gun and assault weapons, using thousands of bullets—in one case, 700 rounds of ammunition on one whale. IWC nomenclature categorizes this slaughter as "aboriginal subsistence whaling."

At the end of the twentieth century, a new threat to the gray whale surfaced from a small Washington State Native American tribe, the Makah, who petitioned the IWC to be granted a quota of five gray whales annually (the petition actually asked to be allowed to strike up to ten whales to capture at least five the first year of their quota) so that they could revive a long-abandoned hunt. Whales and whaling are central to the Makah oral and artistic tradition and tribal identity. The Makah, however, have not killed whales in over seventy years and no longer remember how to do it. (The United States government later supplied equipment and trainers.) A majority of tribal elders opposed the hunt, but an aggressive group within the Makah

actively pursued and got a quota. Encouraged by the National Marine
Fisheries Service, the Makah also sought advice and support from the
Russians, Japanese, and Norwegians as well as other tribes to the north
and "wise use" groups.

The Makah kill the gray whales from cedar canoes backed up
by a powerboat and scuba divers. The whale is harpooned, then dis-
patched with a .50 caliber bullet. There is little mention of the rigorous spiritual preparations of the whaling crews chronicled in their
traditions, and the tribe cannot cite nutritional need. The whaling is
done in or near the Olympic Coast National Marine Sanctuary, from
whose regulations the Makah are exempted. This area is favored by a
cetaceans dubbed "resident whales," gray whales who appear to stop
in Washington waters rather than continuing north to the feeding
grounds of Alaska. What consequences the hunt will have on whale-
watching enterprises along the Northwest coast, on the Makah, and
on the resident whales is yet to be seen.

The lives of whales are not random. They are loyal to their breeding and feeding areas, their migratory paths and sheltered bays, and
have social structures so visible and remarkable even the open-boat
whalers were aware of them. They do not adapt as humans adapt. For
most of the historic time shared by whales and humans, the human
population was small and the whales many. They could outrun us; they
could hide; they could fight back. That changed in the nineteenth century, and with technological innovations, whaling became a holocaust
in the twentieth. Now we are many, with sophisticated weapons of
pursuit and death, and they are few, still plying the same waters for
the same ends, a least navigable craft among the huge and magnificent
flotillas crowding the waves. To assure their continued existence into
the twenty-first century, surely it would be a wise use of sea law to
extend to the whales a right of passage.

The Language of Animals

Barry Lopez *(1998)*

The steep riverine valley I live within, on the west slope of the Cascades in Oregon, has a particular human and natural history. Though I've been here for thirty years, I am able to convey almost none of it. It is not out of inattentiveness. I've wandered widely within the drainages of its eponymous river, the McKenzie; and I could offer you a reasonably complete sketch of its immigrant history, going back to the 1840s. Before then, Tsanchifin Kalapuya, a Penutian-speaking people, camped in these mountains, but they came up the sixty-mile-long valley apparently only in summer to pick berries and to trade with a people living on the far side of the Cascades, the Molala. In the fall, the Tsanchifin returned down valley to winter near present-day Eugene, Oregon, where the McKenzie joins the Willamette River. The Willamette flows a hundred miles north to the Columbia, the Columbia another hundred miles to the Pacific.

The history that preoccupies me, however, in this temperate rain forest is not human history, not even that of the highly integrated Tsanchifin. Native peoples seem to have left scant trace of their comings and goings in the McKenzie valley. Only rarely, as I hear it, does someone stumble upon an old, or very old, campsite, where glistening black flakes of a volcanic glass called obsidian, the debitage from tool-making work, turn up in soil scuffed by a boot heel.

I've lingered in such camps, in a respectful and deferential mood, as though the sites were shrines; but I'm drawn more to the woods in which they're found. These landscapes are occupied, still, by the wild animals who were these people's companions. These are the

296

descendants of animals who coursed these woods during the era of the Tsanchifin.

When I travel in the McKenzie basin with visiting friends, my frame of mind is not that of the interpreter, of the cognoscente; I amble with an explorer's temperament. I am alert for the numinous event, for evidence of a world beyond the rational. Though it is presumptuous to say so, I seek a Tsanchifin grasp, the view of an indigene. And what draws me ahead is the possibility of revelation from other indigenes—the testimonies of wild animals.

The idea that animals can convey meaning, and thereby offer an attentive human being illumination, is a commonly held belief the world over. The view is disparaged and disputed only by modern cultures with an allegiance to science as the sole arbiter of truth. The price of this conceit, to my way of thinking, is enormous.

I grew up in a farming valley in southern California in the 1950s, around sheep, dogs, horses, and chickens. The first wild animals I encountered—coyotes, rattlesnakes, mountain lion, deer, and bear—I came upon in the surrounding mountains and deserts. These creatures seemed more vital than domestic animals. They seemed to tremble in the aura of their own light. (I caught a shadow of that magic occasionally in a certain dog, a particular horse, like a residue.) From such a distance it's impossible to recall precisely what riveted my imagination in these encounters, though I might guess. Wild animals are lean. They have no burden of possessions, no need for extra clothing, eating utensils, elaborate dwellings. They are so much more integrated into the landscape than human beings are, swooping its contours and bolting down its pathways with bewildering speed. They travel unerringly through the dark. Holding their gaze, I saw the intensity and clarity I associated with the presence of a soul.

In later years I benefited from a formal education at a Jesuit prep school in New York City, then at New York University and the universities of Notre Dame and Oregon. I encountered the full range of

Western philosophy, including the philosophy of science, in those classrooms and studied the theological foundations of Christianity. I don't feel compelled now to repudiate that instruction. I regard it, though, as incomplete, and would say that nothing I read in those years fundamentally changed what I thought about animals. The more steeped I became in the biology and ecology of animals, the more I understood about migration, and the more I comprehended about the intricacy of their neural impulses and the subtlety of their endocrine systems, the deeper their other unexplored capacities appeared to me. Biochemistry and field studies enhanced rather than diminished my sense that, in Henry Beston's phrase, animals were other nations.

If formal education taught me how to learn something, if it provided me with reliable structures (e.g., *Moby Dick,* approaching the limit of calculus, von Clausewitz's tactics) within which I could exercise a metaphorical imagination, if the Jesuits inculcated in me a respectful skepticism about authority, then that education gave me the sort of tools most necessary to an examination of the history of Western ideas, a concept fatally flawed by an assumption of progress. I could move on from Gilbert White's *Selbourne* to Thoreau's *Walden.* I could trace a thread from Aristotle through Newton to Schrödinger. Or grasp that in the development of symphonic expression, Bach gives way to Mozart who gives way to Beethoven. But this isn't progress. It's change, in a set of ideas that incubate well in our culture.

I left the university with two ideas strong in my mind. One was the belief that a person had to enter the world to know it, that it couldn't be got from a book. The other was that there were other epistemologies out there, as rigorous and valid as the ones I learned in school. Not convinced of the superiority of the latter, I felt ready to consider these other epistemologies, no matter how at odds.

When I moved into the McKenzie valley I saw myself beginning a kind of apprenticeship. Slowly I learned to identify indigenous plants and animals and birds migrating through. Slowly I began to expand the basis of my observations of their lives, to alter the nature of my assumptions. Slowly I began to recognize clusters of life in the valley as opposed to individual, isolated species. I was lucky to live in a place too steep for agriculture to have developed, too heavily wooded to be good for grazing, and too poor in commercial quantities of minerals for mining (though the evidence that all three occurred on a small scale is present). The only industrial-scale impact here has come from commercial logging—and the devastation in parts of the valley is as breathtaking a sight as the napalmed forests of the Vietnam highlands in the 1960s. Pressure is building locally now to develop retirement real estate—trailer parks, RV parks, condominiums; but, for the moment, it's still relatively easy to walk for hours across stretches of land that have never been farmed, logged, mined, grazed, or homesteaded. From where my house sits on a wooded bench above the McKenzie River, I can look across the water into a four- or five-hundred-year-old forest in which some of the Douglas-firs are more than twenty feet around.

Two ways to "learn" this land are obvious: enter it repeatedly and attentively on your own; or give your attention instead—or alternately—to its occupants. The most trustworthy occupants, to my mind, are those with no commercial ties, beings whose sense of ownership is guided not by profit but by responsible occupancy. For the valley in which I live, these occupants would theoretically be remnant Tsanchifin people and indigenous animals. To my knowledge, the Tsanchifin are no longer a presence; and the rational mind (to which many of us acquiesce) posits there is little to be learned from animals unless we discover a common language and can converse. This puts the emphasis, I think, in the wrong place. The idea shouldn't be for us to converse, to enter into some sort of Socratic dialogue with animals. It would be to listen to what is already being communicated. To insist on a conversation with the unknown is to demonstrate impatience and to imply that any such encounter must include your being heard.

To know a physical place you must become intimate with it. You must open yourself to its textures, its colors in varying day and night lights, its sonic dimensions. You must in some way become vulnerable to it. In the end, there's little difference between growing into the love of a place and growing into the love of a person. Love matures through intimacy and vulnerability, and it grows most vigorously in an atmosphere of trust. You learn, with regard to the land, the ways in which it is dependable. Where it has no strength to offer you, you do not insist on its support. When you yourself do not understand something, you trust the land might, and you defer.

When I walk in the woods or along the creeks, I'm looking for integration, not conversation. I want to be bound more deeply into the place, to be included, even if only as a witness, in events that animate the landscape. In tracking a mink, in picking a black bear scat apart, in examining red alder trunks that deer have scraped with their antlers, I get certain measures of the place where I live. In listening to the songs and tones of Swainson's thrushes and to winter wrens, to the bellows of elk, I get a dimension of the valley I couldn't get on my own. In eating spring chinook, in burning big-leaf maple in the stove, in bathing in groundwater from the well, in collecting sorrel and miner's lettuce for a summer salad, I put my life more deeply into the life around me.

The eloquence of animals is in their behavior, not their speech. To see a mule deer stot across a river bar, a sharp-shinned hawk maneuver in dense timber, to watch a female chinook build her nest on clean gravel, to see a rufous hummingbird extracting nectar from foxglove blossoms, to come upon a rubber boa constricting a shrew is to meet the world outside the self. It is to hear the indigenes.

We regard wild creatures as the most animated part of the landscape. We've believed for eons that we share a specific nature with them, different from the nature of wild berries or lightning or water. Our routine exchanges with them are most often simply a verification of this, reaffirmations that we're alive in a particular place together at a particular time.

Wild animals are like us, too, in that they have ancestors. When I see river otter sprawled mid-stream on a boulder in the noon sun, I know their ancestors were here before the fur trappers, before the Tsanchifin, before *Homo*. The same for the cormorant, the woolly bear caterpillar, the cutthroat. In all these histories, in the string of events in each life, the land is revealed. The tensile strength of the orb weaver's silk, the location of the salmon's redd, the shrew-moles' bones bound up in a spotted owl's cast, each makes a concise statement.

Over the years and on several continents I've seen indigenous people enter their landscapes. (I say *enter* because the landscape of a semi-permanent camp or village, as I have come to understand it, is less intense, less numinous.) Certain aspects of this entry experience seem always to be in evidence. Human conversation usually trails off. People become more alert to what is around them, less intent on any goal—where to camp that night, say. People become more curious about animal life, looking at the evidence of what animals have been up to. People begin to look all around, especially behind them, instead of staring straight ahead with only an occasional look to the side. People halt to examine closely things that at first glance seemed innocuous. People hold up simply to put things together—the sky with a certain type of forest, a kind of rock outcropping, the sound of a creek, and, last, the droppings of a blue grouse under a thimbleberry bush. People heft rocks and put them back. They push their hands into river mud and perhaps leave patches of it on their skin. It's an ongoing intercourse with the place.

Learning one's place through attention to animals is not solely a matter of being open to "statements" they make about the physical, chemical, and biological realms we share. A more profound communication can take place. In this second sphere, animals have volition; they have intention and the power of influence; and they have the capacity to intervene in our lives. I've never known people who were entirely comfortable addressing such things. However we may define "consciousness" in the West, we regard it as a line of demarcation that separates human nature from animal nature. A shaman might cross back and forth, but animals, no.

In my experience indigenous people are most comfortable in asserting a spiritual nature for animals (including aspects of consciousness) only when the purpose of the conversation is to affirm a spirituality shared by both humans and animals. (They're more at ease talking about animals as exemplars of abstract ideals, as oracles and companions, and as metaphorical relations.) When someone relates something previously unheard of that they saw an animal do, something that demonstrates the degree of awareness we call consciousness, the person is saying the world still turns on the miraculous, it's still inventing itself, and that we're a part of this. These observations keep the idea alive that animals are engaged in the world at a deep level.

The fundamental reinforcement of a belief in the spiritual nature of animals' lives (i.e., in the spiritual nature of the landscape itself) comes from a numinous encounter with a wild creature. For many indigenous people (again, in my experience) such events make one feel more secure in the "real" world because their unfolding takes the event beyond the more readily apparent boundaries of existence. In a numinous encounter one's suspicion—profound, persistent, and ineluctable, that there is more to the world than appearances—is confirmed. For someone reared in the tradition of the cultural West, it is also a confirmation that Rationalism and the Enlightenment are not points on a continuum of progress but simply two species of wisdom.

Whenever I think of the numinous event, and how vulnerable it is to the pincers of the analytic mind, I recall a scene in a native village in Alaska. A well-meaning but rude young man, a graduate student in anthropology, had come to this village to study hunting. His ethnocentric interviewing technique was aggressive, his vocabulary academic, his manner to pester and interfere. Day after day he went after people, especially one older man he took to be the best hunter in the village. He hounded him relentlessly, asking him why he was the best hunter. The only way the man could be rid of the interviewer was to answer his question. He ended the assault by saying, "My ability to hunt is like a small bird in my mind. I don't think anyone should disturb it."

A central task facing modern Western cultures is to redefine human community in the wake of industrialization, colonialism, and, more recently, the forcing power of capitalism. In trying to solve some of the constellation of attendant problems here—keeping corporations out of secondary education, restoring the physical and spiritual shelter of the family group, preserving non-Western ways of knowing—it seems clear that by cutting ourselves off from nature, by turning nature into scenery and commodities, we may cut ourselves off from something vital. To repair this damage we can't any longer take what we call "nature" for an object. We must merge it again with our own nature. We must reintegrate ourselves in specific geographic places, and to do that we need to learn those places at greater depth than any science, Eastern or Western, can take us. We have to incorporate them again in the moral universe we inhabit. We have to develop good relations with them, ones that will replace the exploitative relations that have become a defining characteristic of twentieth-century Western life, with its gargantuan oil spills and chemical accidents, its megalithic hydroelectric developments, its hideous weapons of war, and its conception of wealth that would lead a corporation to cut down a forest to pay the interest on a loan.

In daily conversation in many parts of the American West today, wild animals are given credit for conveying ideas to people, for "speaking." To some degree this is a result of the pervasive influence of Native American culture in certain parts of the West. It doesn't contradict the notion of human intelligence to believe, in these quarters, that wild animals represent repositories of knowledge we've abandoned in our efforts to build civilizations and support ideas like progress and improvement. To "hear" wild animals is not to leave the realm of the human; it's to expand this realm to include voices other than our own. It's a technique for the accomplishment of wisdom. To attend to the language of animals means to give yourself over to a more complicated, less analytic awareness of a place. It's to realize that some of the so-called equations of life are not meant to be solved, that it takes as much intelligence not to solve them as it does to find the putative answers.

A fundamental difference between early and late twentieth-century science in the cultural West has become apparent with the emergence of the phrase "I don't know" in scientific discourse. This admission is the heritage of quantum mechanics. It is heard eloquently today in the talk of cosmologists, plasma physicists, and, increasingly, among field biologists now working beyond the baleful and condescending stare of molecular biologists.

The Enlightenment ideals of an educated mind and just relations among differing people have become problematic in our era because the process of formal education in the West has consistently abjured or condemned non-Western ways of knowing, and because the quest for just relations still strains at the barriers of race, gender, and class. If we truly believe in the wisdom of Enlightenment thought and achievement—and certainly, like Bach's B-Minor Mass, Goethe's theory of light, or Darwin's voyage, that philosophy is among the best we have to offer—then we should consider encouraging the educated mind to wander beyond the comfort of its own solipsisms, and we should extend the principle of justice to include everything that touches our lives.

I do not know how to achieve these things in the small valley where I live except through apprenticeship and the dismantling of assumptions I grew up with. The change, to a more gracious and courteous and wondrous awareness of the world, will not come in my lifetime, and knowing what I know of the modern plagues—loss of biodiversity, global warming, and the individual quest for material wealth—I am fearful. But I believe I have come to whatever I understand by listening to companions and by trying to erase the lines that establish hierarchies of knowledge among them. My sense is that the divine knowledge we yearn for is social; it is not in the province of a genius any more than it is in the province of a particular culture. It lies within our definition of community.

Our blessing, it seems to me, is not what we know, but that we know each other.

GRIZZLY FEARS

GLENDON BRUNK *(1999)*

It has been close to thirty years now since I had my first serious encounter with a grizzly. I was just a kid, in my early twenties, crazy for the wild and adventure, staying in an old cabin thirty miles southeast of Fairbanks on the Tanana River, building my own log cabin just downstream. Late August as it was, the nights were starting to get dark for a few hours, a contrast to the round-the-clock sunlight of full summer. The head of my bed was about three feet from the cabin's only door, a rickety wooden slat affair that admitted huge drafts of frigid air in the winter. I'd been asleep only an hour or so when I awoke suddenly to my dog barking, the unmistakable, gut-bending whoof of a husky badly scared. I lay quietly then, eyes wide, staring up into the blackness. The dog yelped once and ran behind the cabin. I sat up. Suddenly something big hit the cabin door, rattling it like a sheet of kraft paper. Then came a low, insistent growl, a terrifying sound with enough big creature in it to send adrenaline pummeling through my veins.

That was back in my dedicated hook 'n' bullet days when I never went anywhere without some kind of a gun. I shucked my arms out of my sleeping bag and grabbed the 30.06 leaning up against the wall by the head of my bed. I pushed the safety off and jacked the bolt. With a sinking feeling I felt the bolt miss the shell. (Over the summer months the clip spring had weakened enough so that it would not push the top shell up high enough for the bolt to receive it.)

I felt helpless, terrified. I scrambled out of bed, then stumbled around in the dark with my useless rifle pointed at the door, hollering "Get the hell out of here!" Finally, after a couple more swats at the door, the creature left and made the sad mistake of going upriver to my neighbor Denis's place. Denis, a huge man from Minnesota, known locally (never to his face, of course) as Grizzly Den, was a fellow who would kill just about anything he could get his sights on, damn the seasons, the species, or any ethics that might be involved. The animal entered Denis's compound and tried to crawl into the corral with his skidding horse. Denis's sled dogs, all thirty of them, began baying. Denis leaped out of bed, naked as a tortellini, and from his front porch shot at a hazy black silhouette.

The next part of the story is a testimony to the youthful impetuousness and testosterone overload that most of us young male Tanana dwellers were victims of then. Denis and his (reluctant) wife came down and got me, and off we went through the moonless night, stumbling along by the pale light of a hissing Coleman lantern, following the dull rust spatters of a blood trail, accompanied here and there by the unmistakable prints of a large bear. We followed the trail a hundred yards up along the riverbank before it cut into the woods. We'd made about fifty slow yards in the woods when the world suddenly erupted. Brush rattled and snapped beyond the reach of the lantern light. Agonized, angry roars beat against the trees like the devil's own voice. We held our rifles ready for the charge, for a snarling fury to erupt from the darkness. But none came. And then as suddenly as it had begun, it ended. The woods around us were completely silent.

We were at least smart enough to give up the pursuit at that point. We went back to our respective cabins. The next morning Denis and I got up at first light and picked up the trail again. When we approached the spot where we'd heard the roaring, the ground all around was gouged and ripped; small trees were scarred and broken like grass stems. At the base of a big spruce we found him, an old boar grizzly, shot hard, up high and behind the lungs, stretched full out on his stomach, his head twisted grotesquely off to his right and up under his leg. Blood froth rimmed his mouth. His canines were broken and dangling from their roots. That bear had given up life in great agony. I remember thinking that the way his head was twisted up under his leg like that, it looked like he had been ashamed to die the way he had.

He was a big bear, record book, but old and thin, missing back teeth; there was no way he would have made the winter. The outside toes on his right front foot were gone, most likely lost to a trap at some early point in his life. Those missing toes were the clear signature of a bear that had raided cabins up along the Salcha River for years. Glad as I was that he hadn't come into the cabin with me, I remember feeling sad and wishing he could have had a better, more dignified death.

I try now to recall how I felt standing there in the dark woods with that bear roaring his death throes. It's strange, but I don't recall any fear. I felt fear in the cabin, I guess because I felt so helpless. But in the woods, all I can remember is calmness, a feeling of being exactly where I wanted to be. Mixed with it, too, was a sense of exhilaration. This same mix of feelings I've experienced other times, always when I've been in the most danger. There may be some grand psychological explanation for it. If I had to label it, though, I would call it a swift, exacting moment when one's life finally comes to some essential connection, some place where the dread of one's own mortality is temporarily exorcised. Our ancestors, in less predictable and insulated-from-nature times, must have often visited this place. I would guess, for the most part, their lives were a great deal richer for it.

I started thinking seriously about fear and grizzly bears not long ago when I was attempting to see as much of the Bob Marshall Wilderness as I could. "The Bob," as they call it in western Montana, is a pretty piece of country, about as wild, I suppose, as it gets in the Lower 48. When people asked me what I was up to and I told them I was exploring the Bob, I couldn't help but note how routinely predictable their responses were: "There's grizzlies in there, you know," or "You're going in there with all those bears?" These were mostly reasonable people, too, wilderness travelers some of them. But their first reaction, consistently, returned to the fact that the place might harbor killer bears. The notion seems to cling like an unwanted houseguest, that grizzly bears inhabit every possible nook and cranny of the Montana (and Alaska) wildernesses, and if you don't watch out real careful you're going to end up dead, looking like you've been tackled by . . . well, by a grizzly bear.

For sure, there are some grizzlies in the Bob. I must emphasize "some," because relative to most places I've traveled in Alaska, the Bob is a regular bear desert. In close to 200 miles of walking trails, as well as a fair amount of off-trail wandering, I've seen only a couple of definite grizzly signs, and not one grizzly in the flesh. Yet I have been assured by Chris Servheen, former head of the federal Grizzly Bear Recovery Program, that an estimated 400 grizzlies reside in the whole ecosystem, which includes Glacier National Park. But they're not in the Bob Marshall Wilderness in elbow-scraping numbers, certainly not bountiful enough that you need to carry heavy artillery or spruce up your will before you leave town. From what I know about bears I'd say that in the Bob they're living in some pretty confined and remote pockets, and that they'd much prefer we human types just leave them alone. So people's fear of them is for the most part unfounded.

Not that the fear is all bad. As I told one friend when she asked me whether I was afraid of bears: "Sure I'm afraid of bears. But I'm sure glad they're out there, because it keeps a lot of people out of places they'd be in otherwise." I didn't add that in my mind, fear is one essential, integral, unmitigated part of the true wilderness experience.

I think it was Doug Peacock, the grizzly guru of the West, who said, "It's not really wilderness unless there are things out there big enough to eat you." Peacock was alluding to the idea that a little reasonable, solidly grounded fear is what makes life worth living: zest, it's called. You want safe and predictable nature, go hang out at the San Diego Zoo or Disney World. Buy stock in some newly formed virtual reality company. Try golf. Leave the few, hard-pressed, and harassed grizzlies left in North America alone.

Of course, fear is a relative thing. Like most things we think about, the thinking is usually a lot more scary than the actual fact. For certain, our irrational fears keep a lot of us from doing some pretty wonderful things. Our fear of bears (or anything else, for that matter) leads most of us to all kinds of stop-short-of-enjoying-life-fully decisions—like an acquaintance of mine in California who was reluctant to visit Montana because he'd heard a grizzly had walked through the streets of "some town out there." The fact that the town was Gardiner, a tiny burg up on the very northern boundary of Yellowstone Park, had nothing to do with it. In his mind there were bears, dozens of them, battling over the turf in downtown Missoula and Great Falls. I have to mention again that he was from California, where some real serious turf wars are going on in the streets he inhabits. (And I'll ignore the irony of a place they still call the Golden Bear State, where they managed to eliminate the last villain grizzly somewhere around the turn of the twentieth century.)

There are a lot of emotional knee-jerks around the subject of bears—all bears—but especially grizzlies. For example, the author of a letter to the editor published last year in Missoula's daily paper expressed outright disgust because the U.S. Fish and Wildlife Service was considering reintroducing bears into the Bitterroot Wilderness of Idaho. He related that his nephew was elk hunting in Wyoming, just "walking up a trail, and was attacked by a grizzly. He went into the fetal position and tried to act dead. His gun was nearby, but every time he reached for it, the bear hit him again."

Now in my mind that sounds like a pretty smart bear, batting a guy for reaching for a gun. Not that I want to demean the terror the young man must have felt, or the pain that he no doubt endured from lacerations that took over 200 stitches to close. The most important point, though, runs deeper than the subject of one person having a nightmare experience with a bear. It relates to something else the letter writer had to say: "It would be a crying shame and, yes, stupid to lock people out of these beautiful areas because of fear."

There it is again, the old "f" word. If the Fish and Wildlife Service put grizzly bears back in the Bitterroot, some people automatically assume that it becomes off-limits for most of the human population. I understand the reasoning, but to me it seems out of place relative to some of the things we accept daily in this society. I'm wondering how many roads the guy stays off because somebody once died in a car accident. Or how many lakes he won't swim in because somebody drowned there. I once heard an Alaska Fish and Game official say that more people are killed by man's best friend in any given year in Alaska than are ever killed by bears.

The point is, most of our fears run irrational. We fear grizzly bears more than some things that truly deserve a good dose of horror, like our own society's corruption and violence. But I suppose, given our modern relationship with nature, it's understandable. Grizzly bears are one of the few wild elements left, in a society determined to create predictability and homogeneity and that very rarely delivers us nature at its most horrible, unpredictable, uncaring, demeaning, and nondiscriminating best. Grizzlies are a reminder of the dark side of things, of Momma Nature beating on the door, shoving the real goods right in our face. What with all our technological marvels, all our wise notions of dominance and security, the message still comes through: you slip up just a little bit, buddy, and you're hosed.

I've had a couple dozen encounters with grizzly bears since that first one on the Tanana River. I must hasten to add that even though I've killed several black bears for their meat, I've never killed a grizzly. The best I can figure is that some instinct kept me from doing it. Maybe somewhere in my youthful subconscious I knew a truth about myself, and I saved myself from killing an animal I was sure to have deep regrets about when I finally made the decision to quit hunting altogether. Yes, I quit hunting. There are no complicated philosophical explanations for it. All I can say is that the sorrow of killing simply began to outweigh the pleasure of the hunt. I say this, and at the same time I must admit that the old killer instinct is never far below the surface; it can rise easily and entirely when the circumstances are right.

I think that it's important for us to fear bears. We live in a world of natural disasters—tornadoes, for example. But nobody ever cautions me about going back to my boyhood home in Indiana because they have tornadoes there. And I've personally known several people killed by tornadoes. In contrast, I've never personally known anyone killed by a bear, even though I've lived a whole lot longer in bear country. Twenty-five million people live in California, with an ironclad guarantee of multiple earthquakes, and more people are moving there every day. Yet you talk to Californians, and most are totally nonchalant about earthquakes.

The difference with bears is that they just seem a lot more personal, not abstract and distant like weather or plate tectonics. A bear is a living thing, furry and fast, with teeth and beady little eyes and long toenails, a creature clearly not feeling all warm and fuzzy about the presence of human beings. Our response over the centuries has been to eliminate things that we perceive as a threat to us. We've figured for a long time that if we can just snuff out enough nature we can make the world safe for civilization. Today, of course, it's old news that if we choose to, we can exterminate a whole species. Gone. Done. Kaput. We win.

But not really. Perhaps—a highly cautious and qualified perhaps—a slight majority of people are beginning to realize that "civilization" is not about getting the world safely sterile. A few years ago the Idaho Fish and Game Department commissioned a poll regarding the reintroduction of grizzlies in the Bitterroot Mountains on the border of Idaho and Montana. In response to the poll there were some lame comments, like "They'll do away with game, and the hunters do a good enough job of that already," or "It's not practical," or "Unnecessary when they're in Alaska." And another that did a masterful job of reordering history with a Zen flare: "Since they're not there now then it's not meant to be."

The good side of the poll, though, seems to present a hopeful paradox. Even though the vast majority of people fear grizzly bears, most would still like to see them back in wild areas. Of the national respondents, 77 percent were in favor, 73 percent in the region in favor, and 62 percent locally. Of those who disapproved, in all cases over half did so because of safety concerns. It's noteworthy that the farther away from the Bitterroot the people lived, the more they were in favor of reintroduction; no doubt this says something about the reality of bears actually being in your backyard. But the fact that over 60 percent of local residents supported it says a whole lot about changes under way in the wild West. One of the respondents summed it up quite simply: "The bears belong in the mountains."

July 17, 1987, the Brooks Range in Alaska's Arctic National Wildlife Refuge, my favorite place on Earth. Tom Ballantyne, my wilderness partner of many seasons, and I have been out for over three weeks now. In that time we've seen plenty of grizzly signs. On one occasion we surprised a young boar grazing contentedly among a small herd of caribou on a tundra hillside. Two days earlier we saw a bear move high above us on a mountain ridge, then disappear into low clouds. We know we are overdue to see more.

Today we follow a westward compass bearing, hoping to gain a pass that will take us back to the broad gravel wash of the Canning River (the western boundary of the refuge) thirty miles away, where eight days earlier we cached our raft and the bulk of our gear. Today we use the compass because we move through a surrealistic, drizzling, white-on-gray cloak of fog, a separation from anything familiar. As we move, odd forms emerge like ghosts to metamorphose into rocks or hillsides. We move slowly, attentively, concerned that one of those forms might indeed become a living bear.

Eventually we gain the pass. But on top we can't figure where to turn; the country appears to fall away too steeply on all sides to trust a descent in the fog. We talk it over and decide our only choice is to camp and wait.

Early the next morning the fog clears enough for us to resume our journey. We climb down into a beautiful green Shangri-la of a valley. At noon we stop and eat lunch in the steep-walled canyon of the creek we've been following. We are about done with lunch when we spot a big grizzly standing on the canyon rim just across from us. The bear is no more than a hundred yards away, yet clearly doesn't see us. We watch it poke around in a little ravine that runs down the canyon wall. Tom and I whisper to each other, trying to decide whether or not we should announce ourselves. Suddenly our presence becomes a moot point. The bear turns quickly and begins to climb the mountain, throwing worried glances downstream over its shoulder. We watch it climb high above us until it comes to a heavy talus slope. There, like a tired dog, it turns round and round several times before it finally beds down in the rocks.

We can't figure what spooked that bear. But when we climb out of the canyon the source quickly becomes evident. A quarter mile away another grizzly chases two caribou downslope and across the creek, then up through a steep break in the canyon wall on the far side. The caribou easily outdistance the bear, a fact that obviously perturbs the bear badly. As it climbs the far slope it swings its head back and forth in an exaggerated, irritated way. Everything in its body language indicates an animal that has had enough of losing.

We know we have to get upwind from it; we want it to get our scent if it spots us, not to mistake us for more caribou. So we start moving cautiously along the opposite side of the valley, doing our best not to attract the bear's attention. We are doing fine it seems. But just as we get directly opposite the bear, it swings its head up and looks hard at us. In the next instant it breaks for us, coming way too fast, in that rolling, flowing, ground-eating gait only a grizzly possesses.

We know we have to gain some high ground fast, to do our best to get ourselves between the wind and the bear. But a couple of middle-aged guys running across rough tundra with heavy packs is no ballet performance. We stumble and trip across the hillside. A steep-sided ravine drops sharply ahead of us. We plunge over the edge, pant and claw our way up the other side, concerned that the bear might catch us down in there where there is damn little maneuvering room.

When we make the top there is no sign of the bear. We keep moving and make the rise. There we quickly turn in the direction we expect it to show, dropping our packs in the same motion.

The wind is at our backs now. Tom pulls out his camera and gets ready to photograph the charge. I crank a slug into the chamber of the shotgun I carry. At that instant the bear appears over the edge of the canyon, coming for us at a dead run.

It takes a lot longer to tell it than it actually took. Tom's motor drive begins whirring. I pull the shotgun up and hold it on the bear's chest. As it closes on us we both holler. Just as I'm ready to pull the trigger, the bear computes the situation—smell, sound, sight—and suddenly, frantically veers off and away from us. It is astounding how immediately its whole demeanor changes, how quickly it goes from bold aggression to absolute panic. The bear heads uphill away from us, sprints up a forty-five degree slope, an incline that would have me wind-broke in a few seconds. In the next moment it disappears over the top of the ridge.

As it is with any close call with a bear, a grand mix of emotions— joy, terror, relief—boils through one like a storm. That particular bear, though, left me with something else. I remember it very distinctly. Seeing his bold male (my assumption) swagger turn to witless panic,

Tom and I beheld how a human presence can so easily elicit terror in the most awesome of creatures. Witnessing his fear I felt embarrassed and deeply sad, embarrassed for the bear and embarrassed for my own species, sad for the legacy we modern humans have sown among wild creatures. We have done so much to alienate the world we live in.

It took that close call, though, for me to have an epiphany of sorts. It took cranking a slug into the chamber of my shotgun, readying myself to shoot, before I finally came face to face with the kind of "nonhunter" I was. There I was owned by my own fear. There I was still depending on a firearm for protection. I was struck by the hard irony of it: for me to be in this wilderness place I loved, I was prepared to kill one of the creatures that absolutely defined its wildness. I had to ask myself that day, was the experience of being there really worth that kind of sacrifice?

It seems to me there are two types of fear: legitimate fear and projected fear. Legitimate fear, like the fear I felt when the bear tried to get in the cabin with me, is real: there is a clearly definable threat to some aspect of one's life, either carried from past experience or felt in the present moment. Projected fear, on the other hand, is fear of the future, a fantasy of what *might* go wrong. Projected fear is the cause of so much bigotry, intolerance, violence, and suffering in the world. Humans may be the only species on the planet with the capacity to project fear: to imagine what might go wrong, and then to create elaborate defense mechanisms—be they psychological or mechanical—to prepare for the possibility.

There's so much irony in it all. I won't say I begin to understand the intricacies of the position we humans have forcefully taken on this planet. But I will say that it seems in wanting to have it our own way, in seeking what's missing in our overly civilized spirits, we so often tend to project fear on those attributes of nature that would seem to sustain us most, the very qualities that would lead us home to the missing parts, the wild, unscrubbed, unruly, arrogant, and, at the same time, soft nature that is ultimately us.

We modern humans choose to fear the bear within us. We live in terror of those wild, untamed, restless places within and without. They wake us at night and keep us running scared during the day. Most of us don't seem to understand how our fears control us. Instead, we push against them until our souls bleed. We run scared to the shopping centers and movie houses, drown ourselves in a hundred addictions, all under the misperceived notion that such activities will somehow provide solace. There's more sad irony to it all: the more we run from our fears, the farther away from our essential, longing selves we're taken.

I don't mean to infer that an experience with wilderness and bears is the only route home. But I will say that the combination is certainly one of the shortest paths I know of. Like that trip Tom and I took up in the Arctic. The bears were there for us and we knew they were there, so there was no more running from the shadow. We were incapable of escaping our deepest cravings and fears, and in the process we could begin to discover that we truly were alive. We were alive because we were forced to come face to face with our own mortality. And if I'm to understand anything about human psychology, it's that peace can begin to enter one's life when one accepts the inevitability of one's mortality; that's when real spiritual healing begins to take place. In my mind, then, this is the only argument that's needed for the protection and restoration of primal wilderness: give us untamed places so that we may have the opportunity to come home to ourselves.

To this end, I would add, may grizzly bears always roam the Earth. And all the other fearsome creatures, too. Let's hear it for killer sharks and vipers and poisonous spiders. Unfurl the flag for crocodiles and sea snakes. Up with lions and tigers and rampaging elephants. Three cheers for panthers. And let's not forget polar bears. You want terror, those white demons creeping across an ice floe like a stalking cat, thinking you're a ring seal, now that can turn the hardest heart to

jelly. Hold on, all you wild terrifying predators—keep scaring us, because there's some hope that the tide of human consciousness is turning. I see evidence. Like what one of the interviewees in the Bitterroot
grizzly reintroduction poll had to say: "I support it because I can't think
of any reason not to." Now that kind of thinking I like.

Afterword

EARTH VERSE

Wide enough to keep you looking
Open enough to keep you moving
Dry enough to keep you honest
Prickly enough to make you tough
Green enough to go on living
Old enough to give you dreams

—GARY SNYDER

ABOUT THE CONTRIBUTORS

DAVID ABRAM is a cultural ecologist and philosopher who lives in the inter-mountain West. He is the author of *The Spell of the Sensuous: Perception and Language in a More-Than-Human World,* for which he received the Lannan Literary Award for Nonfiction. An accomplished sleight-of-hand magician, David has lived and traded magic with indigenous magicians in Indonesia, Nepal, and the Americas.

CONNIE BARLOW is a science writer, conservation activist, and founding member of the Epic of Evolution Society. Her most recent books are *Green Space, Green Time: The Way of Science* and *The Ghosts of Evolution.* She now lives in the Lower Hudson Bioregion of New York State.

WENDELL BERRY is a farmer and writer of essays, poetry, and novels. His many literary works include *The Unsettling of America; What Are People For?; Another Turn of the Crank; Life Is a Miracle;* and *Jayber Crow.* His farming works include the ongoing restoration of an eroded hillside farm near the Kentucky River.

GLENDON BRUNK, who spent twenty-five years in Alaska, teaches environmental studies and environmental writing and literature at Prescott College in Prescott, Arizona. His first book, *Yearning Wild: Exploring the Last Frontier and the Landscape of the Heart,* was published in 2001.

DAVID A. BURNEY is an associate professor in the Department of Biological Sciences at Fordham University in the Bronx, New York. His research interests include the causes of extinction and prehistoric landscape transformation in Madagascar, Hawaii, the West Indies, Africa, and North America.

J. BAIRD CALLICOTT, who offered the world's first course in environmental ethics in 1971, is professor of philosophy at the University of North Texas. His many books as either author or editor include *Earth's Insights: A Multicultural Survey of Ecological Ethics from the Mediterranean Basin to the Australian Outback,*

In Defense of the Land Ethic: Essays in Environmental Philosophy, and *For the Health of the Land: Previously Unpublished Essays and Other Writings by Aldo Leopold.*

JOHN DAVIS is the founding editor of *Wild Earth* journal and a cofounder of the Wildlands Project. He is biodiversity program officer for the Foundation for Deep Ecology and also works for the Eddy Foundation, which is based near his home in the Adirondack Mountains of New York.

R. WILLS FLOWERS is an entomologist whose interests range from Neotropical mayflies to the insect communities of longleaf pine forests. He has been a professor at Florida A&M University in Tallahassee since 1975.

DAVE FOREMAN is one of America's best-known conservation leaders. He has worked as a Washington, D.C., lobbyist for the Wilderness Society, has served on the Sierra Club board of directors, and cofounded *Wild Earth* journal and the Wildlands Project, where he serves as publisher and chairman, respectively. He is the author of a novel, *The Lobo Outback Funeral Home,* and two works of nonfiction: *The Big Outside* (with Howie Wolke) and *Confessions of an Eco-Warrior.*

WALT FRANKLIN is a manic fly fisherman, naturalist, teacher, and writer who works for the environmental integrity of his corner of the Susquehanna watershed of New York State.

PETER FRIEDERICI had a childhood ambition to open a natural history museum. This passion lives on in his writing, which brings together a keen vision and his training as a field biologist. His book of essays *The Suburban Wild* is set in the North Shore of Chicago where he grew up. He now lives in Arizona.

LYANDA LYNN HAUPT, an avid birder, is a natural history writer and instructor. She is the author of *Rare Encounters with Ordinary Birds* (Sasquatch Books, 2001). She and her husband live in Seattle, where they are raising a toddler and three chickens.

SANDY IRVINE, who holds a graduate degree in rural planning and reforestation, now earns his bread by teaching media studies at the City of Sunderland College in England. A prolific writer on green issues, he is coauthor of *A Green Manifesto,* was formerly an associate editor of *The Ecologist,* and was a founder and coeditor of the quarterly magazine *Real World* for eight years. He is a member of the British Green Party.

JosÉ Knighton is a poet, hiker, and bioregionalist who manages the Back of Beyond bookstore in Moab, Utah. He is author of *Canyon Country's La Sal Mountains Hiking and Nature Handbook, Coyote's History of Moab,* and assorted poetry chapbooks from his own Compost Press. *Harper's* magazine has published his work in its "Readings" section.

Anne LaBastille is a wildlife ecologist and author who lives in the Adirondack Park. Her writings include two books about her international conservation work, *Mama Poc* and *Jaguar Totem,* and a popular trilogy, the *Woodswoman* series, describing her life in a log cabin in the Adirondacks.

Gary Lawless is co-owner of Gulf of Maine Bookstore in Brunswick, Maine, and editor/publisher of Blackberry Books. A teacher, activist, and widely published poet, he has served as poetry editor for *Wild Earth* since 1991. His books include *First Sight of Land* and *Caribouddhism,* which was recently published in Italy as *Caribouddhismo.*

Barry Lopez is the author of a dozen books, including *Desert Notes, Of Wolves and Men, Arctic Dreams* (for which he won a National Book Award), and *About This Life: Journeys on the Threshold of Memory.* He lives in Oregon's McKenzie River Valley.

Christopher Manes is a philosopher, writer, and attorney presently practicing law in Southern California. His books include *Green Rage: Radical Environmentalism and the Unmaking of Civilization* and *Other Creations: Rediscovering the Spirituality of Animals.*

Paul S. Martin, an originator and leading proponent of the Overkill Hypothesis for end-Pleistocene extinctions, is emeritus professor of geosciences at the University of Arizona's Desert Laboratory. Since the 1950s, he has investigated prehistoric biotic changes in arid regions, especially the extinction of large animals in the late Pleistocene. He is coeditor of *Packrat Middens: 40,000 Years of Biotic Change* and the classic *Quaternary Extinctions: A Prehistoric Revolution.*

Mollie Yoneko Matteson is a conservation activist, writer, and wildlife biologist who has studied wolves and coyotes in the Greater Yellowstone Ecosystem. She presently lives in Oregon, where she is collaborating with her husband, George Wuerthner, on the forthcoming book *Welfare Ranching: The Subsidized Destruction of the American West.*

BILL MCKIBBEN, a former staff writer for the *New Yorker,* is an environmental journalist who writes often for the *New York Review of Books, Doubletake,* and other periodicals. His books include *The End of Nature, Maybe One,* and *Hope, Human and Wild.* He presently lives in Vermont with his wife, the writer Sue Halpern, and their daughter.

STEPHANIE MILLS was launched to national prominence in 1969 when she vowed in her college commencement speech to never have children. Since that time she has been an outspoken writer, lecturer, and advocate for wild nature. Her books include *Whatever Happened to Ecology?, In Service of the Wild, Turning Away from Technology: A New Vision for the 21st Century,* and *Epicurean Simplicity.*

KATHLEEN DEAN MOORE is chair of the Philosophy Department at Oregon State University in Corvallis. Her essays have appeared in many publications, and have been collected in two books: the award-winning *Riverwalking* and *Holdfast: At Home in the Natural World.*

GARY PAUL NABHAN is an ethnobotanist and director of the Center for Sustainable Environments at Northern Arizona University. He is the author of *Coming Home to Eat, The Desert Smells Like Rain, Gathering the Desert, The Forgotten Pollinators* (with Stephen Buchmann), *Plants and Protected Areas* (with John Tuxill), and many other works of natural history.

RODERICK FRAZIER NASH is emeritus professor of history and environmental studies at the University of California, Santa Barbara. His many books include *The Rights of Nature: A History of Environmental Ethics, American Environmentalism: Readings in Conservation History,* and *From These Beginnings: A Biographical Approach to American History.* His classic work, *Wilderness and the American Mind,* originally published in 1967, is now in its third edition.

REED F. NOSS is a leading thinker in conservation planning at regional and broader scales, and a cofounder of the Wildlands Project. He is science editor of *Wild Earth,* an international consultant on biodiversity issues, past president of the Society for Conservation Biology, and former editor of *Conservation Biology.* He is coauthor of *Saving Nature's Legacy* (with Allan Cooperrider) and *The Science of Conservation Planning* (with Michael O'Connell and Denis Murphy), and he has published more than 150 articles in the scientific and popular press on biodiversity conservation.

DOUG PEACOCK, inspiration for Ed Abbey's famous hero Hayduke, is a writer, naturalist, and close friend of grizzly bears (though he has been charged twenty-five times, each time he has reached an amicable truce with his would-be ursine devourers). His books include *Baja!* and *Grizzly Years: In Search of the American Wilderness.*

PATTIANN ROGERS has published eight books of poetry, most recently, *Song of the World Becoming: New and Collected Poems 1981–2001* (Milkweed Editions, 2001). She has won numerous awards and fellowships, including two NEA grants, a Guggenheim Fellowship, and a Lannan Poetry Fellowship. The mother of two grown sons and a daughter-in-law, she lives with her husband, a retired geophysicist, in Colorado.

JAMIE SAYEN, a creative and tenacious conservation activist in northern New Hampshire, is the founder of the Northern Appalachian Restoration Project, publisher of its regional newspaper, *The Northern Forest Forum,* and author of the book *Einstein in America*. He is presently writing a book on the ecological and cultural history of the Northern Forest.

FLORENCE R. SHEPARD is professor emerita at the University of Utah, an essayist, and a scholar who now divides her time between Utah and Wyoming. She is the author of, among other works, *Ecotone* and is editor of *Encounters with Nature: Essays by Paul Shepard,* a collection of works by her late husband.

GARY SNYDER is a poet, bioregional activist, scholar, and visionary. His books include *Turtle Island, The Practice of the Wild, A Place in Space, Mountains and Rivers without End,* and *A Gary Snyder Reader.* His place in space is Kitkitdizze in the Yuba watershed, Shasta bioregion (Northern California).

LOUISA WILLCOX has been working to protect American wildlands and wildlife for over two decades. She coordinates the Sierra Club's Grizzly Bear Ecosystems Project in Bozeman, Montana; is a board member of the Wildlands Project, the Rocky Mountain Ecosystem Coalition, and the Park County Environmental Council; and serves on the steering committee of the Yellowstone to Yukon Conservation Initiative (Y2Y).

ROBIN W. WINKS is Randolph W. Townsend Jr. Professor of History and chair of the history department at Yale University. He serves on the board of the National Parks Conservation Association and has visited all units in the National Park System. He writes on various facets of European and American history, including the development of the American conservation ethic and public lands policy. His books include *Frederick Billings: A Life, Laurance S. Rockefeller: Catalyst for Conservation,* and the Pulitzer Prize-nominated *Cloak and Gown: Scholars in the Secret War 1939–1961.*

HOWIE WOLKE is a longtime wilderness activist in the northern Rockies. He was a field organizer for Friends of the Earth in the 1970s, cofounded Earth First! in 1980, and through the 1990s worked to protect the roadless wildlands of the Greater Salmon-Selway Ecosystem. He is the author of *Wilderness on the Rocks* and coauthor (with Dave Foreman) of *The Big Outside.* He operates his wilderness guiding service, Big Wild Adventures, out of his home in the Bitterroot Valley of Montana.

DONALD WORSTER is the Hall Distinguished Professor of American History at the University of Kansas. He is the author of *A River Running West: The Life of John Wesley Powell; Rivers of Empire: Water, Aridity, and the Growth of the American West; Nature's Economy: A History of Ecological Ideas;* and other works of environmental history.

PHOEBE WRAY was the founder (in 1973) and for many years executive director of the Center for Action on Endangered Species in Ayer, Massachusetts, an international nongovernmental organization specializing in public information and education. She continues to serve as senior consultant, attending International Whaling Commission meetings and writing on environmental issues for the popular and environmental press. She is a professor at The Boston Conservatory.

KEN WU is campaign director for the Western Canada Wilderness Committee (Vancouver Island Chapter). A graduate of the University of British Columbia's ecological science program, he melds his interests in conservation science and philosophy in his work to protect imperiled wildlands in Canada.

GEORGE WUERTHNER is a conservation activist, ecologist, photographer, and author who has written over twenty books on America's wild places, including

The Adirondacks: Forever Wild, California's Sierra Nevada, and *The Grand Canyon: A Visitor's Guide.* He has been a vocal critic of livestock grazing on public lands, served on the boards of directors of several regional and national conservation organizations, and presently is the board president of RESTORE: The North Woods.

NETWORKS OF PEOPLE PROTECTING NETWORKS OF LAND: ABOUT THE WILDLANDS PROJECT AND *WILD EARTH*

The Wildlands Project is an international, member-supported non-profit conservation organization that melds conservation science and wilderness advocacy.

We are ambitious. We live for the day when grizzlies in Chihuahua have an unbroken connection to grizzlies in Alaska; when wolf populations are restored from Mexico to the Yukon to Maine; when vast forests and flowing prairies again thrive and support their full assemblages of native plants and animals; when humans dwell on the land with respect and affection.

Toward this end, the Wildlands Project is working to restore and protect the natural heritage of North America. Through advocacy, education, scientific consultation, and cooperation with many partners, we are designing and helping implement systems of interconnected wilderness areas that can sustain the diversity of life.

Wild Earth—the quarterly publication of the Wildlands Project—inspires effective action for wild nature by communicating the latest thinking in conservation science, philosophy, politics, and activism, and serves as a forum for diverse views within the conservation movement.

The Wildlands Project
P.O. Box 455
Richmond, VT 05477
Phone: 802-434-4077
Fax: 802-434-5980
www.wildlandsproject.org

ACKNOWLEDGMENTS

First and foremost, this book would not have been possible without the literary, intellectual, and artistic contributions of the writers, scientists, artists, and activists whose work we have been privileged to publish in *Wild Earth* journal through its first decade. The contributors represented in this anthology are but a small part of that generous group.

I am deeply indebted to two great conservationists and mentors, Dave Foreman and John Davis, who founded *Wild Earth* journal in 1991. Their good influence and friendship have changed the course of my life. With *Wild Earth,* they hoped to forge links between wilderness activists and conservation biologists. That marriage of advocacy and science has been a fruitful one, and the journal has prospered. The other founding board members—including Mary Byrd Davis, who did the bulk of the work setting up *Wild Earth's* business infrastructure; political scientist and attorney David Johns, who helped with legal issues; and ecologist Reed Noss, a leading thinker in conservation planning and unflinching advocate for wilderness—were central also to the journal's birth and continuing vitality. Other board members, including Katie Alvord, Barbara Dean, Stephanie Mills, and Kris Sommerville, have been invaluable through the years, as have our volunteer poetry editors Art Goodtimes, Gary Lawless, and Sheila McGrory-Klyza.

I am grateful also to many *Wild Earth* colleagues with whom I have argued over punctuation and grammar, met (and missed!) deadlines, and discussed the pressing issues facing the conservation movement. They are too numerous to acknowledge comprehensively, but Marcia Cary, Kathleen Fitzgerald, Erin O'Donnell Gilbert, and Monique Miller were central to the organization's survival during their years with *Wild Earth,* and much of the credit for the journal's present good health goes to current staffers Josh Brown, Kevin Cross, Jennifer Esser, Lina Miller, and Heidi Perkins.

My wonderful family has been extraordinarily patient with my long hours of paper pushing for wilderness, which has too often kept us from adventures in the big wild.

Finally, I extend thanks to Emilie Buchwald, Hilary Reeves, Laurie Buss, Dale Cooney, and the rest of the excellent team at Milkweed Editions, and to Lynn Marasco, for her good work. When Emilie broached the idea for this book, I was skeptical, but soon was won over by the prospect of collecting in one volume some of the best writings of *Wild Earth*'s first ten years, and communicating to a wider audience the bold thinking in conservation science and advocacy we've long featured in the journal. Moreover, I realized that any financial return that might result from book sales could be directed to land protection work in the Adirondacks.

For several years, *Wild Earth* and Wildlands Project staff have been working with local landowners and partners (including the Eddy Foundation, Adirondack Nature Conservancy, Adirondack Council, Boquet River Association, and others) to secure a key wildlife movement corridor in the eastern Adirondack Mountains, just across Lake Champlain from our Vermont office. *Wild Earth* has raised money through its Buy Back the Dacks fund to purchase (from willing sellers) private lands within the project area that are critical wildlife habitat. All royalties from the sale of this book will be channeled through the Buy Back the Dacks fund to keep this beautiful and ecologically rich landscape forever wild. For information about this effort or to make a tax-deductible contribution to the Buy Back the Dacks fund—and thereby to wildlands protection in the Adirondacks—please contact us.

—TOM BUTLER

CONTRIBUTOR ACKNOWLEDGMENTS

David Abram, "Returning to Our Animal Senses," *Wild Earth* 7, no. 1 (Spring 1997): 7–10. Copyright © 1997 by David Abram. Reprinted with permission from the author.

Connie Barlow, "Rewilding for Evolution," *Wild Earth* 9, no. 1 (Spring 1999): 53–56. Copyright © 1999 by Connie Barlow. Reprinted with permission from the author.

Wendell Berry, "Conservation Is Good Work," in *Sex, Economy, Freedom and Community* (New York: Pantheon, 1993): 27–43. Copyright © 1992 by Wendell Berry. Reprinted with permission from Pantheon Books. Originally published in *Wild Earth* 2, no. 1 (Spring 1992).

Glendon Brunk, "Grizzly Fears," *Wild Earth* 9, no. 1 (Spring 1999): 16–21. Copyright © 1999 by Glendon Brunk. Reprinted with permission from the author.

David A. Burney and Paul S. Martin, "Bring Back the Elephants!" *Wild Earth* 9, no. 1 (Spring 1999): 57–64. Copyright © 1999 by David A. Burney and Paul S. Martin. Reprinted with permission from the authors.

J. Baird Callicott, "A Critique of and an Alternative to the Wilderness Idea," *Wild Earth* 4, no. 4 (Winter 1994/1995): 54–59. Copyright © 1994 by J. Baird Callicott. Reprinted with permission from the author.

John Davis, "A Minority View: Rejoinder to 'Island Civilization,'" *Wild Earth* 1, no. 4 (Winter 1991/1992): 5–6. Copyright © 1991 by John Davis. Reprinted with permission from the author.

R. Wills Flowers, "Night and Fog: The Backlash Against the Endangered Species Act," *Wild Earth* 2, no. 3 (Fall 1992): 6–9. Copyright © 1992 by R. Wills Flowers. Reprinted with permission from the author.

Dave Foreman, "Around the Campfire," *Wild Earth* 1, no. 1 (Spring 1991): 2. Copyright © 1991 by Dave Foreman. "Wilderness: From Scenery to Nature," *Wild Earth* 5, no. 4 (Winter 1995/1996): 8–16. Copyright © 1995 by Dave Foreman. Reprinted with permission from the author.

Tom Butler is director of education and advocacy for the Wildlands Project and edits its award-winning periodical, *Wild Earth,* which covers wilderness and biodiversity conservation efforts across North America. An activist for more than fifteen years, Butler has worked for *Wild Earth* since its inception in 1991 and became the journal's editor in 1997. He lives with his family in the foothills of Vermont's Green Mountains in a house he designed and built. He is an avid paddler, backcountry skier, and birder who admits that his passion for these pursuits is considerably greater than his skill.

More Books on The World As Home from Milkweed Editions

To order books or for more information, contact Milkweed at (800) 520-6455 or visit our website (www.worldashome.org).

SWIMMING WITH GIANTS:
MY ENCOUNTERS WITH WHALES, DOLPHINS, AND SEALS
Anne Collet

THE PRAIRIE IN HER EYES
Ann Daum

BOUNDARY WATERS:
THE GRACE OF THE WILD
Paul Gruchow

GRASS ROOTS:
THE UNIVERSE OF HOME
Paul Gruchow

THE NECESSITY OF EMPTY PLACES
Paul Gruchow

A SENSE OF THE MORNING:
FIELD NOTES OF A BORN OBSERVER
David Brendan Hopes

ARCTIC REFUGE:
A CIRCLE OF TESTIMONY
Compiled by Hank Lentfer and Carolyn Servid

THIS INCOMPARABLE LAND:
A GUIDE TO AMERICAN NATURE WRITING
Thomas J. Lyon

A WING IN THE DOOR:
LIFE WITH A RED-TAILED HAWK
Peri Phillips McQuay

THE BARN AT THE END OF THE WORLD:
THE APPRENTICESHIP OF A QUAKER, BUDDHIST SHEPHERD
Mary Rose O'Reilley

ECOLOGY OF A CRACKER CHILDHOOD
Janisse Ray

OF LANDSCAPE AND LONGING:
FINDING A HOME AT THE WATER'S EDGE
Carolyn Servid

THE BOOK OF THE TONGASS
Edited by Carolyn Servid and Donald Snow

HOMESTEAD
Annick Smith

TESTIMONY:
WRITERS OF THE WEST SPEAK ON BEHALF OF UTAH WILDERNESS
Compiled by Stephen Trimble and Terry Tempest Williams

THE *CREDO* SERIES

BROWN DOG OF THE YAAK:
ESSAYS ON ART AND ACTIVISM
Rick Bass

WRITING THE SACRED INTO THE REAL
Alison Hawthorne Deming

THE FROG RUN:
WORDS AND WILDNESS IN THE VERMONT WOODS
John Elder

TAKING CARE:
THOUGHTS ON STORYTELLING AND BELIEF
William Kittredge

AN AMERICAN CHILD SUPREME:
THE EDUCATION OF A LIBERATION ECOLOGIST
John Nichols

WALKING THE HIGH RIDGE:
LIFE AS FIELD TRIP
Robert Michael Pyle

THE DREAM OF THE MARSH WREN:
WRITING AS RECIPROCAL CREATION
Pattiann Rogers

THE COUNTRY OF LANGUAGE
Scott Russell Sanders

SHAPED BY WIND AND WATER:
REFLECTIONS OF A NATURALIST
Ann Haymond Zwinger

OTHER BOOKS OF INTEREST TO THE WORLD AS HOME READER

ESSAYS

ECCENTRIC ISLANDS:
TRAVELS REAL AND IMAGINARY
Bill Holm

THE HEART CAN BE FILLED ANYWHERE ON EARTH
Bill Holm

SHEDDING LIFE:
DISEASE, POLITICS, AND OTHER HUMAN CONDITIONS
Miroslav Holub

CHILDREN'S NOVELS

TIDES
V. M. Caldwell

NO PLACE
Kay Haugaard

THE MONKEY THIEF
Aileen Kilgore Henderson

TREASURE OF PANTHER PEAK
Aileen Kilgore Henderson

THE DOG WITH GOLDEN EYES
Frances Wilbur

CHILDREN'S ANTHOLOGIES

STORIES FROM WHERE WE LIVE—THE CALIFORNIA COAST
Edited by Sara St. Antoine

STORIES FROM WHERE WE LIVE—THE GREAT NORTH AMERICAN PRAIRIE
Edited by Sara St. Antoine

STORIES FROM WHERE WE LIVE—THE NORTH ATLANTIC COAST
Edited by Sara St. Antoine

ANTHOLOGIES

SACRED GROUND:
WRITINGS ABOUT HOME
Edited by Barbara Bonner

URBAN NATURE:
POEMS ABOUT WILDLIFE IN THE CITY
Edited by Laure-Anne Bosselaar

VERSE AND UNIVERSE:
POEMS ABOUT SCIENCE AND MATHEMATICS
Edited by Kurt Brown

POETRY

TURNING OVER THE EARTH
Ralph Black

BOXELDER BUG VARIATIONS
Bill Holm

BUTTERFLY EFFECT
Harry Humes

FIREKEEPER:
NEW AND SELECTED POEMS
Pattiann Rogers

SONG OF THE WORLD BECOMING:
NEW AND COLLECTED POEMS 1981–2001
Pattiann Rogers

THE WORLD AS HOME, the nonfiction publishing program of Milkweed Editions, is dedicated to exploring our relationship to the natural world. Not espousing any particular environmentalist or political agenda, these books are a forum for distinctive literary writing that not only alerts the reader to vital issues but offers personal testimonies to living harmoniously with other species in urban, rural, and wilderness communities.

MILKWEED EDITIONS publishes with the intention of making a humane impact on society, in the belief that literature is a transformative art uniquely able to convey the essential experiences of the human heart and spirit. To that end, Milkweed publishes distinctive voices of literary merit in handsomely designed, visually dynamic books, exploring the ethical, cultural, and esthetic issues that free societies need continually to address. Milkweed Editions is a not-for-profit press.

JOIN US

Milkweed publishes adult and children's fiction, poetry, and, in its World As Home program, literary nonfiction about the natural world. Milkweed also hosts two websites: www.milkweed.org, where readers can find in-depth information about Milkweed books, authors, and programs, and www.worldashome.org, which is your online resource of books, organizations, and writings that explore ethical, esthetic, and cultural dimensions of our relationship to the natural world.

Since its genesis as *Milkweed Chronicle* in 1979, Milkweed has helped hundreds of emerging writers reach their readers. Thanks to the generosity of foundations and of individuals like you, Milkweed Editions is able to continue its nonprofit mission of publishing books chosen on the basis of literary merit—of how they impact the human heart and spirit—rather than on how they impact the bottom line. That's a miracle that our readers have made possible.

In addition to purchasing Milkweed books, you can join the growing community of Milkweed supporters. Individual contributions of any amount are both meaningful and welcome. Contact us for a Milkweed catalog or log on to www.milkweed.org and click on "About Milkweed," then "Why Join Milkweed," to find out about our donor program, or simply call 800-520-6455 and ask about becoming one of Milkweed's contributors. As a nonprofit press, Milkweed belongs to you, the community. Milkweed's board, its staff, and especially the authors whose careers you help launch thank you for reading our books and supporting our mission in any way you can.

Interior design by Dale Cooney.
Typeset in Bembo 11/15.5
by Stanton Publication Services.
Printed on acid-free 55# Frasier Miami Book Natural recycled paper
by Friesen Corporation.